THE BOND OF BEING

THE BOND OF BEING

An Essay on
Analogy and Existence

BY

James F. Anderson

GREENWOOD PRESS, PUBLISHERS
NEW YORK

DEO OPTIMO MAXIMO
EIUSQUE GENETRICI BEATAE
MARIAE VIRGINI PERPETUAE

ACKNOWLEDGMENTS

I CAN hardly hope to thank adequately those teachers and friends without whose patience and wisdom and inspiration this book would either not have been written at all or would certainly have been immeasurably less worthy of its theme. To Father Gerald B. Phelan, who initiated me into the study of St. Thomas over a decade ago, and who to me is still teacher as well as friend, I am exceedingly grateful; the book has in large measure grown out of the many stimulating discussions on analogy I have had with him. Especial thanks also are due Professor Yves Simon of the University of Chicago, who read the entire manuscript and offered numerous helpful suggestions and criticisms.

For permission to quote passages from various works, I am indebted to The Clarendon Press, Oxford; E. P. Dutton & Co., New York; Charles Scribner's Sons, New York; Harcourt, Brace and Co., New York; The Marquette University Press, Milwaukee; and to Dr. Ignatius Smith, O.P., Editor Emeritus of *The New Scholasticism*. I wish to thank Dom Illtyd Trethowan, O.S.B., the Editor of *The Downside Review*, Bath, England, for permission to incorporate in this volume parts of an article of mine. And last but not least, I am grateful to The University of Toronto, which through the kind agency of Professor Fulton H. Anderson has allowed me to make use of my doctoral thesis in the preparation of this book.

JAMES F. ANDERSON

University of Notre Dame
South Bend, Indiana

FOREWORD

A PHILOSOPHY inspired by the thought of St. Thomas
Aquinas cannot but be, at bottom, metaphysical, and its
metaphysics inevitably centers upon the primacy of *esse,*
the exercise of the act of existing. By his insistence upon
the primordial importance and significance of the *"esse"*
of all that, in any manner whatsoever, *is* (and consequently
may be known and said, *"to be"*) St. Thomas' philosophical
thought reveals itself as incorrigibly existential. Not—God
forbid!—in the sense in which that adjective is applied to
those anti-Hegelian thinkers, Christian or atheistic, from
Kierkegaard to Sartre and Gabriel Marcel, who are known
today as "existentialists"; but in the sense that *"esse"* is
the root-cause and ultimate source of the *being* of all that
is, as well as of the intelligibility of everything in the universe and of the God who made it. In a word, according to
St. Thomas, nothing *is,* and nothing "is-intelligible," in
the last analysis, except in terms of (or in function of, if
you prefer) the dynamic act of existing which is its "esse."

It was a novelty in philosophy, as Etienne Gilson has
pointed out,[1] that a philosopher, presumably in the Aristotelian tradition, should suggest that there could be an
"act" which was not a *"form,"* at the root of all being and
all intelligibility, and consequently, of all knowledge, human, angelic, or divine. But that is exactly what St.

[1] E. Gilson, *L'Être et l'Essence,* pp. 78–141, especially pp. 100 ff.

vii

Thomas did. He insisted that the being and intelligibility of "*what is*" rest upon "*esse,*" not on "*essentia.*" On the other hand, he vehemently resisted the Platonic tendency to reify human abstractions and make mind the measure of reality. For St. Thomas, God is that measure. And God is not essentially "*Mind*" but "*Esse.*" God alone *is* "Esse"; all else *has* "esse." Being Himself *Ipsum Esse,* God gives *esse* to all that is and to each in proportion to its quiddity. In addition to the act or "form" by which whatever *is,* is made to-be-*what-it-is,* and thus take its proper place in the ranks of being, there is a further and ultimate act which makes it *to be, to exist,* and without which no being would or could be a "what" of any kind. That act is *esse* and it gives existence to each and every being that is, and gives it in the exact measure required by each being's nature. Thus the universe is "peopled by individual acts of existing. Or rather it is made up of them" [2] and each of these acts is proportionate to the individual being which exercises it.

Consequently when St. Thomas applied his mind to expressing, in human language, the "mystery of being," he had recourse to analogy, which is simply Greek for proportion. Nothing is more frequently encountered in St. Thomas' discussions of metaphysical questions than those distinctions and explanations based on the proportionate exercise of the act of existing (*esse*) by the beings under consideration, each according to its own mode of existing. Analogy, in the thought of St. Thomas, was thus no mere "method." It was a metaphysical fact. Beings *are* analog-

[2] E. Gilson, *op. cit.,* p. 117.

ical or, if you will, exercise the act of existence each in proportion to its nature or essence; and, consequently, the metaphysician who aims at dealing with beings as they *are,* and in so far as they *are,* is inescapably obliged to deal with them analogically. Analogy is a way of understanding what is only because it is the way what is, is.

Questions like those concerning the one and the many, the true and the false, good and evil, and the whole host of problems raised by the doctrine of participation demand for their solution an understanding of the intrinsic analogicity of being as such, and the essential variety of modes of existing. And it is in this wise that St. Thomas tackles these problems.

There exists no treatise by St. Thomas *"De analogia,"* but the concept of analogy is implicitly present, as it were, *in actu exercito,* whenever the Angelic Doctor deals with such or similar questions.

Although St. Thomas gave little attention to the philosophical analysis of the doctrine of analogy,—since as a "Christian teacher" (*Doctor Christianus*) he was more interested in "using" philosophy for Christ than in justifying it before men—yet he wrote much that a student of his writings could elaborate into a philosophical interpretation of his thought.

That is precisely what Professor Anderson has done in this book. His treatment of this subject, however, is not merely analytical nor is it divorced from metaphysical problems which have emerged in the course of history. On more than one occasion he points to the doctrine of analogy as most relevant in solving difficulties that have arisen in the attempts of philosophers throughout the ages to grapple with "the mystery of being."

This book deserves assiduous study. It is packed with metaphysical insights and should prove thoroughly rewarding to the careful reader.

GERALD B. PHELAN

The Mediaeval Institute
University of Notre Dame

CONTENTS

CONTENTS

Part Three

SYMBOLIC ANALOGY OR ANALOGY OF METAPHOR

Part Four

ANALOGY OF PROPER PROPORTIONALITY

CONTENTS

INTRODUCTION

A. Statement of the Problem

"There is no word . . . which is used more loosely, or in a greater variety of senses, than Analogy." [1] This remark, made toward the middle of the last century, is not a whit less true today. A glance at "analogy" in any unabridged dictionary and a quick review of the uses of the term to be found even in a small sampling of modern logical, psychological, mathematical, and scientific books will yield sufficient evidence of the tangled meanings of this word. "Analogy" enjoys a certain vogue among intellectuals, particularly philosophers. But generally their use of the term seems not to be governed by any rational rule. Yet there are indications of a growing sense of the importance of analogy; the term appears, often mysteriously, in a surprisingly large number of the really deep books of recent years. Analogy is central in our philosophical knowledge of things, central, too, in our conceptions of the nature of God. This is so because there is an analogy in the existence of things, linking them all, even the most diverse, to one another.

More and more thinkers are coming to recognize this fact, however vaguely; but among those who recognize it, there exist very different ideas about what analogy is: what

---

[1] J. S. Mill, *A System of Logic* (London, 1868), II, 86. Mill's *Logic* was first published in 1843.

it means in itself, what it means for human knowledge. And among those who concede, and even insist upon, the intellectual value of analogy, we find radical disagreements. Note, for instance, such counter-statements as these: Analogy is a metaphysical category; analogy is not any kind of category; analogy is a form of logical argument; [2] analogy is not a form of argument (or a form of anything whatever); analogy is a dialectical concept, whose chief function is a hierarchizing one; [3] analogy, basically, is not any sort of concept; analogy is a mathematical principle, useful in metaphysics and especially in cosmology; analogy is not a mathematical principle and it has no proper use in cosmology at all.

Now although in the lingo of philosophers "analogy" sometimes has about it an aura of almost unintelligible mystery, the word does evoke in everyone's mind a vaguely similar notion, the notion of resemblance or likeness. Everybody understands that "analogy" is a kind of likeness. Everybody understands also that likeness is or implies some sort of relation. But there are as many kinds of likeness as types of things like one another, and as many types of relation as kinds of things related. Then where in this whole realm of likenesses and relations does analogy come in? This is our problem: What sort of likeness is analogy, and what role, if any, does it have in philosophy? What role does it have in *existence?*

---

[2] This is now, and for some years has been, the most commonly held opinion.

[3] This conception has its roots in Plato, and is developed interestingly by some modern philosophers. But it is still formally a logical view and therefore has no proper place in a discussion of the metaphysics of analogy, which this book purports to be.

B. Notes on Some Common Uses of Analogy

The purpose of these notes is simply to clear the ground for the discussion of philosophical analogy. They are not to be considered as so many treatises. Each of the following topics (Popular Analogies, Analogy in Logic, Analogy in Science, Analogy in Mathematics) deserves a separate treatise. This is especially true of the last three. Here are vast problems that are not even broached. These large subjects have received only an abridged treatment. But the following summary observations are designed to serve merely as general approaches to the doctrine of analogy in philosophy. They do sketch a line of development toward that doctrine, however, and they should be read in that light.

1. POPULAR ANALOGIES

In ordinary everyday speech "analogy" may express almost any sort of likeness. There seems to be no set rule to tell us when to say "analogy" and when to say "resemblance" or some similar word. For instance, we say that father and son are "like" each other, not that they are "analogous"; but the elephant's trumpet and man's hand are "analogous" and not "similar." It is true that in some cases "resemblance" is used to designate a certain likeness of form or quality or kind, whereas "analogy" is applied to similarities of relations or functions. Although this distinction is only a matter of usage and is in no sense definitive, one might suggest that it could serve as a handy rule of thumb.

In biology, for example, analogous organs are defined

in terms of similarity in function (coupled with difference in origin or phylogenetic history), homologous organs in terms of similarity in origin or phylogenetic history alone.[4] When Darwin speaks of "analogical resemblances" he means precisely those external similarities which arise from adaptation to environmental conditions.[5] So here we find the notion of analogy linked with the idea of similarity in function or behavior. But unfortunately there are other fields of knowledge to which our "rule" cannot be consistently applied. Thus in modern psychology we find the term "analogies of sensation" used as a synonym for synesthesias, that is, associations between certain sensations or sense-perceptions; for example, the association of color with sound (color-hearing), of personal likes and dislikes with numbers, etc.[6] Everyone experiences and manufactures such "analogies." Poetry and fiction abound in them. But obviously they consist merely in likenesses which are in the main only subjective.

"Analogy" also has been used to indicate that kind of primitive logic which is characteristic of undeveloped stages of human mentality: the habit, deeper than the language of words and underlying their use and formation, of comparing things with one another, of tracing resemblances and noting contrasts.[7] Although in this sense "analogy" designates a mental function, in the underlying

---

[4] Cf. J. M. Baldwin, *Dictionary of Philosophy, Psychology and Scientific Method* (New York, 1911), I, 40 ff.; A. Lalande, *Vocabulaire technique et critique de la philosophie* (Paris, 1928), I, 45, (D), (C).

[5] *Origin of Species* (1st ed., 1859), chap. 13, pp. 427 ff.

[6] Cf. Baldwin, *op. cit.*, II, 654 f.

[7] Cf. J. Jastrow, *Fact and Fable in Psychology* (Boston and New York, 1900), p. 236, in chapter entitled "The Natural History of Analogy."

substantive meaning of the term, "analogy" here signifies that imperfect likeness between things, whether real or imaginary, on the basis of which comparisons can be made. Of course in our practical life we continually use such "analogies," and they are generally a reliable guide, allowing us to invent associations between things and aiding us thereby in classifying them empirically with a view to their use. Analogy in this vague and loose everyday sense has been aptly termed "popular analogy." [8]

The comparisons commonly used by literary people and by teachers are merely a more sophisticated type of the same thing. But imaginative comparison can play havoc if it is allowed to enter the philosophical field.[9] It is evident that illustrative and imaginative comparisons can be called analogies only in a very imprecise sense. Nor do the linguists help us with their expositions of "analogy-formations," or associations of linguistic forms,[10] for they conceive analogy as simply likeness of external (verbal) form.

In fact, the only common meaning that can be abstracted from the cases of "analogy" reviewed thus far is the idea of likeness in general. And since things are like only because they are different, it follows that in each case

[8] M. T-L. Penido, Le rôle de l'analogie en théologie dogmatique, p. 13. Leibnitz saw a sort of "analogy" between the knowledge, reason, understanding of brute animals, and some men. (Nouveaux essais, Bk. III, in Erdmann, Opera phil., 1841: pp. 311–312a, 391b).

[9] The notion of God as an immense container holding everything in the universe, as the Ocean of Being, the All, is a case in point. (Cf. P. M. de Munnynck, O. P., "L'Analogie métaphysique," pp. 130 f.)

[10] E.g., see Otto Jespersen, Language, Its Nature, Development and Origin, pp. 70, 93 f., 128–30, 164, 290; Baldwin, Dict. of Phil., Psych. & Scientific Method, pp. 41 f.; G. Middleton, An Essay on Analogy in Syntax (London: Longmans, 1892), pp. 7–11.

"analogy" has meant likeness mingled with unlikeness: a certain dissimilar similarity or similar dissimilarity. It cannot be claimed that this sweeping idea brings us very close to an accurate understanding of analogy. It may be said that no such understanding is possible because the word has no clear meanings. But, quite apart from the definite evidence to the contrary that is to be found in dictionaries, it is reasonable to assume that this word would not have been invented had there been no specific use for it.

The logicians, obviously, ought to be able to tell us something clear and definite.

2. ANALOGY IN LOGIC

In the *Prior Analytics* (Bk. II, chap. 24) Aristotle distinguishes argument by example (παράδειγμα) from induction on the one hand and from syllogism on the other, stating that in the case of παράδειγμα the argument does not proceed from the part to the whole, nor from the whole to the part, but from the part to the part. In short, he reduced the paradigmatic type of argument to an inference by partial induction which proceeds from one or more facts not to a universal conclusion, but to a particular conclusion based on some resemblance between the cases or facts. To use his own illustration: The war between the Thebans and the Phocians was a destructive enterprise; but these two are neighboring peoples (the point of resemblance); hence a war of the Athenians against the neighboring Thebans would be a destructive enterprise. Aristotle remarks that such argument is more rhetorical than scientific. Essentially it is only a method of persuasion by example.[11] Logically it is only a way of arguing from an observed resemblance to the probability of a conclusion based on that resemblance. Aristotle uses a fitting analogy when he says that example is related to induction as the enthymeme to syllogism.[12]

Now Aristotle never uses the term ἀναλογία in dealing with this type of argument. Yet it is precisely what is now commonly called the "argument from analogy" or "reasoning from analogy." For example, Ueberweg simply calls Aristotle's παράδειγμα "the inference of analogy" or "inference from analogy."[13] Maritain likewise sees in "reasoning by analogy" essentially nothing more than in Aristotle's *exemplum:* an imperfect induction which concludes from the particular to the particular in virtue of a resemblance.[14] It can yield no necessary conclusions.

Most modern books on logic contain no suggestion that there may be a type of analogical reasoning which would not consist in arguing from partial resemblances or in manipulating figures of speech. The rhetorical argument, based on a "loose identity of relations," that is, on a metaphorical proportion (colony : mother country : : child : mother), is discussed,[15] and divergent views of the argu-

---

[11] *Rhetorica, I,* 1357 b25–1358 a3.
[12] *Anal. Post.* I, 1.
[13] *System of Logic,* pp. 491–505.
[14] *An Introduction to Logic,* p. 286. Maritain points out that reasoning by resemblance has nothing to do with analogical *knowledge.* In a sense it is true that reasoning from resemblance is an element in all inductive reasoning: for even induction by simple enumeration would not be possible unless the instances enumerated had some common character, some points of resemblance to one another (cf. L. S. Stebbing, *A Modern Introduction to Logic,* p. 249).
[15] H. W. B. Joseph, *An Introduction to Logic,* pp. 495 ff.

ment by analogy are presented; but it seems to be generally agreed that analogical reasoning is not conclusive. The conflicting opinions of Bernard Bosanquet and of F. C. S. Schiller are instructive on this point.

Bosanquet insists that "analogy is essentially an argument about the significance of a type." [16] But it is evident that he has in mind merely the old argument from resemblance. Despite his view that "in analogy the examples or the properties are to be weighed and not counted," [17] like the rest, he holds that analogical argument is inconclusive: "the formal defect of analogy . . . is expressed by the 'probably' inserted in the conclusion, which indicates a coherence under conditions not precisely known"; [18] and indeed "analogy," he says, is never demonstrative.[19] Mr. F. C. S. Schiller, on the other hand, holds that, if "analogy" is not demonstrative, then no argument is.

Schiller maintains that "every argument . . . is really analogical," and that, if analogical argument is not "formally valid," no argument can be formally valid.[20] Every argument, he holds, is really analogical because it is based on similarity or partial identity between "cases" of a "law" or "rule"; that is, every argument is analogical because it is based on resemblance, whether it proceeds from a number of cases to a law or rule (induction) or in the reverse order (deduction). But no two cases are absolutely identical. Hence every argument from case to case must rest on

---

[16] Bernard Bosanquet, *Logic*, II, 87, in chap. 3, entitled "Analogy."
[17] *Ibid.*, p. 100.
[18] *Ibid.*, p. 92.
[19] *Ibid.*, p. 100.
[20] *Formal Logic.*, p. 342. Cf. Schiller's *Logic for Use*, pp. 347–52.

an "analogy." Even if taken in the strict sense of an identity of ratios, he asserts, the analogical argument may still be erroneous, because even here we have to do with cases in relation, and whether or not they are "good" cases depends upon whether or not they are identified as cases of A. This, however, "is merely the risk which . . . all reasoning takes."

Even as regards analogy taken in the strict sense of identity of ratio, we can have no absolute assurance, Schiller claims, that the argument based thereon will be true, because our determination of the "cases" of a "law" or "rule," that is to say, of a generic principle (or a universal properly so called) will always entail the possibility of error.[21] Thus it seems to be implied that this common notion, which we may call A, will be a generic idea, serving as the mean in the proportional "analogy" in question: in other words, it appears that when Schiller speaks of "cases" he means members of a genus or class. His "analogy," therefore, would be a likeness of relations between things sharing a common generic notion. If this is so, then Schiller's analogical argument is either the ordinary argument from resemblance or an argument from an identity of ratios between cases which are similar because they share a common generic character. But in either case, that argument will apply only within the order of things which can

---

[21] This argument is patently false if applied to identical ratios in mathematics. Here there is no question of determining "cases" of a "rule" or "law." This use of the term "identity of ratios" is illegitimate. In any instance, if there is such identity, it is either seen or it is not; there is no "risk of error." But I believe Schiller actually had in mind not identity of ratio but likeness of qualitative relations between similar things; in arguing from which there is indeed always ample risk of error.

be ranged in classes or put under laws or rules, and hence considered either as members of the former or as cases of the latter. Nor will it necessarily be conclusive.

However, if being (that which *is* or can *be* in any and every manner) escapes the limitations intrinsic to the nature of the genus or category or class and in this sense transcends them, yet is found in them all intrinsically,[22] and if there is a science which treats of "being as being," its properties and causes, then we should expect to find proportions in that order which would be the real basis of analogical knowledge. But analogical reasoning seems to have been taken as the exclusive province of logic. The majority of modern thinkers make no mention of analogical reasoning in metaphysics. Apparently, if there is such a thing in that science (assuming the latter to exist), it will be as inconclusive as the logicians say it is in logic.

3. ANALOGY IN SCIENCE

It is generally recognized that the role of analogical reasoning in scientific investigation and discovery is a vital one. John Locke was well aware of this fact: "In things which sense cannot discover, analogy is the great rule of probability." He would even apply his "rule of analogy" to speculation about "things above us and our observation." In this way we may attain some probable knowledge. Furthermore, such probability "is the best conduct of rational experiments and the rise of hypothesis . . . ; and a wary reasoning from analogy leads us often into the

---

[22] Every class is limited by differentiating or specifying characters, whereas being (the act, "to be") is proper to everything which is in any way whatsoever.

discovery of truths and useful productions, which would
otherwise lie concealed." [23]

That this is so we have abundant evidence. It is a fact
that "analogy" has been of great value in suggesting experiments, observations, and hypotheses which have led to
important discoveries and even positive scientific conclusions: for example, Descartes' perception of the analogy
between algebraic and geometrical relationships which
led to important discoveries in modern mathematics; and
Franklin's "analogies" between lightning and electricity.[24]
Many important scientific hypotheses grew out of the discovery of unexplained resemblances which appeared too
striking to be accidental.[25] Indeed, it has even been said [26]
that this sort of "analogical inference" is "probably the
most fruitful source of suggestions, of hypotheses, that is,
of tentative inferences. . . ." In short, while "analogy"
is not itself a type of proof, it may lead to both deductive
and inductive proofs.

It is true that analogy, as understood by the modern
scientist, is essentially suggestive, and that "in the more
advanced sciences analogy plays a relatively unimportant
part," whereas in the "less developed sciences" it may be
an extremely significant factor. The point is that "the fin-
ished [scientific] results are supported by inductive evidence," and that "the analogies by which they may have

[23] *An Essay Concerning Human Understanding* (London: Ward, Lock & Co.),
IV, chap. 16, sect. 12, pp. 564 ff.
[24] See the excellent article, "Analogy," by Professor Abraham Wolf in the
Encyclopaedia Britannica, 14th ed., Vol. I. Cf. also J. S. Mill, *A System of Logic*,
II, 92–94.
[25] Cf. L. S. Stebbing, *op. cit.*, p. 255.
[26] A. Wolf, *art. cit.*, p. 865.

been first suggested are no part of the evidence, and are of vital interest only as incidents in the mental history of the builder rather than in the structure of the building." [27]

Almost every modern book on logic or scientific method includes a section on "analogy" or "reasoning from analogy" or the "argument from analogy" or "analogical inference"; the titles vary but the doctrine is in a sense the same. I mean it is essentially the same as regards the conception of the nature of analogy itself. For despite the many differences of opinion concerning the precise character and function of the so-called argument from analogy, it appears on all sides that at least for most modern logicians, philosophers, and scientists, "analogy" primarily and fundamentally signifies resemblance or likeness or partial identity between things or between certain of their characters, properties, or accidents.[28] Of course I am not

[27] *Ibid.* Cf. Joseph, *op. cit.*, chap. 24; and article entitled "Analogy in Logic," by Professors R. Adamson and Josiah Royce, in Baldwin, *op. cit.*, I, 41.

[28] Charles Mercier is a rare exception—and he is a medical doctor! In fact, Doctor Mercier, as far as I know, is the only modern writer on logic who insists that this idea is completely mistaken and who wants "analogy" restored to its original and proper sense of "comparison of ratios." In his *A New Logic* he takes the logicians to task for having introduced the notion of analogy as a comparison between *terms* or *things* based on likeness and for having departed from the only correct meaning of the word, which was that given it by Aristotle and by Euclid, namely, *proportion* (p. 345). Mercier uses the terms *proportion, ratio,* and *relation* synonymously. "Every comparison of relations is an Analogy," he says (p. 347), "and every Analogy is a comparison of relations"; and it is "indifferent to the nature of its terms."

Mercier is of course exclusively concerned with analogy in *logic,* but his observations on the radical difference between inductive and deductive reasoning, in the ordinary sense, and analogical thinking, do not apply merely to logic: "In Induction and Deduction, the proposition, having been stated, is then modified *secundum artem* and appears in the conclusion in a new form. In Analogy, the proposition is stated merely. When it is stated, the reasoning process is complete. The reasoning process is the discernment of likeness, or the discrimination of difference, between two Ratios, and the proposition expresses the likeness or difference; and when the likeness or difference is stated,

suggesting that these thinkers are unaware that analogy also can mean something else. On the contrary Royce lists four senses of the term.[29] But I find the main emphasis put on analogy in the sense above stated.

It is well to point out that in this running commentary on some typically modern notions of analogy, we have witnessed a certain development toward clarity and precision. It will be recalled that we started out with "analogy" in the sense of any sort of likeness at all, even imaginary or fictitious. The notion has now been narrowed down to that of real or objective likeness upon which "wary reasonings," or even happy guesses, of great value for the development of the empirical sciences (and of mathematics) have been and still are based.[30] But, as we have seen, these reasonings, no matter how wary they may be, can never of themselves yield objective certainty. So, although "analogy" has a more definite meaning in the observational or empirical sciences, an element of the vagueness of analogy in the popular sense remains; because "reasoning by analogy" consists simply in passing from some partial resemblance recognized between two or more things or "characters" to other aspects whose resemblance is as yet unexplored.

Basically, most, if not all, empirical hypotheses rest

---

the Analogy is complete; the reasoning process is at an end. This dissimilarity between the process of Analogy and the processes of Induction and Deduction may be the reason why Analogy, as understood in the Aristotelian and Euclidean sense, is excluded from all books on Logic" (p. 349).

[29] *Art. cit.*

[30] J. M. Keynes (*A Treatise on Probability.* London, 1921, p. 241) states: "Scientific method . . . is mainly devoted to discovering means of so heightening the known analogy that we may dispense with the methods of pure induction." "Analogy" has here the usual sense of similarity between things or terms.

upon generalized "analogies." This partly accounts for the element of probability in scientific conclusions arrived at by methods of empirical investigation. And as every scientist knows, in inferring the likeness of certain characters from the likeness of others, there is always the risk of overlooking or neglecting some concealed yet essential traits, only to arrive at resemblances which are in fact merely accidental; a risk inherent in the very nature and procedure of positive science. Partial identity in the order of sensible reality is the type of objective likeness which is the basis of this kind of scientific thinking, and which founds what has been aptly called "experimental analogy." [31]

4. Analogy in Mathematics

Many philosophers and logicians tell us that analogy originally meant something quite different from any of its meanings we have examined thus far. Mill, for instance, lists two senses of the term: "resemblance of relations" ("the primitive acceptation given to it by mathematicians") and "any sort of resemblance." The latter is "the more usual sense." In the first meaning, he says, analogy can serve as the basis of an argument having "no inherent inferiority of conclusiveness." [32] Joseph observes that "analogy meant originally identity of relation," and in the case of mathematics, where the terms and relations are quantitative, reasoning from analogy is necessary, "like any other mathematical reasoning." But analogy in mathematics is "more commonly called proportion." [33] Schiller

[31] Penido, Le rôle, p. 19.
[32] A System of Logic, p. 86.
[33] An Introduction to Logic, p. 492.

states that "arguing by analogy originally meant arguing from an equality or identity of ratios, but it is now commonly taken more laxly as arguing from any sort of likeness. . . ." [34] Wolf points out that analogy originally meant proportion in the quantitative sense, e.g., 3:4 : : 9:12; so that analogy in this sense could serve as a basis for "reliable inferences." [35] Adamson and Royce hold that "all derivative senses of the term bear traces of its original restriction to resemblance in relations." [36] Now "analogy" is simply Greek for "proportion." [37]

In Euclid's *Elements* there is a complete theory of pro-

---

[34] *Formal Logic,* p. 341.

[35] *Loc. cit.,* p. 654. Wolf remarks that in mathematics "analogy" has now been replaced by "proportion," except in Napier's analogies," still used in spherical geometry.

[36] *Art. cit.,* in Baldwin, p. 41.

[37] The word "analogy" comes from the Greek ἀναλογία, which means proportion. But ἀναλογία is itself made up of the preposition ἀνα and the noun λόγος. Greek scholars point out that ἀνα used as a prefix in composition with another word has several shades of meaning. One interpretation is that ἀνα with λόγος has the sense of "according to"; so that, taking ἀνα in the sense of due relation, ἀναλογία will mean "according to due relation" (see *Catholic Encyclopedia* revised. New York, 1936, I, 466). But it is more illuminating to see in ἀνα the notion of a backward relation (and in fact ἀνα in compounds is often used with a reversing force), roughly corresponding to the prefix *retro* in Latin. Λόγος signifies both a concept or an idea and a word expressing a concept or an idea, its equivalent in Latin being either *ratio* or *oratio*, according as λόγος means an idea or concept, or a word expressing an idea or concept. Thus in this strict etymological sense, ἀναλογία signifies a reciprocal relation between ideas: a proportion, a relation of ratios. When preceded by κατα (κατα τὴν ἀναλογίαν) the phrase has the sense of proportionality. Other senses of the term ἀναλογία, implying resemblance, are derived from this primary and strict one. The Latin equivalent, *analogia,* has the same meaning as the Greek original from which it is derived. Quintilian gives as its synonyms *proportio, convenientia, similitudo;* and it may be rendered into English as *proportion,* likeness, resemblance, analogy. (See Liddell Scott, *A Greek-English Lexicon;* Oxford, 1901; and Freund-Loverett, *Lexicon of the Latin Language;* Philadelphia, 1912.) For an excellent translation of Euclid and a penetrating commentary on the whole theory of proportion, see *The Thirteen Books of Euclid's Elements* (Eng. tr. by Sir Thomas Heath), Vol. II, esp. pp. 112–17, 120–24, 131 f., and Heath's *A History of Greek Mathematics* (Oxford, 1921), Vol. I, esp. pp. 325–27, 384 f.

portion which applies to all sorts of magnitudes or quantities. The basic conception of proportion which we find in the *Elements* is that of identity of ratio: it is a precise relation between quantities, whether that relation is geometric or arithmetic; whether it involves lines, surfaces, volumes, whole or "irrational" numbers; in fact, any type of magnitude or quantity, continuous or discrete. The same conception of mathematical proportion is expressed by St. Thomas in the phrase *certa habitudo unius quantitatis ad alteram*,[38] a determinate relation of one quantity to another. The relation may be a simple one, involving only two terms, or a "proportion" involving at least four.[39]

St. Thomas, following Aristotle, uses "analogy" and "proportion" interchangeably.[40] But ordinarily we think

[38] *S. th.*, I, 12, 1, ad 4; cf. *De ver.*, VIII, 1, ad 6; III *Sent.*, I, 1, 1, ad 3; IV *Sent.*, XLIX, 1, 1, ad 6.

[39] To avoid confusion, it is necessary to point out that for Euclid and the ancients generally, *proportion* did not have the same extension as its English derivative. The Latin *proportio*, indeed, includes only two terms (e.g., see St. Thomas, V *Eth.*, V, 940). Hence *proportio* corresponds to our "relation," while our mathematical "proportion" requires at least four terms. Strictly speaking, therefore, "simple proportion" (*proportio simplex*) should be translated by the term "relation," "composite proportion" (*proportio composita seu proportionalitas*) by the term "proportion."
Proportionalitas signifies the "equality of two proportions" (St. Thomas, *loc. cit.*), and hence corresponds to our geometric "proportion," signifying the equality of two relations with respect to the quotient of the related terms (4 : 2 :: 6 : 3). F. A. Blanche remarks ("Note sur le sens de quelques locutions concernant l'analogie dans le langage de Saint Thomas d'Aquin," p. 55) that the Thomistic *analogia proportionalitatis* ought to be called "analogy of proportion," whereas *analogia proportionis* is equivalent to "analogy of relation." This is of course true; but to alter, merely for the sake of verbal exactness, a terminology which has become traditional, might result merely in bringing confusion into the whole doctrine of Thomistic analogy, where "analogy of proportion" means something very different from "analogy of proportionality." (Cf. Penido, *Le rôle*, p. 17.)

[40] For instance, in his Commentary on the *Metaphysics*, we find the expression *proportione vel analogia* (V *Meta.*, VIII, 879; cf. *De ver.*, VIII, 1, ad 6; *S. th.*, I, 12, 1, ad 4); in his Commentary on the *Ethics*, the phrase *secundum analogiam, idest proportionem eamdem*; (I *Eth.*, VII, 96; cf. I *Phys.*, X, 7;

of proportion as belonging primarily and in the strict sense to mathematics, and in particular to geometry. Hence if analogy means proportion, then it seems that, if analogy has any properly scientific application in philosophy, this must consist in some sort of extension of *mathematical* analogy into the domain of philosophical science. One may well ask how any such extension can be valid. Specifically this raises two questions: (1) Where there are no bodies, how can there be any quantity? (2) Where there is no quantity, how can there be any proportions or "analogies" in a truly scientific sense: in any sense other than a merely literary or metaphorical one? Yet if "analogy" does have a properly philosophical role, it clearly cannot be that of even the most suggestive symbol or myth.

Nevertheless, "proportion" signifies a definite, precise, determinate relation of one dimensive quantity (quantity of mass or extension), whether continuous or discrete, to another; for instance, the relation of a surface to a surface or of a number to a number, including the "incommensurable magnitudes." But this is proportion in the "primitive sense"; in technical language, it is proportion according to the first imposition of the name.[41] In this sense "proportion" is univocal: it applies only to the class of dimensive quantities, in respect of which it always has the same meaning, namely, determinate relation of one such

XIII, 9; I *De C. et M.,* XIV, 3-4; *Comp. Th.,* XXVII; *De princ. nat.,* in fine); and in the Disputed Question *on Truth,* the categorical statement that *"according to analogy* means nothing else than according to proportion"—*secundum analogiam, quod nihil est aliud dictu quam secundum proportionem* (*De ver.,* II, 11, c.).

41 Cf. J. M. Ramirez, O.P., "De Analogia secundum Doctrinam Aristotelico—thomisticam," *La Ciencia Tomista,* XXIV (1921), 23.

quantity to another; and this holds whether or not the quantity in question is commensurable or incommensurable in the commonly accepted mathematical sense.[42] It is a question simply of ratio: relation between two dimensive quantities of the same kind. Of course the ratio need not be expressible in exact numerical units. The mathematical notion of ratio, however, is formally univocal.[43]

A genus is predicated of its "inferiors" (the things that come under it or are included in it) *secundum rationem omnino eamdem,* according to a formality identically the same. Thus "living organism" is predicated univocally of horse and of cow, designating the common "form" or "nature" in them both in virtue of which they belong to the same genus. This doctrine of univocal predication is exemplified in ordinary mathematics in the most elementary way. For instance, in a typical proportion (or proportionality) such as $6:2 :: 21:7$, it is evident that the common notion realized in both relations (triplicity) is univocal. There is no need to multiply examples. It is clear that all mathematical concepts in the domain of classical mathematics, at least, are univocal, because they apply only within the order of dimensive quantity, whether continuous or discrete; and in this sense of the term quantity is

---

[42] Cf. Heath, *History* . . . , I, 384, *et alibi passim.*

[43] St. Thomas, IV *Meta.,* I, 535 ff.; cf. X *Meta.,* III, 1966. Although there are "degrees" in the actual understanding of the meaning of any term, if that term is generic, it is formally or essentially univocal, because it then designates the same formal character in the things of which it is predicated. Thus, although there will always be diversity as regards the actual ("material") content of ideas present to the mind upon the interior evocation or outward expression of a name, there is, if the term is generic, identity as regards that which the name signifies formally. The psychological is distinct from the logical order.

generic. It is true that mathematical proportions (ratios) and proportionalities (proportions strictly so called) do exhibit a genuinely analogical "form" inasmuch as they bear upon the relations between entities rather than upon the entities themselves. But the terms of those relations are always univocal. If analogical concepts in the proper sense are those which are apt of their very nature to be realized in the order of existence according to essentially diverse modes, then mathematics has nothing to do with such concepts; and mathematical "analogies," consequently, are not true analogies but "univocities" in their guise. Perhaps it is because they look so much like analogies that they are so often mistaken for them.[44]

The object of the foregoing survey of some current and common uses of analogy has been to prepare the way for our inquiry into philosophical analogy.

"Analogy" signifies a certain likeness in difference. Perfect likeness in meaning (conceptual identity) is "univocity"; mere likeness in name (homonymity) is "pure equivocity." It is clear that analogy is a "mean" between these extremes.[45] But it may participate in them in diverse ways, thus giving rise to diverse "modes." These modes are reducible to three: analogy of inequality, analogy of attribution, and analogy of proportionality, the latter

---

[44] It is evident that none of these points have been sufficiently developed. But in dealing with a problem like that of analogy, it is, I believe, impossible to give satisfactory consideration to any single point taken separately. It may not be possible, therefore, to frame significant objections or to ask relevant questions until the entire book, or at least the main expository part of it, has been read.

[45] Cf. St. Thomas, IX *Meta.*, III, 2197; IV *Meta.*, I, 535.

being itself divided into two modes, the one metaphorical, the other proper.[46] This work will treat of those "modes" in that order.[47]

C. Abbreviations Used in the Footnotes

1. REFERENCES TO THE WORKS OF ST. THOMAS [1]

In referring to his Commentaries, the number of the Book will appear before the title, followed by the first subdivision in roman and the others in arabic numerals. In the case of other works, the first division, whether Part, Book, Lecture (or Reading), Distinction, Question, or Chapter, will be indicated in large romans, except where (as in many of the Opuscula) there is only one division,—into

---

[46] Cf. Cajetan, *De nominum analogia*, I, pp. 4 f.; III, p. 25. See below, chap. 22, sect. 3, where the "participation" in question is dealt with in detail.

[47] There are conceivably other modes of analogy having some philosophical significance. The scheme of this whole essay is based on the acceptance of Cajetan's division, not because it is considered exhaustive, nor because it is viewed as the only valid or valuable one, but because it is held to provide the best available framework for sound speculation on this problem. The fact that this division faithfully represents the thought of St. Thomas on analogy alone suffices to render the division suspect in the eyes of some, while validating it in the eyes of others. But all such reactions are in themselves philosophically irrelevant.

The first chapters of the first three parts are primarily expository; in the main, the others are illustrative and critical commentaries upon the analogies in question. But all the chapters of the last part, except two (chapters 20 and 21), are primarily expository. The expository chapters are of course intrinsically the most important because it is in them that the doctrine of analogy itself is presented and expounded. The other chapters, being in the category of illustration, commentary, and criticism, are, so to speak, extrinsic to the doctrine itself. They are included for the purpose of elucidating the various modes of analogy by indicating their role, for weal or woe, in actual philosophies and in certain common types of philosophical systems. Some theological examples also are introduced, but only in order to illustrate or clarify philosophical points.

[1] The majority of references in this book are to these works. In order to simplify those references as much as possible, the name of "St. Thomas" will usually be omitted from them.

Chapters or Headings or Topics—in which case romans will be used. Titles of works also will be abbreviated. The following should make this system clear.

Title of Work	*Example of Reference Used*
Commentary on the "Metaphysics" of Aristotle [2]	I *Meta.,* I, 1 (First Book, lecture 1, number 1)
Commentary on Aristotle's "Nichomachean Ethics" [3]	I *Eth.,* etc. (Same system)
Disputed Questions, *De anima* [4]	*De an.,* etc. (Same system)
Commentary on Aristotle's "Physics"	I *Phys.,* I (First Book, lecture 1)
Commentary on Aristotle's "Posterior Analytics"	I *Anal. Post.,* I (Same as above)
Commentary on Peter Lombard's "Sentences"	I *Sent.,* I, 1, 1, ad 1 (First Book, distinction 1, question 1, article 1, reply to first objection)
Disputed Questions, *De potentia Dei*	*De pot.,* I, 1, ad 1 (Question 1, article 1, reply to first objection)
Disputed Questions, *De veritate*	*De ver.,* etc. (Same system)
Disputed Questions, *De malo*	*De malo,* etc. (Same system)
Opusculum, *On Dionysius' "De divinis nominibus"*	*De div. nom.,* I, 1, 1, (Chapter 1, lecture 1, number 1)
Opusculum, *On Boethius' "De Trinitate"*	*De Trin.,* I, 1, c. (Question 1, article 1, body of the article)
Opusculum, *On Boethius' "De Hebdomadibus"*	*De Heb.,* I (Chapter 1; no further division)
Opusculum, *De ente et essentia*	*De ente,* I (Chapter 1; no further division)
Opusculum, *De principiis naturae*	*De princ. nat., in fine* (i.e., towards the end; no chapter or other divisions)

[2] For references to paragraph numbers, see Cathala edition (Taurini: Marietti, 1935).

[3] For references to paragraph numbers, see Pirotta edition (Taurini: Marietti, 1934).

[4] For references to paragraph numbers, see Pirotta edition.

Title of Work	Example of Reference Used
Quodlibetal Questions	Quodl., I, 1, 1, ad 1 (First "Quodlibetum," question 1, article 1, reply to first objection)
Summa theologica	S. th., I, 1, 1, c. and ad 1. (Part One, question 1, article 1, body of the article and reply to first objection); or S. th., I-II, etc. (First Section of Part Two)
Summa Contra Gentiles	C.G., I, 1 (First Book, chapter 1)

2. REFERENCES TO OTHER WORKS (BOOKS AND ARTICLES) LISTED IN THE BIBLIOGRAPHY

To eliminate needless repetition of details, only the titles of such works are given, along with the book or volume or chapter number (where necessary), and the page reference. Other pertinent information—periodical in which found, place where published, date of publication, number of edition, etc.,—is given in the Bibliography. In most cases, titles are abbreviated after the initial reference, although some very long ones have been abbreviated from the start. Titles of books are italicized; for titles of articles quotation marks are used.

Part One

ANALOGY OF INEQUALITY

CHAPTER I

WHAT THIS ANALOGY IS

1. A Difficulty about the Doctrine of Univocity

ACCORDING to the doctrine of univocity, that which is formally signified by a generic or specific term is identically the same in respect of all things to which it properly applies. This proposition appears extremely questionable. How can one possibly be sure that any concept is perfectly "univocal" in that sense? For it is obvious that different people at different times, or even the same people at different times, do not have absolutely the same understanding of that which is designated by any term. Sufficient refutation of this theory seems to be supplied by the mere consideration of the multiple associations which the same word has for the same person at different stages of his life. Since there is all manner of diversity in the actual apprehension of the meaning of a term, what grounds are there for the assertion of any rigid or static "univocity" in our concepts?

This difficulty, however, rests on a confusion between the material and the formal aspects of knowing. For materially (psychologically) speaking, no two cognitive acts have an identical content, but formally (logically), some cognitive acts have an identical formal object. It is true that we have no perfect comprehension of anything; yet we do have some definitive knowledge of some aspects of generic things. Thus, irrespective of the diversity of content in the actual conception of any generic or specific object, a basic, formal univocality is supposed if the concept has been grasped at all. Were this not so, ordinary conversation would be impossible. For instance, the statement, "this is a typewriter," would be unintelligible if the word typewriter were not univocal, that is, if it did not have an identical minimal meaning as applied to all typewriters; for in that case no one could be sure what I was talking about. The "univocal" character of terms (and all universals—generic and specific concepts—are univocal) must be understood formally, as designating, apart from all particular determinations or differences, solely that identical intelligible element or structure which they each denote.[1]

2. ANALOGY OF GENERIC PREDICATION

It does not follow that there is no sort of analogy between the members of one and the same genus. Different species can be validly placed in the same genus provided that each species actually shares the same generic formality. But they are not thereby rendered equal in their actual natures.[2] Thus, whereas all species are alike

[1] This argument simply aims to show that concepts have an objective content independent of the psychological modalities of thought, and that this content, in some cases at least, is univocal. Of course it is not to be inferred that we do not also communicate *analogical* concepts.

[2] As St. Thomas cryptically puts it (*De malo*, II, 9, ad 16), "All animals are equally animals but they are not all equal animals, for one animal is greater and more perfect than another." Cf. *S. th.*, I–II, 61, 1, ad 1.

inasmuch as they share a "character" which is univocally the same, they differ inasmuch as the mode of participation proper to each species is diverse from that proper to every other. Moreover, these diverse modes may constitute a hierarchy, introducing gradation or participation according to varying degrees of perfection.[3] In such cases, then, there will be likeness mingled with unlikeness; hence a certain "analogy." And this is what St. Thomas calls analogy *secundum esse et non secundum intentionem:* analogy according to being but not according to intention.[4]

The example he uses is that of the term "body" predicated of "corruptible" (terrestrial, elemental) bodies and of "incorruptible" (celestial, quintessential) bodies. The illustration is of course borrowed from the physics of his day. But it is only an example and does not affect the point he is making,[5] namely, that a generic idea applies equally and in the same sense to all its inferiors. Thus, the logician, who is concerned only with "second intentions," may say that any genus is predicated univocally of the species under it, disregarding the fact that their actual mode of existence may be essentially diverse. For instance, logically speaking, "body" is univocally predicated of a baseball and of a sphere, though the former has physical matter whereas the latter has only "intelligible matter." From the point of view of logic, there is no reason why things which are actually or physically diverse

---

[3] See the illuminating text in *S. th.*, I, 4, 3, c.

[4] I *Sent.*, XIX, 5, 2, ad 1.

[5] As Dr. Gerald B. Phelan shows (p. 32, in *St. Thomas and Analogy*), one may substitute any other terms provided they illustrate the matter in question; e.g., baseball and sphere.

in genus may not be brought under the same generic concept.[6] For the logician considers essences only in their mental existence in concepts, whereas the natural philosopher and the metaphysician consider essences from the standpoint of their actual existence in things.[7]

Hence, in the case of analogy "according to being but not according to intention," there is analogy inasmuch as there is diversity in mode of realization, but there is no analogy in respect of the formality which is shared or of the intention which is realized diversely. This, therefore, is simply "analogy" of generic predication (*analogia generis*). "Genus is predicated equally of species as regards intention, but not always as regards being";[8] so that things which are diverse in nature may be included in the same *logical* genus.[9]

3. PREDICATION "BY PRIORITY AND POSTERIORITY"

Although as a rule only the most general genera and those akin to them (e.g., quantity and quality, body) are said to be analogous in this sense, every genus, the formal character of which exists more perfectly in one subspecies than in another, can be so termed. There will be degrees of

---

[6] X *Meta.*, XII, 2142, 2144.
[7] St. Thomas, *De Trin.*, VI, 3, c.; cf. *De pot.*, VII, 7, ad 1, *in contrarium;* I *Sent.*, XXXIII, 1, 1, ad 3.
[8] St. Thomas, II *Sent.*, III, 1, 5, ad 3.
[9] From the standpoint of nature, the term "body" predicated of the baseball and the geometrical sphere, is "intentionally" equivocal (i.e., it is analogical), because such things do not have a common matter; but, logically speaking, they are generically one. See St. Thomas, *S. th.*, I, 13, 10, ad 4, with I, 51, 1 and *De ver.*, XIV, 9, ad 4, where it is pointed out that intentional equivocity (*aequivocum a consilio*), as distinguished from pure equivocity (*aequivocum a casu*), is an analogical mode of predication. Cf. Cajetan, *De nom.* II, 20, notes 3, 4, and p. 21; St. Thomas, VIII *Phys.*, VIII.

perfection, therefore, in this sharing. Consequently the common generic term will be predicated "by priority and posteriority" (*per prius et posterius*) in the order of perfection.[10]

Cajetan remarks [11] that it is "now" customary to suppose that we are using synonymous expressions when we say that something is predicated "by priority and posteriority" and that it is predicated "analogically"; but this usage, he points out, is incorrect, because the former is wider in scope than the latter. That is to say, while all analogical predication is by priority and posteriority, not all such predication is properly analogical. Then is the sort of predication by priority and posteriority which we have in analogy of inequality authentically analogical? In a sense, the remainder of this Part will be devoted to solving that problem; yet an adequate (even though incomplete) solution of it will require an exposition of all the major philosophical modes of analogical predication.

4. Is ANALOGY OF INEQUALITY THE BASIC ANALOGY?

Likeness arises from communication in form; and when things communicate in the same form according to identically the same formality, there is perfect likeness; in other words, identity in essence. But "univocity" signifies identity in meaning, which, in turn, is based on identity in essence: that which is signified as univocal is that which is identical in essence; and things identical in essence are said to be perfectly alike. Basically, therefore, where there

[10] Cf. Cajetan, *De nom.*, I, 7 f.
[11] *Ibid.*, pp. 8 f.

is univocity, there is in this sense perfect likeness, and conversely.

We have said that analogy is a "mean" between equivocity and univocity. But if "equivocity" is mere likeness in name—homonymity—(for example, "pen" said of an enclosure for swine and of the instrument used for writing), then this formula seems nonsensical; for there are no purely "equivocal" concepts; there are only equivocal names and, presumably, the word "mean" designates a middle term or concept standing between two other types of concept. Which is true. But to say that "equivocity" signifies mere homonymity is to say that is signifies sheer conceptual diversity; because an equivocal term predicated of two or more objects is a term which signifies diverse concepts in each case. Therefore analogy is a mean between equivocity and univocity, in the sense that it participates in these extremes. Equivocity imports sheer diversity; univocity, sheer identity; analogy, a certain identity in diversity.[12]

This general, rough notion of the meaning of analogy seems to apply very well to "analogy of inequality," which does indeed entail a certain measure of diversity along with a definite element of identity. For this "analogy" consists precisely in that kind of imperfect likeness which arises from the unequal participation of things in a common generic character.

One of the basic assumptions of a certain type of philosophy ordinarily called "idealism" is that the ultimate terms of our knowledge are universal ideas. These ideas

[12] See chap. 22, sect. 3.

are usually named "categories." They are concepts having a high degree of generality; they are class-notions, genera. If, in the last analysis, human knowledge does revolve around and lead up to certain "ideal," categorial objects, then analogy must fundamentally be analogy of inequality, that is to say, analogy of generic predication.

To determine whether or not this is the case, it is evidently necessary, first of all, to give some satisfactory answer to the question of the orders or degrees of knowledge.

CHAPTER II

"ANALOGIA GENERIS" IN SCIENCE AND MATHEMATICS

1. THE FIRST TWO DEGREES OF ABSTRACTION

THE philosophic significance of analogy of inequality has been generally ignored, even by scholastic authors.[1] But this "analogy" obtains throughout an immense area of human knowledge; for it is found (or there is a basis for it) wherever there are specific or generic notions realized diversely in diverse things. This, for example, is the case in what are called the natural sciences.

All such sciences "operate" within the order of sensible nature. Although they aim to abstract from the strictly contingent and particular features of things and to envisage only those qualities, properties, and functions which are susceptible of empirical or experimental analysis, verification, and measurement, they remain within the realm of φύσις: the order of things composed of matter and form. But there is no science of the particular as such, of things in their concrete singularity. Science grasps the sin-

---

[1] This "analogy" is usually disposed of in a few short paragraphs, and very often not mentioned at all. As far as I know, Cajetan wrote more on it than anyone up to his time (d. 1534), namely, five paragraphs, about three small pages (in his *De nom. anal.*, I, 6–9). (An excellent brief exposition of the doctrine is found in G. B. Phelan's *St. Thomas and Analogy*, pp. 27 f., 30–35. But of course the wide scope of the topic and the time allowed for the lecture made it impossible for the author to delve into the philosophic implications of this pseudo-analogy.)

gular, indeed; but only through the universal. The universals of natural science, however, must be drawn from the material composites with which it deals; and they are therefore relative to those composites. The universality of those concepts, therefore, will not extend beyond the domain of φύσις.

Although the genus is not itself matter, it is abstracted from matter, and, although the "difference" (*differentia*) is not itself form, it is abstracted from form.[2] In natural substances, of course, matter does not exist apart from form nor form apart from matter: they are indissolubly bound together in the *res naturae* whose properties and operations natural science explores. Thus genus "is to" difference in the logical order, as matter "is to" form in the physical order. No properly generic or differential concept, therefore, can overstep the boundaries of the "physical" order.

The various sciences are specified (and hence differentiated from one another) by their formal objects. It is the business of "formal abstraction" to assign to each science its proper object.[3] Thus the philosophy of nature treats of the actions and passions of bodies, the laws of generation and corruption, of movement; and in this case what Maritain calls "the objective light under which a science attains its object"[4] is that type of intellectual "visualization"[5] whereby sensible nature itself is considered apart

2 St. Thomas, *De ente*, III.

3 There is a very important text on this point in the *Summa theol.* of St. Thomas: I, 85, 1, ad 2 (quoted by N. Balthasar in his *L'être et les principes métaphysiques*, p. 51, note 2.) Cf. J. Maritain, *Les degrés du savoir*, p. 75.

4 *Sept leçons sur l'être*, p. 89. Cf. Cajetan, *In I S. th.*, I, 3.

5 Philosophical abstraction consists properly not in subtraction or even in

from particular sensible things. This is the "first degree of abstraction." [6]

Leaving aside the various kinds of subordination or subalternation involved, it is clear that all the natural sciences somehow fall under that single science called by the ancients *physica*—the science of φύσις, that is, the science of sensible nature. But if *physica* itself falls under the first degree of abstraction, then so likewise will all the positive sciences of sensible nature. The latter accent the *sensible* aspects of nature and are devoted to the problem of determining their observable traits, whereas the philosophy of nature, as a philosophy, accents the *being* aspect of sensible nature. Nevertheless, in both cases, that which is interrogated and explored is nothing other than "sensible and mobile being." [7]

But neither in natural philosophy nor in the natural sciences is there to be found any higher concept than the generic in the strict sense of the term, because in neither case is a level of abstraction apart from *all* matter attained.[8] For, although *physica* abstracts from particular sensible matter (e.g., from *this* flesh and *these* bones in *this* animal), it does not abstract from *common* sensible matter—from

---

extraction, but rather in "inspection," in considering one aspect of a thing without considering other aspects, "aspect" meaning not the way we look at a thing but the way the thing, so to speak, looks at us. (Cf. Maritain, *op. cit.*, pp. 85 ff.)

[6] *Ibid.*, p. 91.

[7] Cf. Maritain, *Degrés*, pp. 77 f. See his "Tableau des sciences," p. 79.

[8] The generic concept strictly so called is univocal because its signification is limited to those types of being which are composed of matter (including "intelligible matter") and form. Our concepts of the predicamental accidents are univocal only so far as the latter are conceived as generic determinations of these orders of being. (See below, note 11.)

matter considered precisely and exclusively as subject to sensible qualities but not to this or that particular sensible quality in this or that particular thing.[9]

Now mathematics (on its speculative or theoretical side) requires a higher degree of abstraction than natural science or even than the philosophy of nature, because it abstracts from all sensible matter, common as well as individual. Mathematics does not, however, soar beyond "common intelligible matter"; it does not abstract from substance "according as it is subject to quantity."

The presence of quantity in substance is ontologically prior to that of sensible qualities, quantity being the first accident of corporeal substance. Thus quantities such as numbers, dimensions, and figures can be considered apart from, that is, they can be abstracted from, sensible matter; but they cannot be conceived separate from the notion of substance-as-subject-to-quantity. This would require abstraction even from common *intelligible* matter—from extension, from matter considered precisely as subject to three dimensions, without any concrete determinations whatever. But mathematical entities can be conceived independently of this or that substance; and to do so is to abstract them from *individual* intelligible matter, from matter considered as subject to three dimensions (as extended) in this particular material thing. In virtue of its "elevation" above the realm of sensible matter and even of individual (though not of common) intelligible matter,

---

[9] Cf. St. Thomas, *S. th.*, I, 85, 1, ad 2; Cajetan, *loc. cit.*; Maritain, *Sept leçons, loc. cit.*, and *Degrés*, p. 71.

mathematics, then, falls under the "second degree of abstraction." [10]

If intelligibility is proportionate to immateriality, it follows that we shall not be able to form any concept superior to the generic unless we can reach a still higher level of intellectual visualization and see things in their pure intelligibility, apart from all matter. But to view things in this way is to consider solely the being in them; to direct the mind's eye upon the "is" of things and upon that alone (following the apprehension of that object, technically called *ens in quantum ens*, the "transcendental" characters of being will unfold).

Only on this level do we form and employ concepts higher [11] than the generic. Indeed, on this level, which is

[10] See Maritain, *Degrés*, pp. 71–73, 279–84; *Sept leçons*, pp. 91–93. Cf. Cajetan, *loc. cit.*, and John of St. Thomas, *Logica*, II, 27, 1.

[11] "Higher" is of course only a metaphor. But some such metaphor seems unavoidable. A concept "higher than" the generic is not higher precisely because it is "more universal"; such a concept is in fact less *of* a universal than a univocal concept. It is "higher" because it is not limited to the "physical" nor to the mathematical modes of being. I refer not only to *the* transcendentals, but to all concepts transcending these orders.

Now it seems that we can have an analogical unity within a univocal unity. For instance, the division of the virtues is analogical (e.g., see *S. th.*, I–II, 61, 2, ad 1). But virtue falls under *habitus*, and *habitus* under the "first species" of quality (cf. Aristotle, *Categoriae*, chap. 8); and quality, presumably, is a category, which as such is univocal. But this is not an instance of analogy within univocity, because quality as divided into its "four species" clearly has no univocal unity but only an analogical unity in the proper sense of the term. It seems that we ought to have "analogy of inequality" here, arising from the division of a genus into its species; but the fact is that we have proper analogy. How can this fact be accounted for? Only, it seems to me, by adverting to a further fact, namely, that some of the predicaments have a transcendental amplitude. This is obviously the case with respect to substance, quantity, and relation. It appears to me no less clear in the case of quality. A predicamental accident is univocal only as a generic determination of that which is composed of matter and form. Hence, on this view, quality is generic and thus univocal, strictly speaking, only with respect to determinations flowing from

that of metaphysics, no strictly generic concept can work, if for no other reason than that we are here altogether outside the order of matter, even of that intelligible matter which mathematical quantity is.

Since the so-called analogy of inequality consists in the unequal participation of diverse things or characters in an identical generic or specific formality, it is most commonly exemplified in the sphere of cosmology and of the natural sciences.

A great deal even of what is called definitive scientific thought is based on correspondences which are themselves only refinements of the garden variety of analogies: vague, imperfect likenesses, by analysis rendered progressively less vague and hence more "scientific." Fundamentally, such are the numerous morphological or functional classifications, the comparative studies in anatomy, psychology, grammar, and so on.

Classification is a matter of putting species under genera. Hence, wherever we have to do with things which can be classified, we must operate with generic and specific concepts; and we are then in the categorial order. But that order is the order of univocity. As we have seen, genera, classes, or categories are formally univocal. Comparisons made within this realm, therefore, are not so much analogies as "univocities." They are not bona-fide analogies, because they have nothing to do with concepts which are intrinsically and formally analogical in the sense of

material forms. Consequently analogical unities like that of virtue can exist within quality: not within quality taken as a genus in this strict and restricted sense but taken broadly, as a determination flowing from any (finite) type of form.

being capable of realization, in different ways, in the order of existence. On the contrary, they employ concepts which are intrinsically and formally univocal.

2. On Ipsum Esse Commune Omnibus

If "analogy" of inequality (or of generic predication) is the basic type of analogy, then analogy must be defined in terms of imperfect likeness in the categorial order. There is a significant distinction, however, between specific or generic likeness and analogical likeness. It is this distinction which St. Thomas applies, for instance, to the various types of agent: "If, therefore, there is an agent not contained in any genus, its effect will still more distantly reproduce the form of the agent; not, that is, so as to participate in the likeness of the agent's form according to the same specific or generic formality, but only according to some sort of analogy; just as being itself is common to all things—*sicut ipsum esse est commune omnibus.*" [12]

The emphasis is to be placed on that *ipsum esse* which is common to all things; for if metaphysics bears on the very act of being itself, then we shall have to look there for metaphysical analogy. But in that quest we have advanced only a short way. At this stage it would be well to introduce some examples with a view to gaining a clearer and fuller understanding of analogy of inequality. For while this "analogy" belongs by nature in the categorial order and is therefore found properly in cosmology, in the natural sciences, and in comparative studies, it is, I believe, also discoverable in certain great metaphysical

12 *S. th.,* I, 4, 3, c.

systems, both ancient and modern, in some recent philosophies, and in a certain type of thinking in natural theology.

The following chapters aim at illustrating the *implicit* role of "analogy of inequality" in Platonic ontology, in Plotinus, in Spinoza, in Bradley and Höffding, and in a kind of anthropomorphic method in natural theology. These analyses are made from a strictly limited point of view and with a strictly limited object. They are not offered as representations of the integral philosophies of any of these thinkers, and still less as summary "refutations." They are solely intended to illustrate what happens when a pseudo-analogy usurps the place of analogy proper.

CHAPTER III

A CRITIQUE OF PLATONIC ONTOLOGY

1. THE WAY OF ASCENT

IF THERE is any argument which may be called typically Platonic, it is the "henological argument." To ascend always from the many to the one, from the composite to the simple, is the constant goal of Platonic "dialectic." A guiding principle of Plato's thought is the conviction that the existence of degrees of any reality or perfection implies the existence, in some sense, of that reality or perfection itself: that which is "more or less" demands that which *is* in the highest degree. The relative, in any order, presupposes the absolute; but to speak of various degrees is to speak of multiplicity, and multiplicity is the mark of imperfection or of perfection more or less great. Furthermore, if the same character is found in several things, it is impossible for each of them to possess it *by* itself. But that which a thing does not possess by itself, it receives from another. In other words, it shares that thing or "participates" in it.[1] For "nothing imperfect is the measure of anything." No instance of equality is equality itself, no embodiment of beauty is beauty itself; and so of all other things. In a typically humorous and lofty discourse in the

---

1 See, for example, Socrates' great speech in the *Republic*, VI, 507b.

Phaedo,[2] Socrates says: "I . . . simply and singly, and perhaps foolishly, hold and am assured in my own mind that nothing makes a thing beautiful but the presence and participation of beauty in whatever way or manner obtained; for as to the manner I am uncertain, but I stoutly contend that by beauty all beautiful things become beautiful."

Socrates' uncertainty about the manner in which things participate in their Ideas or Forms (εἴδη) reaches a climax in the *Parmenides,* where Plato brings up his heaviest dialectical artillery and lays siege to his own theory of ideal types. However, Plato apparently never abandoned that theory but to the end stoutly contended that relative things *are,* and become that which they are, only "by" their absolutes. Socrates never tires of arguing that all multiplicity points to a higher unity.

Similarly St. Thomas argues that, if a single character is found to be common to several things, this necessarily results from a single cause. That which is common to a number of things cannot be caused by those things themselves because each thing considered in itself is distinct from every other—and diversity of causes produces diversity of effects.[3] In fact, he attributes this argument to Plato himself, "who wished that, prior to every multiplicity, there should be some unity, not only in number but also in the nature of things."[4]

The diverse cannot be the *raison d'être* of the one. By

---

[2] 100d. (In Jowett's translation of the *Dialogues of Plato,* 1892 edition, II, 246.) All quotations from Plato will be taken from this work.

[3] *De pot.,* III, 5, c.

[4] *Ibid.*

this principle Plato ascended from the multiplicity of particulars to the eternal types or forms of things, to the Ideas of eternal and absolute truth, beauty, justice. But he did not fail to see that the diversity of eternal essences, Ideas or Forms, itself presented the same problem and called for the same solution: those "eternal objects" themselves had to be reduced to a supreme unity. The many, always and everywhere, demand the one.

2. THE IDEA OF THE GOOD

This One, the Form of forms, Plato called the Idea of the Good, or simply the good—the "sun" of the intelligible world.[5] As visible things are seen only when the sun shines upon them, so truth is known only when the mind is illuminated by the Idea of the Good; which is "the author of science and truth, and yet surpasses them in beauty." [6] We must go even further and say that, as the sun is the cause of generation, so the good is the cause of the being and essence of all things; "and yet the good is not essence, but far exceeds essence in dignity and power." [7]

There follows what has been called [8] "the most important single text for the whole of Plato's epistemology," namely, that famous passage at the end of this book (*Rep.*

---

[5] *Rep.*, 508e; Jowett, III, 209.

[6] *Rep.*, 508e–509a; *ibid.*, p. 210.

[7] *Rep.*, 509b; *ibid.* Of course every translator has a slightly different version of this celebrated text (as of most others), but the meaning is clear and scholars are in substantial agreement. (It is true that Jowett's renderings are sometimes more "literary" than strictly accurate. But we are concerned only with some of the broad structural features of the Platonic system and not with exegetical details.)

[8] A. E. Taylor, *Plato* (London: Archibald Constable & Co. Ltd., 1908), p. 53.

VI) on the four grades of cognition.[9] Here we find that "dialectic" holds the highest rank in the order of knowledge. Its objects are "ideas" or "forms" themselves, and it considers them without the aid of sensible representations, such as are used in geometry and arithmetic and the "sister arts." The dialectician will make use of the axioms of mathematics as hypothetical starting points from which he may rise to the first principle, that is unhypothetical; then from this principle he will descend "by successive steps" to the knowledge of its consequences, proceeding always from Ideas to Ideas, without any sensible aids. The principle in question, of course, is the Idea of the Good. But before asking what this Idea is, we should simply ask: What is any Idea in Plato?

3. Professor Taylor and the Ideas

Concerning the nature and function of the Ideas, there are many theories: theories probably almost as various as the philosophies held by the different commentators themselves. But I shall deal exclusively with the commentary of Professor A. E. Taylor.[10]

He holds that "what Plato calls an 'idea' we should now call the 'signification' or 'intension' of a class-name, as distinguished from its 'extension,' " the latter being what

[9] 511 a-e; in Jowett, III, 211–13.
[10] I have singled out Taylor's excellent little study of Plato, not because I think it is in every way correct on this point (on the contrary, I think his theory of the nature of the Ideas is, from the historical point of view, wrong), but because I believe his interpretation is in all essentials speculatively right. Taylor's large work on Plato—*Plato: His Life and His Work*—contains detailed exegetical studies of the Dialogues. For his over-all appreciation of Plato's philosophy, his essay on Plato is far more serviceable, and for that reason no references are made to the larger work.

Plato refers to when he speaks of "the many things which partake of" the one idea, that is, the one class-concept.[11] Consequently, in the numerous texts where Plato contrasts the unity of the "idea" with the multiplicity of things which participate in it or partake of it, he is in reality contrasting the intension of a class-name with its extension. Indeed all the celebrated Platonic metaphors, such as "partaking of," "participating in," having "communion with," being "present to," "imitating" or "copying" ideas—these are all "intended to express one and the same relation, viz., that which subsists between the subject and the predicate of such propositions as 'Socrates *is a* man,' 'ABC *is a* triangle,' the relation, that is, between the individual member of a class and the class to which it belongs." [12]

Therefore it was in answer to the question, Of what nature are the objects cognized by the universal propositions of science and how are they related to the particular perceptions of our senses? that Plato advanced his theory of ideas—"which is thus, according to its author's intention, neither 'dogmatic' metaphysics nor poetical imagery, but a *logical doctrine of the import of universal propositions*," in fact, "*primarily a theory of predication*." [13]

It is clear, however, that the theory of Ideas was not intended by its author to be a *logical* doctrine in any of the usual modern senses of the term logic, whether instrumentalist, idealist, positivistic, voluntarist, symbolic, or

11 Taylor, *Plato*, pp. 41 f.
12 *Ibid.*, p. 46.
13 *Ibid.*, p. 38. Italics mine.

any other.[14] Their inventor did not intend that they should be interpreted as general names merely, or as "instrumental" signs; as "useful fictions," or as a priori forms having a purely "regulative" value in science; still less did he imagine that they were logico-mathematical, or syntactical symbols; Plato had nothing of that sort of thing in mind. If the Ideas were "logical" at all, they were so only in the sense in which the universal λόγος of the ancients could be said to be logical.[15] The Ideas are for Plato objects "distinct from" and "independent of" the mind, *"about* which it has knowledge"; they are themselves "things," indeed, *entia realissima.* Therefore the doctrine of Ideas is a "conceptual realism." [16]

[14] Surely neither Aristotle nor St. Thomas understood it to be a logical doctrine. Thomas' definition of logic is substantially the same as Aristotle's, namely, that "art which is directive of the act of reason itself, by which man proceeds in an orderly way, with facility and without error, in the very act of reason itself" (*Anal. Post.,* I, 1). For Aristotle and St. Thomas logic remains within the order of second intentions; and for them, second intentions of course have no subsistent reality.

The "order of essence" cannot be identified with the order of "intentional being"; since intentional being is first of all *esse intentionale,* a mode of existence. (Cf. Yves Simon, *Introduction à l'ontologie du connaître;* Paris, 1934, pp. 18 ff.) Moreover, to say that logic remains within the "conceptual" order is ambiguous. For the "objective concept" (object-of-the-concept) of first intention is an intelligible aspect of the thing known and is therefore real inasmuch as it is identifiable with the thing; and the "mental concept," being a disposition of the soul, is a psychological *reality.* But, on account of the intentional existence which they have in the mind, objects ("objective concepts") acquire in the mind properties which they cannot possess in the real—for example, the properties of being a subject, a predicate, a middle term. These properties are "second intentions," known in and through mental concepts. (Cf. John of St. Thomas, *Logica,* II, q. 1 ff.)

[15] Just as, analogically, they could speak of a "reason" *in* things, so analogically (by improper analogy—see Part Three), they could speak of a "logic" in things.

[16] Taylor, *Plato,* pp. 43-45. Taylor advocates this designation so that Plato's theory will not be confused with idealism in the Berkeleyan sense or with that type of "theological idealism" according to which the Ideas are thoughts

Now "Ideal-realism" would be more appropriate, since in Plato's view the Ideas were *entia realia,* not *entia rationis* in the Thomistic sense or in any sense in which the two are opposed to each other. Plato does not distinguish between these two orders of being. There is a tendency in Plato, and in Platonism generally, to mistake logical properties of real beings for real properties of real beings.

Absolutely speaking, it is doubtless true that "By the Ideas . . . Plato means the system of terms or concepts of fixed and determinate intension which would form the contents of an ideally perfect science in so far as it is completely and rigidly 'scientific,' the system of universal meanings"; [17] "a world of exactly defined *logical concepts,* each standing in immutable relations to the rest." [18]

This statement seems true speculatively but false historically. For if Plato's Ideas are *in fact* only intentions (universals) and if intentions as such have no being *in rerum natura,* then his theory of Ideas is actually a logical doctrine. But if the foregoing exposition is correct, this is not true historically.[19]

So, while it is misleading to call the doctrine of Ideas a

---

in the divine mind or "creative conceptions of God." Professor Taylor maintains that for Plato it is the Ideas (and not the soul, or even God) which constitute *ens realissimum* (*loc. cit.*).

[17] Taylor, *Plato,* p. 42.

[18] *Ibid.,* p. 53. Italics mine.

[19] It should be pointed out, however, that Professor Taylor is here considering the Platonic system speculatively and absolutely. He is asking not, What did Plato himself actually have in mind when he propounded his theory of Ideas? but, What is the speculative import of that theory? Of course the speculative judgment in such cases presupposes the historical judgment. (It is impossible to understand the meaning *of* Plato without having first understood *Plato's* meaning.) Hence the crucial importance of the history of ideas. Nevertheless the speculative order is formally diverse from the historical.

"conceptual realism," the term does express an important truth. Making due allowance for the equivocations involved in the use of the words "concept" and "logic," the following is a fine interpretation of what this Realism is: "We may say that the recognition of the 'good,' as the supreme source from which the 'Ideas' derive their being, would appear to mean that the whole body of true *scientific concepts* forms an organic unity in which each member is connected with the rest teleologically by the fact that some of them point forward, or logically lead up to it, while it, in its turn, leads up to others. The *objective unity* of the system of scientific concepts is thus the counterpart of the unity of aim and purpose which it is the mission of philosophy, according to Plato, to bring about in the philosopher's inner life." [20]

4. The Idea of a "Dialectical" Metaphysics

We have already seen that in the *Republic* Plato makes dialectics the highest of the sciences. According to this doctrine, therefore, if metaphysics (a queen of the human sciences) exists, it must be a dialectical science. Of course the Aristotelian concept of dialectics is radically different from the Platonic. But they have this in common: they both operate in the order of essence, of intelligible form. "Dialectical," even in a Platonic sense, does not properly characterize metaphysics as a *science*. This point is implicitly contained in St. Thomas' comparison between the ·metaphysician, the dialectician, and the sophist.[21]

20 *Plato*, pp. 60 f. Italics mine.
21 *In IV Meta.* IV 573–74. "Dialectics" is here taken as being synonymous with "logic" and hence as including not only dialectics in the strict sense, viz.,

If we consider wherein they resemble one another, we find, St. Thomas says, that the dialectician (or logician) and the metaphysician have this in common, that it pertains to them both to consider all things. But if so, then they must consider all things in some single aspect wherein they all agree; for of one science there is only one subject, and of one art, one matter. But, since there is nothing which is common to all things except *being,* it is evident that the subject matter of dialectics (or logic) is being and the universal characters of being as such (i.e., the transcendentals); and these things also fall within the province of the metaphysician or philosopher. Thus the metaphysician and the dialectician (or logician) consider the same subject.

Now, being is twofold: being of reason and being of nature. The former is the sort of being which is proper to logical intentions or concepts, such as the intentions of genus, species, and the like. These are not found in nature

---

"inventive logic," but also "judicative logic." Thus the argument of this section seeks to show that according to Aristotelian-Thomistic doctrine, a "dialectical" metaphysics, that is to say, a metaphysics which, whether explicitly or implicitly, is at the same time a science of logic, is impossible.

Since we are not concerned here with the sophist, we will not transcribe what is said about him. In fact, we are concerned only with those statements which apply both to the dialectician strictly so called (who argues from "probable reasons" alone) and also equally to the "judicative" logician, who considers only necessary arguments and judgments. For though "dialectics" in the sense here used deals with probable arguments and issues only in opinion, this is not true of the science of logic as such. So, for the sake of clarity, I will add the expressions "or logician," "or logic," after the words "dialectician" and "dialectics," where what is said about the latter applies equally to the former. (As for the "philosopher," he is in this text the same as the metaphysician.) In this way, far from misinterpreting the thought of St. Thomas, we will be able to center our attention exclusively on those statements which apply to logic as such, to all logic, having eliminated everything which applies only to that department of logic called "dialectics." Not a literal translation but an accurate paraphrase of the points in question will be given.

but only in the mind. It is this kind of being (*ens rationis*) which is the proper subject of logic. However, there is a certain parallelism between the two orders of being, since all things of nature are possible objects of reason. Consequently the "subject matter" of logic is conterminous with that of philosophy or metaphysics. But the philosopher proceeds from the reasons in *things,* the dialectician (or logician) from the reasons in the *mind,* that is, from principles extrinsic to the things themselves.

Although logic is in a sense "the art of arts," [22] one should not lose sight of the fact that it considers things not as they are in reality, but only as they exist "in reason." For *ens rationis,* the proper or formal object of logic and also therefore of dialectics, is being, considered precisely as known, not as being. When we consider things in themselves, therefore, we are not in the order of logic. Logic is a reflexive art: the mind turns back upon itself to answer the question: What is that being which is "being-known," and what is the order in it? In other words, the logician studies being in its vital relations of reason found within concepts, and the relations of formal concepts to one another. The logician of course presupposes real being; but he does not consider it *as* real but only as known; [23] he is

22 I *Post. Anal.,* I. Here St. Thomas points out that the art of logic is a *rational* art, not only because it proceeds according to reason (which is common to all the arts), but because it deals with the act of reason itself as its proper subject; and therefore seems to be *ars artium* because it directs us in that very act from which all the arts proceed.

23 He sees being as reflected in his own mind and therefore considers not "first" but only "second" intentions: he considers not that in the thing which is envisaged through the concept and toward which the mind first *tends,* namely, the object-of-the-concept (the so-called objective concept), but the object-of-the-concept considered reflexively, precisely as a thing to be *known.* (See Maritain, *Degrés,* pp. 792 f., in his *Annexe* on the Concept, where he

exclusively concerned with the role which being plays in and for knowledge. The being of the logician is a being "reflected or derealized." [24] Hence the calamitous error of attempting to make logic (or "dialectics") a science of the real. For to convert being into a logical entity is to "derealize" being, divest it of its reality; and to confuse logic with metaphysics, or to propose to construct a metaphysic out of logic, is to rob metaphysics of all real content, thereby at the same time undermining the basis of logic itself.

5. LOGICISM IN PLATO

So flexible and diffuse is Plato's thought that it is notoriously difficult to arrive at any perfectly definite conclusions about specific points of his doctrine. But we can grasp the general outlines and discern the main tendencies. The strain of "logicism" in his thought is not so pronounced as in the majority of his Neoplatonist heirs, and by no means so apparent as in Hegel. [25] But it exists at least vir-

brings together and comments upon numerous important Thomistic texts relating to the theory of the concept.)

[24] Maritain, *Sept leçons*, p. 43.

[25] See his *Science of Logic*, Eng. tr. (London, 1929), I, 81 f. Hegel made being indistinguishable from nothing, because he made it a genus and hence had to eliminate from it all determinations; that is, he simply dropped out everything that actually *is*, since all that actually exists is in some way determinate and exclusive of everything else. As I remarked elsewhere (*The Thomist*, October, 1941, p. 586), "Hegel's Pure Being is 'being' grasped by that type of abstraction whereby the mind abstracts universal wholes from their singular embodiments, passing thus to universals more and more 'wide' and less and less 'deep.' It is, indeed, the ultimate term of this abstractive process—a mere *ens rationis*"; and "As Hegel clearly saw, being-in-general, in the highest degree abstracted from every determination whatsoever, is equivalent to our thought of 'nothingness.'" Unlike Plato, Hegel went on to identify Being and Non-being in Becoming, thus planting the roots of all reality in Becoming. The "dialectical process" or development of reality, therefore, will realize itself by opposition

tually in Plato. In every case, the root cause of this phenomenon is the implicit assumption that essences as such
are the specifying objects of the intelligence. The mind is
naturally at home in the realm of essence, of intelligible
form—of conceptual objects. But existence itself is not
such an object; it is not an idea; it is not given in any idea.

In a second intentional metaphysics, "being" may un-
dergo any number of transformations. For instance, it may
be posited outside knowledge, over and above or beyond;
it may be reduced to the status of an accidental character
of essence, a property of it, or even a "difference." Although this tendency does not assume such an extreme
form in Plato as in many subsequent Neoplatonist or essentialist philosophies (in that of Meister Eckhart, for example [26]), the germ of those later extravagances is to be
found in the doctrine of Ideas. For, as we have noted already, the good (or its Idea or Form) is the cause of the
being and essence of all things known, yet is itself beyond
essence or being.

I do not propose that such language be taken in all lit-
eralness. It seems clear that Plato means only that the good
is not an essence in the sense in which finite participated
essences are such. There is no evidence, so far as I am
aware, that the good is anything other than the Idea or
Form of the good.[27] If, then, the good is an Idea, and if an

---

of Being to Non-being in what should have been an endless progression. (This
last point, I believe, is brought out very clearly by Professor Loewenberg in his
introduction to *Hegel: Selections,* Scribner's series, p. xiv).

[26] See B. J. Muller-Thym, *The Establishment of the University of Being in
the Doctrine of Meister Eckhart of Hochheim* (New York and London: Sheed
and Ward, 1939).

[27] The words εἶδος, ἰδέα, mean "form." According to Taylor (*op. cit.,* p. 43),
Plato called the "concepts of science" *Ideas* simply "because they constitute

Idea is a "form," and if *form* means *essence*, it follows that the good is an essence—the Supreme Essence.

6. On Essence and Existence

Now, essence is that by which a thing is *what* it is, or by which it is constituted in its proper genus or species; it is that by which a thing has being "of such a sort" (*esse quid*).[28] Thus essence is that which limits and divides existence (*esse*); for, though unlimited in *itself*, being is necessarily limited by the nature of that which receives it.[29]

Much confusion may be avoided in metaphysical matters if the fact be kept in mind that these terms "essence" and "existence" do not themselves stand for any *things* at all.[30] They merely designate the two faces which every being presents; for every being both *is* (exists) and is *something* (a subject or thing having existence). The word "existence," therefore, signifies the *act*-aspect of things (the *be* in their being), while essence signifies the subject-aspect of things, their whatness, *that which* they are.

Which of these aspects is the really basic one, the more significant metaphysically? If metaphysics is the science of being as being, there is no doubt that it is the aspect of *esse*. The following propositions, stated in the simplest

---

the forms or types of things in accordance with which the universe of things is constructed."

[28] Cf. St. Thomas, *De ente*, I; Aristotle, *Anal. Post.*, I, 22, 82 b38; *De anima*, III, 6, 430 b28; *Meta.*, VII, 3, 1028 b34.

[29] Cf. *De ente*, VI.

[30] Although we can hardly avoid speaking of essence and existence as if they were realities on their own account, we at least will know that we are speaking incorrectly. Metaphysical terms are necessarily inadequate to express metaphysical realities. Metaphysical language almost never "says" what it means. That is why it is such a fruitful source of error and illusion.

terms, go to the heart of the matter: 1. "The very character of being is derived from the act of being, not from that
to which the act of being pertains"; [81] 2. "Being, or that
which is, *is* only inasmuch as it partakes of the act of
being"; [82] 3. "Being is that whose act it is to *be*." [83] It is
evident, therefore, that it is not in virtue of their *esse* but
of their whatness that things may be categorized—divided
up and put into logical molds called genera and species,
classes or categories. It is essence which is the principle of
limitation, of dividedness, of definitiveness, so to speak,
and hence of *logical* intelligibility.

7. PLATO'S PHILOSOPHY A PHILOSOPHY OF ESSENCE

This mere sketch of one of the crucial distinctions in
metaphysics is sufficient, I think, to make it clear that the
ontology of Plato is an ontology of essence, of intelligible
form. Being, in the proper and full sense, belongs only to
the forms, types, Ideas. In Plato, therefore, what is *in fact*
the order of intentional being has been identified with the
order of the real. If the expression "logical concepts" be
properly qualified, Taylor's appraisal would seem unexceptionable: "The system of Platonic Ideas [is] the true
object of scientific knowledge. It is a world of exactly defined logical concepts, each standing in immutable relations to the rest." [84] But by a sort of logical fatality an

---

[81] St. Thomas, *De ver.*, I, 1, ad 3, *in contr.*: "Ratio . . . entis ab *actu essendi* sumitur, non ab eo cui convenit actus essendi . . . "
[82] St. Thomas, *De Heb.*, II: " . . . ens, sive id quod est, sit, inquantum par-
ticipat *actum essendi* . . . "
[83] Garrigou-Lagrange, O.P., *Dieu: son existence et sa nature* (Paris, 1933),
p. 537. Cf. St. Thomas, XII *Meta.*, I, 2419: "ens dicitur quasi *esse* habens."
[84] *Plato*, p. 53.

essentialist philosophy tends to convert itself into a logicism. Of course there are many kinds of metaphysicized logical systems, the extreme case in modern times being the philosophy of Hegel. The logicism there is explicit; it lies on the surface; it could scarcely be more patent. But it exists also in Plato, even if only implicitly.

Essence is as such "existentially neutral." [85] That is why knowledge of essence does not itself entail knowledge of existence: simply to know *what* a thing is, is not to know whether or not that thing exists.[86] Thus, the formation of concepts is in itself an operation distinct from and neutral with respect to the affirmation or denial of existence, whether actual or only possible. The role of concepts is to make present to the mind the essences or intelligible characters of things.[37] In Plato (in the Platonic tradition as a whole) there is a tendency to limit the object of the intelligence to essences; to consider things not as existent but as intelligible.

In a very significant text,[88] St. Thomas states that "being is limited to divers genera according to a diverse mode of predicating, which itself follows upon a diverse mode of being (*essendi*)." Thus behind the modes of predication and the categories (as such logical) which correspond to them, there is the *esse*—being in exercised act. Indeed, all

[85] Gilson has used this apt phrase in recent lectures in discussing certain essentialist philosophies.

[86] Cf. St. Thomas, *De ente*, IV (ed. Mandonnet, *Opuscula omnia*, I, 157).

[37] See the penetrating article, "Verum Sequitur Esse Rerum," by G. B. Phelan, in *Mediaeval Studies*, Vol. I, 1939, Institute of Mediaeval Studies (Toronto, Canada), pp. 11 f.

[88] V *Meta.*, IX, 890: " . . . oportet, quod ens contrahatur ad diversa genera secundum diversum modum praedicandi, qui consequitur diversum modum essendi. . . ."

predication is "of being": every word is reduced to, or revealed in, the word *is* and its participial form; so that there are as many modes of predication as there are ways in which being is predicated, or in which something is said to *be*.[39]

But it is only in the judgment that we attain the *esse* beyond the *essentia,* that we grasp things under the aspect of actual or possible existence; because judgment is the affirmation or denial of the act of existence of something. The mind, receiving an essence (and hence forming a concept of it), gives to it in the judgment an existence which parallels its existence outside the mind. The act of the intelligence thus terminates and is perfected in the act of existence affirmed or denied in the judgment. To base a philosophy on the first operation of the mind—on "simple apprehension"—is to run the risk of converting that philosophy into an ultra- or a "Platonic" realism. This is the peculiar temptation of the logician.

The logician stops at the essence; he considers everything, even existence itself, as an essence, as a certain intellectual determination. He is concerned with things only *as signified,* as apprehended in concepts. As a logician, he views everything under the aspect of formal causality. He is interested in intelligible relations, not in actuality. "The logician considers the mode of predicating, not the existence of the thing." [40] But the philosopher is primarily con-

---

[39] *Ibid.,* 893: " . . . quot modis praedicatio fit, tot modis ens dicitur."

[40] St. Thomas, VII *Meta.,* XVII, 1658: "Logicus . . . considerat modum praedicandi, et non existentiam rei." This statement is especially significant, I think, in view of the not uncommon notion that the main problem of metaphysics is the problem of predication.

cerned not with things as signified (as conceptualized) but *as things;* not with the being-in-idea but the being-in-itself.

By failing to distinguish between the order of intentional being and the order of the real, a philosophy of essence tends to "reify" logic. Logical concepts are metaphysicized. But these are not thereby lifted above the generic and univocal order. Hence one must not be surprised to find in Plato that "being" is listed among the five chief kinds or classes (γένη), to wit: being, rest, motion, same, other; [41] and that even non-being must be reckoned as a class of being—considering being as a sort of class of all classes.[42] Both being and non-being, then, are generic ideas, intrinsically and formally, notwithstanding their exalted degree of universality.

8. Platonic Participation

Since Platonic ontology is an ontology of essence, Platonic participation will be a participation in essence. But essence is that by which, or on the basis of which, being is, so to speak, split up into species and genera or categories; and is thus the basis of logical classification, definition, and division. Logic itself is wholly within the order of second intentions. Yet to consider being logically is to consider it under an aspect in which it can exist only in the mind. This aspect is given the name of *ens rationis.* The order of

---

[41] *Sophist,* 254c–255e, in Jowett, IV, 387–89. In an essentialist ontology even transcendental notions are, and must be, *conceived as* categories, because such an ontology is formally a dialectic and hence moves in the order of second intentions.

[42] *Ibid.,* 258b–259b, pp. 393 f. "Not-being" is simply another name for difference or "otherness." Thus everything is not-being in respect of everything else in the sense that everything is different from or other than everything else.

ens rationis, however, is the conceptual order, and conception is always "of the essence."

In the *Parmenides* it is suggested that "what is meant by participation of other things in the Ideas, is realy assimilation to them." [43] In the same Dialogue, Parmenides tells the youthful Socrates that "a man must be gifted with considerable ability before he can learn that everything has a class and an absolute essence"; [44] and in the *Phaedo* we read that nothing comes into existence "except by participation in its own proper essence." [45] But a thing's "proper essence" is its εἶδος, Form, Idea. If our previous statements on this point are correct. however, the εἴδη are in fact simply logical concepts.

Participation in essence implies community of essence. To say that a thing "exists," then, is to say that it "participates" in its essence or Idea. But if the Platonic Idea is really a "class," that is to say, a generic or specific concept, then the participation in question is, in fact, purely logical. The community which is the basis of this participation, therefore, must be logical. But that which is only logically common does not *exist actually as common.* Humanity is common to all men, but humanity as such does not exist. No universal exists *as* universal. But that which is transcendental [46] (e.g., being, one) exists as transcendental, that is, as actually common to all things, to all classes or categories, genera, and species of things, and to all individuals

<hr />

[43] *Parm.,* 132d; in Jowett, IV, 52.
[44] *Ibid.,* 135 a-b; p. 55.
[45] *Phaedo,* 101c; in Jowett, II, 247.
[46] This word has acquired so many idealist overtones that its use today almost invites misunderstanding. The "transcendentals" are "immanentals." Far from transcending the real, they are in everything that is.

as well. A universal, as distinguished from a transcendental, is a concept which is basically univocal—apt of its nature to be realized in a plurality of subjects according to an identical formality.[47] But that which is predicated according to an identical formality is predicated univocally.[48] Transcendental terms are *conceived as* univocal universals in an essentialist ontology.

The conclusion seems inescapable that things participate in the Platonic Ideas in the same way as the inferiors of a genus participate in that genus, namely, univocally. For Platonic participation implies community of essence among the things participating and the thing participated. But that which is common *essentially* does not exist actually but only logically, *as common*. And so, at long last, we should now be in a position to take a general view of the ontological universe of Plato to the end of seeing what sort of philosophical analogy, if any, is possible in it.

9. CONCLUSION

For Plato the really real world is the intelligible world, the world of Ideas. This world constitutes a hierarchy, with the Idea of the Good at the top. This Idea is somehow the source of all the rest; beyond it there is no other. The intelligible universe is therefore a system of Ideas, forming an organic spiritual unity governed by a universal *telos*— the Idea of the Good. The Ideas constitute a class, with the Good as its principle. They comprise the order of reality;

---

[47] A genus is predicated of its subordinate species *as a universal whole;* it is predicated as such of each of them, and therefore has an identical formal meaning in each case.

[48] Cf. St. Thomas, *S. th.*, I, 13, 10, ob. 3, and *in corpore;* XI *Meta.*, III, 2197.

the ever-changing world of sense, the order of appearance or of relative non-being. From the Idea of the Good at the top to the Void at the bottom, there is a progressive diminution of being or reality; for the reality of sensible things is a borrowed reality. Indeed, what we call nature itself owes its existence to the influence of the Ideal world upon the Void. All things "participate" in Ideas and "imitate" them.[49] But by the same token, things participate thereby in the source of Ideas—the Idea of the Good—and imitate *it*. This participation is based on community of essence and hence may be considered logically; and, being based on community of essence, it is univocal. For whereas everything has an essence, which is its Idea, that essence or Idea or Form is itself only a member of the hierarchically ordered class of essences, Ideas or Forms. Thus the Idea of the Good—the Essence of essences [50]—is specifically, but in the last analysis not generically, different from the other innumerable Ideas of lesser rank.

If this sketch is true, we have in the Platonic intelligible world one and the same ultimate Essence in which all things participate in various degrees. We have, in other words, "analogy of inequality."

Perhaps at least a partial answer can now be given to the question posed in the first chapter (sect. 3), namely, whether the sort of predication by priority and posteriority which is found in analogy of inequality is properly speaking analogical. The answer must be "no," if by analogy

---

[49] In pedestrian language, the signification of a class-name is extended univocally to all members of that class.

[50] Although it is said to be "beyond" or above essence, the Good is still *conceived as* an essence, as the supreme, transcendent form.

we mean analogy in a metalogical sense. For predication by priority and posteriority is predication according to diverse degrees of some common perfection or reality. If the latter is only logically common, then the predication in question will be univocal. Thus St. Thomas points out [51] that if *more* and *less* arise from a diverse participation of one nature,[52] univocation is not removed. Indeed, to have a true analogy it is not sufficient that there be a basis for predication by priority and posteriority as regards being (*esse*), while there remains equality according to intention. The predication will still be univocal.[53]

A modern writer has an excellent comparison, expressing in vivid terms the sort of gradation we find attaching itself to a univocal notion: "The accomplished artist knows how to make a cord vibrate in such a way as to draw from it a piercing note, which little by little fades away and finally disappears. *The intensity varies, but it is always the same note.*" [54]

---

[51] I *Sent.*, XXXV, I, 4, ad 3.

[52] This is precisely what we have in "analogy" of inequality.

[53] Cf. II *Sent.*, III, 1, 5, ad 3: *S. th.*, I, 77, 4, ad 1. Cf. J. Le Rohellec, C.Sp.S., "De Fundamento Metaphysico Analogiae," *Divus Thomas* (Placentiae, 1926), XXIX, 672 f.

[54] "L'artiste consommé sait faire vibrer une corde de manière à en tirer un son éclatant qui peu à peu s'éteint et meurt—l'intensité varie mais c'est toujours la même note" (Penido, *Le rôle*, p. 55).

CHAPTER IV

THE ABSENCE OF METAPHYSICAL ANALOGY IN PLOTINUS

1. THE HIERARCHY

THE ONE (τὸ ἕν) is the primary source of all things, is the absolutely first principle, anterior to all being—all multiplicity, opposition, difference. The One alone is *simpliciter simplex;* it is, therefore, none of the things of which it is the source, for everything other than the One, even Intelligence or Spirit (νοῦς), entails a multiplicity.[1]

Plotinus uses several metaphors to convey his conception of the nature of the One as the supreme source of all things: it is, for instance, like an infinite spring which feeds all streams yet itself always remains at the same level;[2] or like the life of an immense tree: life circulates throughout the entire plant but the *principle* of that life remains single and immobile; far from dissipating itself in communicating vitality to the tree, it remains immovably "seated" in the roots.

The *raison d'être* of any multiplicity indeed always lies in some unitary principle: we must always go back to an anterior unity until at last, proceeding from unity to unity,

[1] See especially *Enneads*, III, 8, 8; 8, 9, in Plotin, *Ennéades* (ed. by Emile Bréhier, Paris: Société d'Edition "Les Belles Lettres," 1925), III, 163–66.

[2] III, 8, 10; in Bréhier, III, 166. (Hereafter, all page references to Plotinus will be to this edition. Italics used in quotations are mine, and my translations are all made from Bréhier.)

we arrive at the absolute One which cannot be reduced to any ulterior One. Thus, to grasp the unity of a thing is to grasp in it that which is "most potent and most precious." But the absolute One is none of those things of which it is the principle; consequently nothing can be affirmed of it, not even *being* or *substance* or *life*. To apprehend it, we must abstract even from being [3] and pass beyond νοῦς.[4]

Although prior to all reality, the One must somehow fill all things in producing them, yet not so as to *be* that which it produces. The One is everywhere because it is *in* all things, but it is nowhere because it is not in things in the sense of being in any way identical with them: the One, therefore, is all, inasmuch as it is *in* all and the source of all; but the One is nothing, inasmuch as it is *not* any thing.[5] The One cannot be said to live, for it gives life and is not life. Thought, likewise, must be denied of the One: to attribute thought to the One is to destroy its absolute unity and saddle it with a defect.[6]

Intelligence, which is the first hypostasis and marks the first and highest stage of the emanation of the One,[7] is itself only an image of the One. To be sure, that which is generated by the One must in some way be similar to the One: it must preserve a certain resemblance to It, a resemblance such as exists between light and the sun which is its source. But as the sun is not the light which it produces, so the One is not νοῦς. Although νοῦς constitutes the inner reality of all things, it is not to be identified with them.

[3] *Ibid.*, pp. 166 f.
[4] *Ibid.*, III, 8, 11; p. 168.
[5] Cf. III, 9, 4; p. 174.
[6] III, 9, 9; p. 176.
[7] V, 1, 6; pp. 22 f.

"And this is why," says Plotinus, "these things are essences (οὐσίαι), for each of them has a limit and a form; being (τὸ ὄν) cannot pertain to the unlimited; being must be fixed in a determinate limit and a stable state, and for the intelligibles this stable state is definition and form— whence also they derive their reality." [8] Summing up, he declares: "This, then, is what must be believed: there is first of all the One, which is beyond Being; . . . then, following it, Being and Intelligence, and in the third stage, Soul (ἡ ψυχή). Since these three realities are in the nature of things, it is necessary to hold that they are also in us. . . . Hence, our soul is a divine thing; it is of a different nature than sensible being; it is such as the universal soul." [9]

2. EMANATION

The emanation of all things from the One is like the efflux of light and heat from the sun, which loses nothing in imparting itself: from the One to matter and back, there is an unbroken chain. The One is present in all grades of things: It is the δύναμις of all things.[10] It penetrates all things, so that "wherever the third rank is present, there also is the second and first." [11] As the good, the One "is the

[8] V, 1, 7; p. 24. This text is not only characteristically Platonic, it is characteristically Greek. It has often been remarked that in general the ancient Greek philosophers identified the "real" with the definite, the limited, the determinate, and abhorred the "infinite," which they equated with the indefinite. This would afford a partial explanation of the tendency, common to practically all Greek philosophy, to conceive being primarily, if indeed not exclusively, under the aspect of essence, that is, under its divisive, limiting, determining aspect.

[9] V, 1, 10; p. 28.
[10] III, 8, 10; p. 166.
[11] VI, 5, 4; p. 203.

principle on which all depend, to which all aspire, from which all proceed, and which all need," while "in itself it is in need of nothing, sufficient unto itself, desiring nothing—the measure and the term of all things, giving out of itself Intelligence and Being, Soul and Life. . . ." [12]

Nothing in the whole scale of emanated beings is separated by a sharp division from that which precedes it.[13] "The procession thus goes on from the first to the last; each thing remains always in its proper place; the thing engendered has a rank below that of its generator; and each thing becomes identical with its guide, in so far as it follows that guide." [14] ". . . Thus all things are the First (ἐκεῖνος) and are not the First; they are the First because they derive from it; they are not the First, because the latter, in giving them being, remains itself. All things, therefore, are like a single life which stretches forth in a straight line; each of the successive points of the line is different, but the entire line is continuous. It has points forever different, but the preceding point is not lost in that which follows it." [15]

We may consider the whole intelligible world as one magnificent light. But above that light is enthroned the One—an other, a superior light, which, shining forth upon the intelligible world, itself remains immobile. The Being which proceeds from the One does not detach itself from the One, yet is not identical with it.

12 I, 8, 2; p. 116.
13 V, 2, 1; pp. 33 f.
14 V, 2, 2; p. 34.
15 V, 2, 2; p. 35.

It is evident, therefore, that Plotinus is neither a monist nor a pantheist in the strict sense of these terms. Things are distinct, and the One is not identical with any of its manifestations or emanations, nor with them all taken together: the One is not the "world" nor is the world the One. Nevertheless the world and all that it contains share in the same reality and somehow *are* that reality, so far as they can be.

3. Equivocity of All Names of the One

The One is, of course, ineffable (ἄρρητον): "Whatever you say, you say *something:* but that which is beyond all things, even beyond the venerable νοῦς and beyond the truth which is in all things, has no name; for (if it had a name) that name would be something other than it; whereas it is not *any* thing and has no name because nothing is predicated of it as of a subject." [16]

The One is indeed superior to all that we call being and is too sublime and too great to be given that name; and evidently the term νοῦς is inappropriate also, for, among many other reasons, the property of being self-sufficing clearly does not belong to νοῦς. In short, everything that we can say about the One imports some sort of defect, because all the names we use are derived from inferior and hence defective things. But each and every defective thing *shares in the same unity,* and consequently νοῦς does also; yet it remains distinct from that Unity.[17]

We must go still further: it is even false to call the One

16 V, 3, 13; p. 67.
17 V, 3, 17; p. 72.

"The One"; for as Plato says,[18] it is beyond essence.[19] It is the function of names to designate or indicate that which something is, its essence or whatness. But if that "thing" is beyond essence and beyond being and beyond intelligibility, obviously it cannot have any proper name, not even "it": any and every name, then, is purely equivocal.[20]

4. UNIVOCAL PARTICIPATION

The univocal relation of all things to one another and to their source, "the One," is clearly seen in the following text: ". . . the lowest things are naturally in the next lowest, the higher in the next highest and so on up to the first principle, which, having nothing above it, cannot be in another; but it contains all the others, without dividing itself among them, and possesses them without being possessed by them." [21]

The One is indeed not those other things, but they do, Plotinus says, have *identity* with it *in the measure in which* they can enter into contact with it.[22] When things participate in the One, it is in the One *as a whole:* to participate in the One is not to receive a portion of it but to share in that single Reality in so far as the limited nature of the sharer allows.[23]

Plotinus stresses time and again that the One is present everywhere as a single, identical Power. So likewise is Being. As the image of a thing, like a light which grows

---

18 *Parm.,* 141c; *Rep.,* VI, 509b.
19 V, 4, 1; p. 78.
20 Cf. V, 5, 6; p. 118.
21 V, 5, 9; p. 101.
22 V, 6, 6; p. 118.
23 VI, 4, 8; pp. 187 f.

dim, ceases to exist if it is separated from that thing, so it is impossible for a thing which derives its substance from another to subsist in separation from its source. Thus the powers which derive from the universal Being, could not exist apart from it. That Being, therefore, will be present everywhere as a single identical reality, present simultaneously to all things, in its entirety and without division.[24] That which is capable of being present to it, Plotinus says,[25] is present to it in the measure that it *can* be. It is present not locally, however, but as a transparent medium is present to light; and *"all being is but a single being."* Like Being, Soul is everywhere the same: unique, undivided, total.[26]

As we have seen, this is in the highest degree true of the One. But if the ultimate reality (the One) is everywhere the same (unique, undivided, and total), then it is a univocal perfection; consequently all things will participate in it univocally, according to the same formality, in diverse degrees. Numerous texts could be adduced to prove this point. I will quote only one, which is remarkable for its clarity and completeness: "If it were objected that after the One there is an other being, let us point out that that being is itself simultaneous with the One, that it is 'round about' it and related to it as its product and in contact with it; so that *that which participates in that being posterior to the One participates also in the One itself.* There are numerous beings in the intelligible world; beings of first, second and third rank; but they are all attached to a unique

24 VI, 4, 9; p. 189.
25 VI, 4, 11; p. 191.
26 VI, 4, 12; pp. 192 f.

center; thus, just as the radii of a sphere are not separated from one another by intervals and are all simultaneous with themselves, so the beings of the first and second rank are precisely *there* where the beings of the third rank are found." [27]

The "primitive nature" or "primordial All" is present everywhere "like a single life." [28] But all things subsist entirely in the supreme unity; all veritable realities, Soul and Life included, derive their being from it and have their end in it.[29]

5. CONCLUSION

"Analogy of inequality" is exemplified in a striking way in the Plotinian universe. For here we are presented with a single, unique Perfection—the super-essential One, which, so to speak, flows over into all things [30] and in which all things participate in diverse degrees. Of course, to say that all things other than the One share in it is not to say that they are parts of it in the usual sense, because the One is absolutely simple. Rather, as we have seen, all things share in the One as in a perfect, an undivided, unique Thing; and they essentially *are* that One so far as their limited natures allow or in the measure in which they are capable of entering into "contact" with it. In other words, the relation of participation in Plotinus is not at all that of a part to a whole in the ordinary physical sense of these terms, but of an imperfect thing to a single perfect Thing.

Nevertheless, as for Plato, so for Plotinus, ontological

[27] VI, 5, 4; pp. 202 f.
[28] VI, 5, 12; p. 211.
[29] VI, 5, 12; concluding paragraph, p. 212.
[30] The generation of things is a kind of overflow, οἷον ὑπερερρύη; V, 2, 1.

participation is based on community in essence; hence to participate in a thing is to *be* that thing *essentially*, to share in its essence, so far as the imperfect character of the thing participating admits. For St. Thomas, however, such participation requires diversity in essence; in this sense, therefore, to participate in a thing is *not* to be that thing essentially. Thus for St. Thomas, all things share *proportionately* in being—not in being *qua* essence but in being *qua esse*. Such participation is analogical in the proper sense, whereas Platonic and Plotinian participation is formally univocal.

This point cannot be developed here.[31] Suffice it to say that participation in *esse* can be, and is, analogical because it does not imply community of essence but obtains in the case of things absolutely diverse in essence (as God and creatures are), whereas participation in essence does imply community of essence; and that which is common essentially does not exist as common, while that which is common existentially does exist as common.

Plotinian emanation consists in the communication of an identical essence to all things in varying degrees. Hence this emanation establishes a univocal relation between the "First Principle" and the "World." All things which flow from that Principle or are generated by it will participate in its essence and therefore will *be* that essence so far as they can be. The farther we are from the sun, the nearer we are to darkness (matter) and throughout the entire scale of Reality there are infinite shades of light and of darkness. But there is only one light.

31 See Part Four, chap. 22.

CHAPTER V

THE "UNIVOCIST" WORLD OF SPINOZA

DESPITE the vast differences between the philosophies of Plotinus and Spinoza, there is a certain structural resemblance between them. This resemblance consists largely in the fact that in both systems there is ultimately only one Thing in which all things share univocally in varying degrees.

1. ALL TRUE PREDICATION UNIVOCAL

In an important scholion in his *Ethics*,[1] Spinoza argues at considerable length that the intellect and the will of God differ from ours as regards both essence and existence, and resemble ours only in name. In other words, intellect and will as predicated of man and of God are equivocal; they are pure homonyms: "they could no more agree with one another than the celestial constellation of the Dog and the barking animal of that name." Why? Because for Spinoza the predication of the same name of two or more realities requires an actual community of essence between them, else the predication will be purely equivocal. In other

---

[1] Part I, Prop. XVII: "Nam intellectus et voluntas, qui Dei essentiam constituerent, a nostro intellectu et voluntate toto coelo differre deberent, nec in ulla re, praeterquam in nomine, convenire possent; non aliter scilicet, quam inter se conveniunt canis, signum coeleste, et canis, animal latrans" in *Benedicti de spinoza opera*, ed. by G. van Vloten and J. P. N. Land [The Hague, 1882], Vol. I). This work is used for all texts from Spinoza cited in this chapter. Although I have not adhered to them in every particular, I have found J. Wild's translations (in *Spinoza: Selections;* Scribner's, 1930) very helpful.

words, a term is truly predicated of diverse things when, and only when, it is predicated according to a formal char-acter which is identically the same in each of them. For Spinoza, apparently, all true predication is of this type. If between univocity and pure equivocity there is no mean, then there is, in the proper sense, no analogy.

2. No Analogy of Being

The mode of predication, however, follows the mode of being; and there is no properly analogical predication in Spinoza because there is no analogy of being. Let us re-view briefly the basic elements of the Spinozist system.

God is "absolutely infinite being, that is to say, sub-stance consisting of infinite attributes, each of which ex-presses eternal and infinite essence"; [2] substance being de-fined as "that which is in itself and is conceived through itself, namely, that the concept of which does not require the concept of another thing from which it must be formed," [3] and attribute as "that which the intellect per-ceives of substance, as constituting its essence." [4] But God, as substance absolutely infinite, is indivisible; [5] thus, "Be-sides God no substance can be nor be conceived"; [6] "whence it follows most clearly, first, that God is one; that

[2] *Eth.*, I, Def. VI: "Per Deum intelligo ens absolute infinitum, hoc est, sub-stantiam constantem infinitis attributis, quorum unumquodque aeternam et infinitam essentiam exprimit."

[3] *Ibid.*, Def. III: " . . . id, quod in se est, et per se concipitur; hoc est, id cujus conceptus non indiget conceptu alterius rei, a quo formari debeat."

[4] Def. IV: ". . . id quod intellectus de substantia percipit, tanquam ejus-dem essentiam constituens."

[5] I, Prop. XIII.

[6] Prop. XIV: "Praeter Deum nulla dari neque concipi potest substantia."

is, . . . in the nature of things there is but one substance, and it is absolutely infinite." [7]

Moreover, it follows that "whatever is, is in God, and nothing can either be or be conceived without God." [8] Nor can it be said that matter is unworthy of the divine nature, because "outside God, no substance can exist from which He could suffer. All things are in God, and all things which come to be, do so by the laws alone of the infinite nature of God and follow from the necessity of His essence." [9] Indeed, "from the necessity of the divine nature infinite things in infinite modes (that is, all things that can fall under the infinite intellect) must follow." [10] For, "the divine nature possesses absolutely infinite attributes, each of which expresses infinite essence in its own way—*in suo genere*." [11]

Of the infinite attributes of the one substance, we know, according to the *Ethics,* only two: thought (*cogitatio*) and extension (*extensio*). There are no *substances,* then, but only *Substance,* with its attributes, and attributes with their modes. But an attribute is only an aspect of substance itself, conceived as if constituting the very essence of substance. Indeed "each attribute must be conceived through itself." [12] It follows, therefore, that, "although two attributes may be conceived as really distinct, that is to say, one without the aid of the other, nevertheless, we cannot conclude that they constitute *two* beings or two different sub-

[7] *Ibid.,* Coroll.
[8] Prop. XV.
[9] *Ibid.,* Schol.
[10] Prop. XVI.
[11] *Ibid.,* Demonstr.
[12] Prop. X.

stances. For it is of the nature of substance that each of its attributes be conceived through itself, since all the attributes which substance possesses *were always in it together;* nor could one be produced by another; on the contrary, every single attribute expresses the reality or being of substance." "It is far from absurd, therefore," Spinoza continues, "to ascribe to one substance a number of attributes; because nothing in nature is clearer than that each being must be conceived under some attribute, and the *more* reality or being it has, the more attributes it possesses which express necessity or eternity or infinity; and consequently nothing is clearer, too, than that absolutely infinite being is necessarily defined as we have shown . . . , [namely] as consisting of infinite attributes, each of which expresses a certain eternal and infinite essence." [18]

From the fact that all things are in God and must be conceived through Him, it follows that He is their cause. But to say that outside God there can be no substance is to say that outside Him nothing can exist which *is in itself.* Evidently, therefore, God is the immanent and not the transitive cause of all things.[14]

As for modes, they are merely "affections" of substance, or "that which is in another thing, through which also it is conceived." [15] And whether they be infinite [16] or finite,[17] each mode expresses in its own way the nature or essence of God Himself, the sole substance; "for, besides substance

---

[18] *Ibid.,* Schol.
[14] Prop. XVIII: "Deus est omnium rerum causa immanens, non vero transiens."
[15] *Eth.,* I, Def. V.
[16] Cf. *Eth.,* I, Props. XXI–XXIII.
[17] Cf. Prop. XXV, Coroll. XXVIII.

and modes, nothing exists . . . , and modes are nothing but affections of God's attributes." [18] "Whatever exists, expresses the nature or essence of God in a certain and determinate manner; that is to say, whatever exists expresses the power of God, which is the cause of all things, in a certain and determinate manner. . . ." [19] Thus both thought and extension are attributes of God expressing His infinite and eternal essence: "Thought is an attribute of God, or God is a thinking thing (*res cogitans*)"; "extension is an attribute of God, or God is an extended thing (*res extensa*)." [20]

It seems probable that the distinction between attributes and modes in Spinoza breaks down, making his attributes in reality modal, that is, limited aspects of substance.[21] For if no attribute can perfectly express God's *complete* essence, to that extent it must be limited in reality or being, since a thing lacks being in the measure that it falls short of the One Reality. *Omnis determinatio negatio est.*

The point is that for Spinoza there is really only one Thing: the absolute infinity of Being—Substance or God. Other "things" are real in the measure that they *have* being (or substance) and things are more or less real in the measure that they embrace in their own natures more or less being. For instance, what is called "falsity" is merely

[18] Prop. XXVIII, Demonstr.
[19] Prop. XXXVI, Demonstr.
[20] *Eth.*, II, Props. I, II.
[21] Cf. *Spinoza: Selections,* ed. by J. Wild Scribner's, 1930), p. xxiv, in Introduction.

"privation" of knowledge.[22] Nothing positive in itself, "it is," as Professor Wild well says,[23] "simply the lack of fulness or completeness which characterizes everything in various degrees, short of the infinite being of God which alone is perfectly and completely real." "The point cannot too often be stressed," Wild continues, "that Spinoza's God is really an immanent God who exists only in and through his modes and includes them rather than simply transcends them. . . . His God is not outside things but always active and immanent in them to the degree in which they themselves embody reality." In Spinoza's own words, "the *more* reality or being a thing possesses, the more attributes belong to it." [24]

3. ANALOGY OF INEQUALITY AGAIN

There are degrees of being or reality. But God has absolutely infinite being or reality; hence He has absolutely infinite attributes, each of which, along with its modes, expresses the infinite reality of God in its own way; and it does so precisely because it *is* that infinite reality in its own way, according to the nature of the being it itself has and is, and in the measure that it itself *is* Being or Substance or God.

Whatever is, is in God; but to be *in* God, for Spinoza, is necessarily to be *of* God. For God is substance, and substance is being, and being is reality; and there is none

22 *Eth.,* II, Prop. XXXV.
23 *Op. cit.,* p. xxxvii, Introduction.
24 *Eth.,* I, Prop. IX: "Quo plus realitatis aut esse unaquaque res habet, eo plura attribua ipsi competunt."

other. If, therefore, there are any realities, they must be "parts" of the One Reality, not of course in the physical or material sense but in the sense of being quidditative participants in it.

Moreover, if whatever is, expresses in its own way and its own kind (*suo modo, in suo genere*) the one infinite and eternal substance, it does so only because it *is* in its own way and its own kind that very substance; for it cannot *express* it unless, in some degree, it *be* it.

In an essential aspect of its metaphysical structure, this philosophy is characterized by the unequal participation of all things in a common univocal perfection: the one Substance, the infinite, immanent God.

CHAPTER VI

TWO RECENT CASES

1. MR. BRADLEY: THE ABSOLUTE AS *Summum Genus*

IF WE pass on to the nineteenth century British philosopher, F. H. Bradley, we shall find some interesting and I think very clear illustrations of the point we are endeavoring to make in this Part.

In many respects Bradley's kinship with Plotinus is evident.[1] In a sense, Bradley took the Plotinian universe, "dialecticized" it *à la* Hegel, and converted it into a radical monism. But I shall not here attempt a comparative study. Let it be said at the outset merely that for Bradley reality is the all-embracing Whole with respect to which all else is appearance: "Reality in the end belongs to nothing but the single Real." "For take anything . . . which is less than the Absolute," Bradley argues, "and the inner discrepancy at once proclaims that what you have taken is appearance. The alleged reality divides itself and falls apart into two jarring factors"—the "what" and the "that." [2]

---

[1] W. R. Inge in his *The Philosophy of Plotinus* (2 vols.; Longmans, Green and Co., 1923) notes many points of similarity between them. (E.g., II, 39 f., 70, 104, note 1; I, 113, 210.) But his work, in many ways excellent, is marred by an ill-advised attempt to Christianize that great pagan. For instance, Inge attributes to Plotinus the doctrine of creation. (Vol. II, pp. 118 f., 179. See also I, 10–15.)

[2] *Appearance and Reality* (Oxford: Clarendon Press), ninth impression, authorized and corrected, 1930; chap. 26, p. 403.

Indeed, "Existence is not reality, and reality must exist. . . . Existence is, in other words, a form of the appearance of the Real." [3] Thus Bradley's One Reality, like that of Plotinus, is beyond being. Moreover, "Goodness, like Truth, is a one-sided appearance. Each of these aspects, when we insist on it, transcends itself." He goes on, with a typical rhetorical flourish: "By its own movement each develops itself beyond its own limits and is merged in a higher and all-embracing Reality." [4]

Nevertheless there are degrees in the participation of the One Reality, which is everywhere and in all things: "The Absolute is present in, and, in a sense, it *is* alike each of its special appearances; though present everywhere again in different values and degrees." [5] This doctrine of "degrees" is put very strongly:

> The Absolute is each appearance, and is all, but it is not any *one as such. And it is not all equally,* but one appearance is more real than another. In short the doctrine of degrees in reality and truth is the fundamental answer to our problem. Everything is essential, and yet one thing is worthless in comparison with others. Nothing is perfect, as such, and yet everything in some degree contains a vital function of Perfection. Every attitude of experience, every sphere or level of the world, is a *necessary* factor in the Absolute. Each in its own way satisfies, until compared with that which is more than itself. . . . And thus the *Absolute is immanent alike through every region of appearances.* There are degrees and ranks, but, one and all, they are alike indispensable. . . .
>
> *Appearances without reality would be impossible,* for what then could appear? And *reality without appearance would be nothing,* for there certainly is nothing outside appearances. But on the other

[3] *Op. cit.,* chap. 24, p. 354.
[4] Chap. 26, p. 403.
[5] *Ibid.,* p. 405.

hand, Reality (we must repeat this) is not the *sum of things*. It is the unity in which all things, coming together, are transmuted, in which they are changed all alike, though *not* changed *equally*.[6]

It is difficult to imagine how the theory of monistic immanentism could be more clearly expressed. There is a single reality in all things, a reality which all things themselves are, so far as they can be. Hence the notion of degrees in reality, and in truth. Not only is this the "fundamental answer" to Bradley's problem, it is the very "centre of philosophy" itself.[7] It is not the answer of the analogist, however, but of the "univocist"; it is the old familiar doctrine of the unequal participation of all things in a single univocal Perfection; it is the doctrine of "analogy of inequality."

It is a consequence of this theory that nothing can be attributed properly and formally to the One Reality. Hence, for instance, the impossibility, to Bradley's mind (and herein he is simply being consistent with his own principles), of attributing personality to the Absolute. "A person . . . to me must be finite," he says,[8] "or must cease to be personal." Bradley, indeed, appears to sense the need for a type of predication which would allow the ascription of absolute perfections to the Absolute without entailing anthropomorphism. But he has no doctrine that will permit him to do so.

Personality implies finitude, he argues, and nothing finite can be attributed to the Absolute: "For me it is suffi-

[6] *Ibid.*, pp. 431 f.
[7] Cf. chap. 27, p. 488.
[8] *Essays on Truth and Reality* (Oxford, 1914), p. 449 (in chap. 15, Supplementary note A, "On the Reality and Personality of God").

cient to know, on the one side, that the Absolute is not a finite person. Whether, on the other side, personality *in some eviscerated remnant of sense* can be applied to it. is a question intellectually unimportant and practically trifling." Nevertheless "it is better in this connection to call it [the Absolute] super-personal." [9] (This is indeed better, but only if the name "person" is understood to be analogical and hence attributable formally and properly, and not merely symbolically, to the Absolute.)

Bradley seems to feel the need of which I have spoken, but his own philosophy prevents him from satisfying it. His own doctrine stands in his way because he conceives the Absolute as the supreme *genus* of all things, hence as a univocal perfection, diffused unequally throughout the entire realm of appearance. What we have already heard Bradley say, I think, makes this clear, but I will add the following by way of confirmation: "Anything, which in any sense can be more than and beyond what we possess [of Reality] must still inevitably be *more of the self-same kind*"; [10] and "on the whole, *higher means* for us *a greater amount of that one Reality,* outside of which all appearance is absolutely nothing." [11]

2. Mr. Höffding: Analogy a Weak Univocity

Among various other meanings which he gives to the term "analogy" (all of which are non-metaphysical), a distinguished philosopher of our own century, Harald

[9] *Appearance and Reality,* chap. 27, pp. 472 f.; cf. *Essays,* p. 436.
[10] *Appearance,* p. 486.
[11] *Ibid.,* p. 488.

Höffding,[12] reiterates the very common notion that analogy merely consists in a lesser degree of identity. Analogy, in other words, is only a species of weak univocity. But his treatment of the problem is worthy of note, not only because it is interesting in itself, and not without originality, but because it exemplifies a widespread phenomenon in modern thought, namely, the de-realization of existence in favor of a logicized version thereof, which alone is believed to be compatible with the "scientific" view of things. This tendency—or rather, this disastrous metaphysical error—in some cases makes itself felt throughout entire philosophical systems. But I am concerned here not with those larger problems, which strike down to the very roots of our intellectual life, but only with the fate of analogy under such a regime as Höffding advocates and represents.

What this regime is (and it is a venerable one) is at least intimated in the following passage: "A considered attempt to discover, through rigorous definition, the diverse grades of similarity and of difference marks the beginning of scientific thought. Plato stands in the history of thought as the first who has demonstrated that there are many ranks of likenesses which present themselves to immediate apprehension, up to that of pure identity, of the Idea of the Good, which alone makes science in the strict sense possible." [13]

This statement, significantly, occurs in a chapter entitled "Analogie und Logik." Indeed Höffding has already

---

[12] See his *Der Begriff der Analogie* (ed. O. R. Reisland; Leipzig, 1924).
[13] *Op. cit.*, p. 29; cf. p. 30.

pointed out that analogy belongs in the "formal categories immediately after Identity." [14] Thus, as a criticist in the Neo-Kantian tradition, he assumes that analogy is essentially logical in character. Despite their "metaphysicized" status in that type of thought, the categories are as such and in reality only logical forms ("second intentions," *entia rationis*), and therefore not metaphysical principles.

Nevertheless analogy, being immediately below Identity, occupies a very exalted position, because Identity (old Parmenides' One, stripped of all mystical accretions) is still "the highest ideal of thought." [15] Now, "the problem of existence, that is, the question concerning the *possibility* of a scientific conception of the world," Höffding declares, "rests precisely on the relation between Totality and Part." [16] Indeed the whole effort of philosophy is essentially a *Drang nach Totalität*.[17] Thus in the most complete "cosmological systems"—those of Parmenides, of Spinoza, of Hegel—Identity, Höffding says, has been the final and the highest point of view. So European philosophy has been guided by a properly "oriental ideal," namely, to grasp all things as one.[18]

But the *Drang nach Totalität* of which Höffding speaks is a *Drang* not toward a truly analogical unity in the real order but toward a univocal unity in the ideal order, toward a Supreme Idea, or Summum Genus. The way of

---

[14] *Ibid.*, p. 2 (in Introduction).

[15] *Ibid.*, p. 29. Parmenidean monism is the perfect example of the univocist error, a "pure" case of ontological univocity.

[16] *Ibid.*, pp. 99 f. Italics mine.

[17] The German translation of Höffding's book on analogy, in which this expression is found, was made by Höffding himself from his own Danish edition published in Copenhagen in 1923.

[18] *Ibid.*, p. 101.

univocity, however, is the way of monism and of pantheism of one degree, of one sort or another; and this way is no better exemplified than in those very systems which Höffding mentions, the systems of Parmenides, of Spinoza and of Hegel. These systems recognize no unity other than that of a genus, be it expanded to include all things; they recognize no analogical unity of all beings in being, but only a univocal unity such as is proper to the inferiors of a class in that class. These are systems which, if we exclude the crude monism of Parmenides, are thus characterized in no insignificant degree by the unequal sharing of all things in a single univocal Substance or Nature or Idea.

CHAPTER VII

THE "VIA AUGMENTI" IN NATURAL THEOLOGY

Not only do we find analogy of inequality cropping up in all those philosophies where the influence of what may be called the Neo-Platonic or essentialist tradition is dominant, we find it also carried over into theology. In that order, most lapses into anthropomorphic univocity are accounted for by the presence of that "pseudo-analogical gradation" which is proper to generic or specific ideas.[1] And it is brought about precisely by the indefinite expansion, in the same line, of univocal created perfections. This is the *via augmenti,* the way of increase.

1. Cajetan's Warning

Cajetan issues a very useful warning against hastily concluding that a term is itself absolutely univocal because it is univocal with relation to some things.[2] We may easily fall into this error, for we are prone to ignore the fact that, as regards their actual use and understanding, "almost all properly analogical names were in the first place univocal and thence by extension were rendered analogical." Cajetan points out that the word "wisdom," for instance, was originally invented to signify human wisdom alone. But

[1] Cf. Penido, *Le rôle,* pp. 20 f.
[2] *De nom.,* XI, pp. 87 f.

when the science of theology was developed and the mind penetrated beyond the sphere of human knowledge to the knowledge of the divine nature, a certain *proportional* likeness between our wisdom and God's was observed, and the term wisdom was therefore extended to signify that in God to which our wisdom is somehow proportional. In other words, "wisdom," which is univocal in respect of men, was seen to be analogical in respect of men and of God. What is true of this name is true of all the other "names of God." Such being the genesis of our analogical attributions, the assumption that analogical notions are simply univocal ones inflated to the ultimate limit is quite "natural" and almost inevitable. It is nevertheless false.

2. THE "ANTHROPOMORPHIC PROPORTION"

It is entirely erroneous to suppose that simply by expanding indefinitely our initial, univocal concepts we shall in the end arrive at the divine perfection. That sort of thinking has no place in metaphysics or in theology; it is a physical or pseudo-physical mode of thought. It would make of theology a quantitative science. In the last analysis almost all anthropomorphisms stem from this attitude of mind.[8]

This term "quantitative" deserves emphasis. Such a "theology" is in fact a mere product of the quantitative imagination: "It is a quantitative type of thought which posits the perfect homogeneity of things, which reduces the diverse to the same, making potency, for instance, a *little* act and man a *little* God; so that if we keep on aug-

[8] Penido, *Le rôle*, p. 21.

menting potency we shall finally arrive at act; and if we push the notion of human nature on to infinity, we shall in the end attain to God." [4] In so doing, "one is professing, whether implicitly or explicitly, the *univocity of being*," thereby in reality affirming that the uncreated perfections of God differ from ours only in degree.[5]

Such a perfection, then, would simply be a higher degree of the same created thing—an infinitely higher degree if you will—a *maxime tale;* yet even so, it would remain univocal. In this way we do not pass beyond the created order; in this way, indeed, "analogy is reduced to inequality." The "anthropomorphic proportion" herein implied may be set down as follows:

$$\frac{A \ (\text{divine})}{a \ (\text{human})} = \frac{\text{superlative}}{\text{positive.}^6}$$

3. Monism and Anthropomorphism

The foregoing proportion marks the type of thinking which in philosophy leads to monism and in theology to anthropomorphism. The classic case of the former is found in the philosophy of Parmenides, or is commonly attributed to him.

In his Commentary on the first book of Aristotle's *Metaphysics* St. Thomas represents the Parmenidean argument as follows: "Whatever is outside being is non-being; and whatever is non-being is nothing; hence, what-

---

[4] *Ibid.*, pp. 64 f.: "Il est une pensée quantitative qui pose la parfaite homogénéité des choses, qui reduit le divers au même: la puissance, par exemple, sera un petit acte, et l'homme un *petit* Dieu; il suit qu'en augmentant la puissance, nous passerons à l'acte; en faisant croître l'homme à l'infini, nous obtiendrons Dieu. Implicitement ou explicitement, on professe *l'univocité de l'être.*"
[5] *Ibid.*, p. 65.
[6] Penido, *loc. cit.*

ever is outside being is nothing. But being is the One; therefore, whatever is outside the One is nothing." [7] This argument implies that being is a genus, and consequently that, if there were anything other than the One Being, it would necessarily have the character of a *differentia* in respect of that One Being. But the *differentia* is extrinsic to the genus. (In other words, the differential concept, e.g., rational, is not included in the generic concept, e.g., animal; for if so, we should have to say that all animals are rational, whereas "animal" signifies animated sensible substance, and nothing else.) Any such determination, any such differential character, therefore, would be outside being and thus would be nothing at all. [8]

But Parmenides, and those who thought similarly, were deceived in this matter because they considered being as if it were both logically one and physically one—properties which belong to a genus but which cannot belong to being. For being is not a genus since it is predicated in many ways of diverse things. [9]

Of course Parmenidean monism is an extreme case, and all later modified versions have recognized a graduated scale of beings under or within the One First Being. But they have retained the notion of being as a generic and hence a univocal unity.

Now, in theology this kind of thinking will give rise to anthropomorphism; for the essence of anthropomorphism lies in the attempt to conceive the uncreated as homogene-

[7] I *Meta.*, I, 138. (See H. Diels, *Die Fragmente der Vorsokratiker*, Berlin, 1912; I, 147 ff. Eng. tr. by J. Burnet, *Early Greek Philosophy* [4th ed.; London, 1930], pp. 173–76.)
[8] St. Thomas, *ibid.*, 138 f.
[9] *Ibid.*, 139.

ous with the created, the infinite Being with the finite, recognizing between the two orders only a distinction of degree.[10]

Equipped solely with univocal ideas, theologians or philosophers who follow this path are thus utterly incapable of parrying the blows delivered by critics of the Kantian or Neo-Kantian school. A great many, therefore, consider it prudent to withdraw from the struggle altogether: it has become too painfully evident that theology as a rationally demonstrative science must simply be abandoned, like any other impossible undertaking; and they are right in doing so. It would be sheer folly and a waste of time for one whose mind is stocked only with univocal notions to become engaged in the pursuit of a "science" which will never make sense in terms of such notions.

4. THE DEMONSTRATION OF GOD'S EXISTENCE

The primary problem of natural theology (the main theses of which are prerequisite to the systematic development of sacred or supernatural doctrine) is the demonstration of God's existence. This problem will forever remain insoluble in terms of univocal ideas. For instance, a philosopher who brings a univocist mentality to the Thomistic proofs will probably imagine that they come to this: there is universal movement or change, hence there is a Mover; there is universal causality, hence there is a Cause; there is a universal teleology or finality, hence there is a Telos or End—as if the term of each series were homogeneous with it.[11] The Being which is the *raison*

10 Cf. Penido, *Le rôle*, p. 67.
11 *Ibid.*, p. 91.

d'être of becoming, causation, contingency, participation, finality, cannot itself be subject to these things. To make these five deficiencies intelligible, a Being which in no way shares them is necessary: "The term which closes the series must be outside the series; it cannot be homogeneous with it." [12] Consequently, if we expect to find a First Being which is Pure Act, necessary, uncaused, unparticipated, absolutely final, hence *essentially diverse* from all things of the created order, then we must leave the *via augmenti* and enter the *via essendi*.[13]

The "proof by degrees" is a general type of argument which, wherever applied, may entail only that weak univocity called "analogy of inequality," and which will do so if in the end the "way of increase" is not abandoned for the sake of the "way of being"; for only that way the way of being, leads out of the order of the univocal into the order of the analogical, wherein alone true metaphysics and true theology can be done.[14]

[12] *Ibid.*, p. 92: ". . . le terme qui clôt la série, doit être hors série, il ne peut lui être homogène." Penido refers to *S. th.*, I, 3, 5, ad 2, where St. Thomas, answering the objection that God is in the genus of substance, points out that, unlike a genus—which must be homogeneous with that of which it is a measure—"*God is not a measure proportionate to anything,* and is called the measure of all things in the sense that everything has being only according as it resembles Him."

[13] Cf. Penido, *ibid.*, p. 93. What this "new" orientation of mind involves is indicated by the following distinction: "Excess is twofold, the one generic, which is signified by the comparative or the superlative; the other extra-generic, which is signified by the addition of the preposition *super*." (St. Thomas, *De div. nom.*, IV, 5 [Vivès, p. 411]; cf. *De pot.*, VII, 7, ad 2-3). Thus God is not properly said to be *most* wise, but *super* wise; and the same applies to all other names attributed to Him.

[14] Father de Munnynck, O.P., observes ("*L'analogie métaphysique*," p. 145) that it is not absolutely true to say that we attribute to the superior object—to God, for example—the actual content of our ideas, while denying their limitations. This purely negative procedure puts us only halfway on the road to knowledge of God. There yet remains the essential determination of the attributes, which are also limitations as compared with the plenitude of being.

5. THE GIST OF PART ONE

This whole Part has been a single, if rather diffuse, commentary upon a type of "analogy" which is not a true analogy at all, but is a pseudo-analogy. Then why has one's attention been invited to it through so many pages? A summing-up may help to justify this lengthy discourse on a subject trivial in itself, yet big with implications.

For, implicitly at least, analogy of inequality ranges through a vast department of human knowledge. Wherever generic or specific notions are found diversely or unequally realized in diverse subjects or things, this "analogy" is covertly at work; it is at work, therefore, throughout the entire order of classifiable things, of composite things.

Although this "analogy" contains a certain participation of true analogy inasmuch as it entails diversity in mode of realization, it is an analogy only improperly so called; it is an analogy which is not formally analogical at all, but formally univocal. It is thus, in fact, *only a sort of univocity* and is therefore *foreign to the nature of authentic analogy.*[15] However, if it has been shown that the pseudo-analogy of inequality deserves more attention than it has hitherto received, that it is in fact a potent source of intellectual evils in philosophy and even in theology, then our apology for this Part will have been sufficient.

Consequently these limitations must likewise disappear. Nevertheless it is still true to say, for instance, that God is good, wise, powerful. But predicates such as these make no sense unless it be realized that they apply to Him analogically, according to *metaphysical* analogy.

[15] Cf. Cajetan, *De nom.,* I, 5 f.

Part Two

ANALOGY OF PROPORTION
OR ATTRIBUTION

CHAPTER VIII

THE NATURE OF THIS ANALOGY

"THERE are many senses in which a thing may be said to 'be'; but all that 'is,' is related to one central point, one definite kind of being, and is not said to 'be' by a mere ambiguity. For everything which is healthy is related to health, one thing in the sense that it preserves health, another in the sense that it produces it, another in the sense that it is a symptom of health, another because it possesses it, another because it is naturally adapted to it, another because it is a function of the medical art. And we shall find many other words used similarly to these. So, too, there are many senses in which a thing is said to 'be,' but all refer to one starting-point." [1]

1. St. Thomas on Proportion and Attribution

In his Commentary on the text just quoted, St. Thomas points out that there are three ways in which a thing may be predicated of other things: (1) in absolutely the same sense (*secundum rationem omnino eamdem*), that is, univocally; (2) in completely different senses (*secundum rationes omnino diversas*), that is, equivocally; (3) in senses partly different and partly not different (*secundum rationes quae partim sunt diversae et partim non diversae*)

---

[1] Aristotle, *Meta.* IV, 1003a–31b 5; Eng. tr. by W. D. Ross (2nd ed.; Oxford, 1928).

—different inasmuch as these *rationes* introduce diverse relations, but one inasmuch as these relations are all referred to identically the same thing. That thing is then said to be predicated *analogically,* that is, *proportionately,* since each term is referred to that one thing according to its relations to it.[2] Here, therefore, we have analogy of simple proportion or of relation in the sense of simple proportion.

This analogy is also rightly called analogy of attribution, because it always involves attribution to a single term.[3] Thus the word "healthy" or "healthful" predicated of such things as diet, medicine, complexion, animal is not predicated univocally because it obviously has a different meaning as applied to each of them. Yet there is always reference to one and the same thing wherein alone health is properly and formally "realized," namely, the living organism or animal. All such objects are called healthy or healthful only in virtue of the relations they have to the health of the animal: a diet is healthful because in certain ways it conserves the health of the animal; medicine, because it produces or helps to produce or restore health; complexion, because it is a sign of health, and so on. Everything healthy or healthful is predicated in reference to one and the same health, that of the animal; for it is the same health which the animal receives, food conserves, medicine restores, and complexion signifies.[4] In this case, therefore, the health of the animal has the character of an end or final cause.

[2] St. Thomas, IV *Meta.,* I, 535.
[3] Cf. *De prin. nat., circa finem.*
[4] IV *Meta.,* I, 537; cf. *De prin. nat., loc. cit.*

Similarly the term "medical" has a different meaning as applied to medical instruments used by doctors, to their medicines (pills, serums, etc.), to medical assistants and orderlies, and to the doctors or skilled medical men themselves. Here, then, is a case of comparing many things to one thing as to an efficient principle or cause. The instruments which doctors use are called medical because they fulfill certain functions in the exercise of the medical art; medicines, because they have certain healing properties; doctors' assistants and orderlies, because they aid the skilled physician in the practice of his art without themselves possessing it, except perhaps only in a rudimentary way; to the physicians themselves, because they possess that art and have a certain mastery of it. The term "medical" thus has a different meaning in each of these cases; but not a completely different meaning, because there is reference throughout to one efficient principle, namely, the art of medicine.[5]

In like manner, there is analogy of proportion in the order of substantiality, where the accident-modes of being are said to *be* by reference to the substance-mode (to being *per se*) as to their subject (quasi-material cause). For an accident is that whose nature it is to inhere in a substance as in its subject.[6] Thus the substance-mode of being is the "prime analogate" for the being of all the accident-modes, which are then called its secondary analogates. So, too, "health," said of the animal, is prime analogate in respect of all other things of which this term can be properly pred-

[5] IV *Meta.* I, 538, with *De prin. nat., loc. cit.*
[6] IV *Meta.* I, 539.

icated; and "medical" as applied to the art of medicine has
the same role with respect to everything else of which it
can be rightly predicated. The essential "notes" of this
type of analogy, then, are two: diversity of relations; identity of the term of those relations.

Analogy of proportion or attribution (which we shall
hereafter simply call analogy of attribution, since this is
the more commonly used designation) is in effect when
the same word is applied to different things according to
a formal signification partly the same and partly diverse—
diverse as regards the diverse modes of relation to the term
of the attribution or attributions, but the same as regards
the term itself. Things are analogous in this way because
they are proportioned to one thing: *proportionantur ad
unum*.[7] In other words, things are analogous by analogy
of proportion or attribution whose name is common, the
notion signified by that name being the same as regards the
term of the attribution but diverse as regards the relations
of the analogates to it.[8]

The single term to which the analogates are all "proportioned" may have the character of any of the four types
of cause. We have already seen examples of three of these
types. In the order of the exemplar or exemplary cause
(which is an extrinsic formal cause), we have the eminent
case of that fundamental analogy between the creature and
God which consists in the one imitating the other so far as
the limited or defective nature of the former allows.[9]

The shortest and simplest formula for analogy of attri-

[7] XI *Meta*. III, 2197.
[8] John of St. Thomas, *Logica*, II, 13, 3 (ed. Reiser; Turin, 1930), p. 484.
[9] St. Thomas, I *Sent*., XXXV, 1, 4.

bution is found in the phrase "according to intention only, and not according to being" (*secundum intentionem tantum, et non secundum esse*); that is, when one intention is referred to several things by priority and posteriority and yet is realized in only one of them; as the intention of health is referred to the animal and to other things in different ways according to priority and posteriority, but exists actually only in the animal.[10]

2. THE PROPERTIES OF THIS ANALOGY

The expression, "according to intention only," means according to pure reference or relation.[11] For intention, like all logical entities, essentially imports reference or relation; and if the adverb "only" is added, we have pure relation, relation alone and nothing else. But pure relation, in turn, means pure attribution, because attribution is simply the relating of an attribute or a predicate to a subject. Thus all predication is rightly called attribution.

The reason for this is indeed a deep one; for the mode of predication is consequent to the mode of being—and every word is ultimately reduced to the word "is" and its participial form. "So many modes of predication, so many modes of being": *quot modis praedicatio fit, tot modis ens dicitur*.[12] The following text brings out clearly the relevance of this absolutely universal principle to the doctrine of attribution: [13] "*Esse* is said in two ways . . . in one way

10 I *Sent.*, XIX, 5, 2 ad 1.
11 Cf. Ramirez, "De Analogia secundum Doctrinam Aristotelico-Thomisticam," in *La Ciencia Tomista*, XXIV (1921), 345.
12 V *Meta.* IX, 893.
13 *Quaest. quodl.* IX, 2, 3, c., Italics mine.

according as it is the verbal copula signifying the composition of any enunciation which the mind makes; *esse* in this sense, therefore, is not something existing in the nature of things but only in the act of the mind composing and dividing [i.e., in the act of judgment]; and thus considered, *esse* is *attributed* to everything about which a proposition can be formulated, whether it be being or privation of being—for we even say that blindness *is*. In another way, *esse* is taken in the sense of the act of being as such, i.e., as that by which something is denominated a being in act, existing in the nature of things; and in this sense *esse* is attributed only to those things which are contained in the ten categories."

The *first* and principal *property* or condition of analogy of attribution is that the notion attributed to a number of things is realized formally only in the prime analogate; it is only by *extrinsic denomination* from the latter that the others receive the common name. This is evident, for instance, in the case of healthy or healthful predicated of animal, of medicine, complexion, food, etc.[14] Of course health exists properly and "formally" only in the animal, and those other objects are denominated "healthy" or "healthful" *extrinsically* from that health, not in virtue of any health inherent in them. (Cajetan,[15] John of St. Thomas,[16] Le Rohellec,[17] Penido,[18] Garrigou-

[14] Cf. *S. th.*, I, 16, 6; IV *Meta.*, I, 539; XI *Meta.*, III, 2196.
[15] *De nom.*, II, 13 f.
[16] *Logica*, II, *ed. cit.*, p. 486.
[17] "De fundamento . . . " in *Divus Thomas* (Placentiae, 1926), Vol. XXIX, p. 87.
[18] *Le rôle*, p. 37.

Lagrange,[19] Manser,[20] Marc,[21] all hold this same doctrine concerning the fundamental property of analogy of attribution.)

From this primary property there follow three additional properties. Of these the first is that the analogous formality is *numerically one,* since it exists only in the one analogate, and not only logically one or one in reason.[22] (This doctrine is drawn directly from St. Thomas.[23]) But in this case the notion of oneness can be understood in two ways: universally and particularly.[24] If the analogates are considered particularly; for instance, if we consider this healthy complexion, this healthful medicine, this healthful food, this healthy animal, then all such things are said to be healthy or healthful by denomination from the health which is in *this* particular animal; and such health

[19] *Dieu,* p. 532.

[20] "Das Wesen der Analogie" in *Divus Thomas* (Fribourg, 1929), Vol. VII, p. 346.

[21] "L'idée thomiste de l'être et les analogies d'attribution et de proportionnalité" in *Rev. néo-scol.,* XXXV (1933), 157–89.

[22] Cf. Cajetan, *De nom.,* II, 15; John of St. Thomas, *Logica,* II, 486; Ramirez, "De analogia . . . ," Part III, *La Ciencia Tomista,* XXV (1922), 26.

[23] See IV *Meta.,* I, 536; *S. th.,* I–II, 20, 3, 3. I shall not enter into the extraordinarily subtle (and sometimes both confused and confusing) discussions which have arisen over a number of St. Thomas' statements on analogy. The aim of this whole study is to discover the principles and to give some intelligible expression to the spirit and essence of metaphysical analogy. Involvement in exegetical details would plague the reader, harass the author, and quite possibly befog the main issues. St. Thomas did not write a treatise on analogy, and as a rule he speaks of analogy explicitly only when he feels he must do so in order to clarify difficult points of doctrine. But he uses the principle of analogy always and everywhere, or nearly so. There is not a single metaphysical or theological argument in St. Thomas where analogy, whether explicitly or implicitly (and most often implicitly), does not come into play. For St. Thomas all properly metaphysical and theological terms are analogical, and the arguments in which such terms occur are therefore also analogical: precisely in what sense has not been shown. That is the object of this book.

[24] Cajetan, *De nom.,* II, 15–17.

is truly and positively one in number. However, if the analogates are considered universally,—for example, if we consider healthy complexion, healthful medicine, health-ful food, healthy animal in general—then, formally speaking, the health by reference to which those things receive a common predication is not numerically one in a positive sense, but negatively or improperly one. For a universal is only logically one, not numerically one, properly and positively speaking.[25]

From this *second property* of analogy of attribution, namely, the fact that the analogous formality is numerically one (whether "positively" or "negatively"), its *third property* or condition is inferred. This consists in the fact that the principal term or prime analogate itself enters into and should therefore always be included in the concepts or definitions of all the other analogates. The reason is clear: those analogates have no title to the common analogous name which is applied to them except through *attribution* to the prime analogate, in which alone that which the term signifies is realized formally. Thus the concept of health as existing in the living organism is nec-essarily included in the concept or definition of complex-ion, medicine, diet, etc., so far as they are said to be healthy or healthful; for to understand what these adjectives mean as applied to such things presupposes an understanding at

[25] Cajetan uses the expression *unum numero negative* to indicate the radical difference in meaning between *unum numero* said of particular sensible or physical qualities, properties, or things, and *unum numero* said of universals, which are not numerically one in a properly mathematical sense but only in a logical sense. Spiritual substances are one in number in a still more radically different sense, and God in the most radically different sense of all. Evidently the term *unum numero* is itself analogical.

least minimal of what is meant by "healthy" said of the living organism. The same holds in all other such cases. In other words: definition is derived from and based on the form; consequently what is realized formally in a thing should be placed in the definition of all other things which receive the same name by extrinsic denomination from or attribution to that thing.[26] St. Thomas is speaking of analogy of attribution and is making the same point when he says that "in analogical terms a name taken in one signification must be placed in the definition of the same name taken in other senses." [27]

A *fourth property* of analogy of attribution follows from the third. Since this analogy entails a plurality of relations, it entails also a plurality of concepts. The common term, therefore, has a different meaning in respect to each of the analogates, and thus in each case involves a different concept. But unlike things which are equivocal merely by chance, all these different significations have a mutual connotation, being all referred to that single thing of which the common name is predicated properly.[28]

3. The Essence of This Analogy

Analogy of attribution may involve only two terms: simple proportion or attribution of *this* to *that;* or more than two terms; in fact, an indefinite number of terms. But regardless of their number, they are all referred to one principal term. Analogy of attribution is thus always *ad*

---

[26] See Cajetan, *op. cit.*, II, p. 17. Cf. *loc. cit.* in John of St. Thomas and Ramirez; in Penido, *Le rôle*, p. 37.
[27] *S. th.*, I, 13, 10, c; cf. I, 13, 6.
[28] Cf. Cajetan, *De nom.*, II, 17 f.; John of St. Thomas and Penido, *loc. cit.*

unum, "analogy of one or of several to *one*" ("analogia unius vel plurium *ad unum*").[29] In analogy of attribution as such, the analogous form exists intrinsically only in the prime analogate, but in the others extrinsically and by denomination. This is the principal condition, the primary constitutive character or property of this analogy. The analogous term, considered simply or absolutely, stands for the prime analogate alone, as everything is denominated through its form; and that which possesses the form simply or absolutely is denominated such simply or absolutely.

But merely to state in abstract general terms the essential character of this analogy would not suffice to make it "concretely" intelligible. Examples are not lacking, however. An interesting case is the term "philosophy" as used by Aristotle.[30] For when Aristotle speaks of "philosophy" *tout court,* he means metaphysics or *first* philosophy. The latter, therefore, is the prime analogate for all the other parts or divisions of philosophical science. Prime analogates of this sort are said to be such antonomastically.[31] As a matter of fact, St. Thomas himself used the word "philosopher" antonomastically in reference to Aristotle. If this were considered a case of *pure* attribution, it would follow

[29] Penido, *op. cit.,* pp. 32–35; cf. Cajetan, *op. cit.,* II, 19 f.

[30] Cf. Ramirez, "De analogia . . . ," p. 27.

[31] "That which belongs to many things in common," says St. Thomas (*S. th.,* II–II, 186, 1, c.), "is attributed antonomastically to that thing to which it belongs par excellence, as the term fortitude, for instance, lays claim to that virtue which maintains strength of soul in the face of dangers, and the term temperance to that virtue which tempers even the keenest pleasures." Moreover, he observes (*op. cit.,* 141, 2, c.) that it is customary to use certain common words to designate only those things which are pre-eminent among things of the same class, the word "City," for example, being taken antonomastically for Rome. (I am indebted to Father Ramirez for indicating these texts.)

that for St. Thomas all other philosophers were philosophers not truly and properly but only *abusively* so called; [32] for they would then be called philosophers only by attribution to and extrinsic denomination from The Philosopher, in whom alone the "virtue" of philosophy was properly realized! Of course St. Thomas did not think of Aristotle in this way. But Averroes did.[33]

A remarkable, not to say monstrous, example of abusive attribution is found in the recent use of the term "leader" in some countries. For if "leader" be taken antonomastically for one man, all other leaders will be such only in an improper sense, only by attribution to and extrinsic denomination from The Leader. The structure of dictatorial regimes exhibits analogy of attribution in the "pure" state, or almost so. In the vast majority of cases, this analogy exists not in a "pure" but in a "mixed" state.[34] Some other type of analogy is at work with it.

This raises a problem (broached by the important sixteenth-century Jesuit theologian and philosopher, Francisco Suarez) which is still hotly debated, and which is in fact of crucial importance for the whole theory of analogy.

[32] See Cajetan, *De nom.* II, 21.
[33] See Gilson, *Reason and Revelation in the Middle Ages* (New York, 1938), pp. 39 ff.
[34] See Maritain, *Degrés*, pp. 822 f.

CHAPTER IX

THE SUAREZIAN QUESTION

1. "Extrinsic" and "Intrinsic" Attribution

For Suarez there are two modes of attribution: *one,* where the denominating form exists intrinsically in one of the terms alone and in the others only through extrinsic relation to that term (as in the case of the word "healthy" which is predicated properly only of the living organism or animal and of other things, solely by extrinsic attribution); *the other,* where the denominating form exists intrinsically in both (or all) the terms, in one absolutely and in the other or others through intrinsic relation to the former. For example, whereas substance is being, in the primary or absolute sense, accident is not designated "being" by extrinsic denomination from the being of substance but from its own proper and intrinsic being, because the whole being of the accident consists precisely in that intrinsic relationship which it has to its substance.[1] The first mode is thus commonly called "extrinsic," the second, "intrinsic" attribution.

Between these two modes, Suarez states in the same text, there are a number of differences. In the "extrinsic" type, for instance, the common name is attributed to the sec-

[1] *Disputationes metaphysicae,* disp. XXVIII, sect. iii, in *Opera omnia* (ed. Vivès, Paris, 1877; Vol. XXVI, p. 17, col. 2). Italics used in all quotations from this work are mine.

ondary object (or objects) signified by it "only improperly and by metaphor, or some other figure"; whereas in the "intrinsic" type, "the denomination is in the highest degree proper, and can even be essential, because it is taken from the intrinsic form or proper nature." Furthermore, in the "extrinsic" type the secondary objects or analogates are "defined through the prime analogate," whereas in the "intrinsic" type it is not necessary that any secondary or posterior analogate be defined through the prime or principal one. Suarez therefore concludes that "the analogy *or* attribution, which the creature has to God under the aspect of being is of the latter sort, that is, it is based on proper and *intrinsic* being, having an essential relation to or dependence upon God." [2]

2. THE REDUCTION OF PROPORTIONALITY TO METAPHOR

Though I shall be anticipating to some extent certain points which belong properly to the last Part of this book, I think it should be said here that for Suarez there is no analogy of *proper* proportionality: "Every veritable analogy of proportionality includes an element of metaphor and of impropriety, just as 'smiling' is said of a meadow through metaphorical transference. . . ." [3] If this is true, then it follows that "there is no proper analogy of propor-

---

[2] *Ibid.*, p. 18 (no. 16), col. 2: "Analogia seu attributio, quam creatura sub ratione entis potest habere ad Deum, sit posterioris modi, id est, fundata in proprio et intrinseco esse habente essentialem habitudinem seu dependentiam a Deo."

[3] *Ibid.*, p. 16 (no. 11), col. 2: "Omnis vera analogia proportionalitatis includit aliquid metaphorae et improprietatis, sicut ridere dicitur de prato per translationem metaphoricam."

tionality between God and creatures." [4] In order to have such an analogy, Suarez argues, it is necessary that the one member (in this case, God) *be* through its very form, properly and absolutely, that which it is designated to be by the common name, whereas the other members (in this case, creatures) will have no proper being of their own and therefore will receive the common name (say, *being*) only in virtue of the fact that they are "subject to a certain proportion or comparison" to the first member. "But this is not so in the present case . . . for the creature is a being by reason of its own being, simply [or absolutely], without taking into consideration any such proportionality, because surely, through that very being which it itself has, it is outside nothingness and has something of actuality." [5]

This last statement is of course true. The creature is a being in its own right; and to perceive that fact it is not necessary to consider any sort of "proportionality" between it and God. But the previous statement is not correct. In analogy of proper proportionality it is not the case that the "secondary members" have no proper being of their own and consequently receive the common predication only in virtue of some "proportion or comparison" with the "primary member." This is true only in the case of analogy of *improper* proportionality or of metaphor.

Between the creature and God there is only a sort of attribution: "attribution of one to another," Suarez says. [6]

[4] *Loc. cit.*: "Analogia proportionalitatis propria non est inter Deum et creaturas."

[5] *Ibid.*: "At vero in praesenti hoc non intercedit . . . creatura enim est ens ratione sui esse absolute et sine tali proportionalitate considerati, quia nimirum per illud est extra nihil, et aliquid actualitatis habet."

[6] *Ibid.*, p. 17 (no. 12), col. 1: " . . . attributio unius ad alium."

The reduction of analogy of proportionality to analogy of metaphor is thus brought about by the identification of the former with analogy of extrinsic proportion or relation; for such, essentially, is the character of metaphorical analogy. For Suarez the only true analogy is analogy of "intrinsic attribution"; it alone is properly analogical and properly metaphysical because it alone applies properly to *being*. Analogy of "proportionality" is merely analogy of extrinsic attribution or relation.[7] In Suarez' opinion these two types of attribution are radically different: there is a vast difference between the oft-repeated "analogy of health," which is based on purely extrinsic relations and thus implies purely extrinsic attribution to a single term, and the "analogy of being," which is based on intrinsic relations and therefore requires intrinsic attribution to *being* in the principal and primary sense.

3. SUAREZIAN ANALOGY AND MODERN SCHOLASTICS

The doctrine of Suarez, summarized above, has exercised an immense influence upon the thinking of "Scholastics" on the problem of analogy, an influence which has continued unabated down to our own times. Pedro Descoqs, S.J., for instance, essentially follows Suarez. Like his master, he draws a distinction between "extrinsic" and "intrinsic" attribution, and apparently supposes that Thomists who hold the "Cajetanist" view deny that in analogy of attribution there is anything intrinsic to the secondary analogates.[8] More recently, Antoine van Leeu-

[7] Cf. *op. cit.*, disp. II; Vol. XXV, p. 78 (no. 24), col. 1.

[8] Cf. Descoqs, *Institutiones metaphysicae generalis*, Eléments d'ontologie, I, 262–64, 268.

wen, S.J., reaffirms essentially the same Suarezian thesis when he proposes intrinsic attribution as against pure extrinsic attribution, asserting that analogy *non secundum esse* cannot be metaphysical.[9] In the case of the analogy of accident to substance, he argues,[10] we have *intrinsic* attribution; whereas in the analogy of healthy to climate, etc., we have *extrinsic* attribution. He therefore proposes (as Suarez had done) that the definition of analogy of attribution be broadened so as to include both types.[11] Emile Laurent, C.Sp.S., likewise maintains that analogy of attribution as such falls outside the field of metaphysics because it is by definition *"non secundum esse."* [12] Its correct name, he holds, is not "analogy of attribution," but "analogy of purely extrinsic attribution," because the concept of attribution or of proportion is essential to analogy as such, and does not characterize one kind rather than another.[13] This positon is clearly Suarezian; as is that of Charles de Moré-Pontgibaud, who reaffirms Suarez' doctrine that intrinsic attribution is the fundamental character of analogy and that proportionality always imports something improper and metaphorical.[14] G. C. Joyce adopts the Suarezian distinction between analogy of "proportion," which he identifies with analogy of "extrinsic attribution," and analogy of "intrinsic attribution." [15] And, although he should not be classed as a "Scholastic," R. L. Patterson appeals to

[9] In his article, "L'analogie de l'être," see pp. 484 f.
[10] *Art. cit.*, p. 486.
[11] *Ibid.*, p. 487.
[12] See his article, "Quelques réflexions sur l'analogie," pp. 169–84.
[13] *Ibid.*, p. 180.
[14] In his article, "Sur l'analogie des noms divins," *Recherches de science religieuse*, XX (1930), 215, 221.
[15] See his article, "Analogy," pp. 415–19.

Father Descoqs in support of his own Suarezian views on analogy.[16]

I mention these writers, not at all that I may summarily dismiss their work (for they have doubtless made some valuable contributions to the theory of analogy), but only in order to indicate in a general way the persistence of the Suarezian influence. They are not all pure Suarezians by any means. If Father Descoqs cannot rightly be called a strict Suarezian, the title would be even less appropriate in the case of van Leeuwen and Laurent, for example; because on certain essential points they appeal to Sylvester of Ferrara, who antedates Suarez by some seventy years.

To make a long story short, those who follow in the tradition of Suarez on this question and deny that the so-called Cajetanist doctrine of analogy of attribution (as formulated not only by Cajetan himself but also by such modern Thomists as Ramirez, Le Rohellec, Penido, Manser, Maritain, and Marc) has any properly philosophical significance, do so because they believe that that doctrine is a theory of pure extrinsicism; that it takes all the reality out of things, so to speak, and leaves nothing but pure extrinsic relations vis-à-vis a single term wherein alone the analogous concept is realized properly. And in a sense this is true. But the very fact that they feel it necessary to posit an "intrinsic" attribution in opposition to "extrinsic" attribution (which the Cajetanists claim essentially characterizes analogy of attribution), bears witness to a confusion of mind on this subject. For the "Cajetanists" do not hold

---

[16] R. L. Patterson, *The Conception of God in the Philosophy of Aquinas*, esp. pp. 248 f.

that there is nothing intrinsic to the secondary analogates but only that they do not realize *formally* the analogical notion as such, their sole title to a common denomination consisting in the fact that they are all linked to a single term which defines them and without which, therefore, they cannot be grasped or conceived at all.

4. THE NON-THOMISTIC CHARACTER OF SUAREZIAN ANALOGY

The Suarezian doctrine of analogy, and in particular the theory of intrinsic attribution, is generally claimed to be Thomistic, to be actually based on the texts of St. Thomas. Of course, even if this were the case, it would not follow that that theory was true. But it is not the case. For St. Thomas holds that, although the analogous concept in analogy of attribution is realized only in the prime analogate, there is something *in* the secondary analogates in virtue of which they are capable of receiving the common denomination. Health, for instance, is not in the medicine, which is a cause of it, nor in complexion, which is a sign of it; but in both medicine and complexion there is *something* by which the former causes and the latter signifies health.[17] Yet at the same time St. Thomas maintains that the intention of health is referred to the animal and to such things as complexion and diet in different ways according to priority and posteriority, but not according to

17 *S. th.*, I, 16, 6, c. In the similarity between proper cause and proper effect lies the foundation of the analogical attribution: the health-causing is called healthy or healthful because the proper cause of health resembles the effect, health.

a diverse act of being (*esse*), because health actually exists only in the animal.[18]

John of St. Thomas makes the same point when he observes that, because of its healing power, the herb is *intrinsically* related to health, but not intrinsically *denominated* healthy; thus, therefore, health in the animal has the character of a form, whereas in respect to the herb it has the character of an extrinsically denominating term.[19] And as Penido rightly says,[20] "attribution, as attribution, does not posit anything else, because it is a pure relation of dependence."

Suarez holds that between the divine being and the created being there exists an analogy of "intrinsic attribution." For the creature is a being-by-participation while God is Being-by-essence; hence the creature participates in being only through dependence upon God and in subordination to Him.[21]

It is of course true that the creature has being only dependently upon the Creator and in subordination to Him; but it is not true that this relation of dependence is that which *primarily* distinguishes these two orders of being. The *relation* itself does not constitute the very nature or being of the creature. As St. Thomas puts it, "although *relation to its cause* does not enter the definition of the thing caused, nevertheless that relation *follows* from the

---

[18] I *Sent.*, XIX, 5, 2, ad 1: "Quia *esse* sanitatis non est nisi in animali."

[19] *Logica*, II, 13, 4 (ed. Reiser, p. 490, *ad tertium*). Cf. Penido, *Le rôle*, p. 37, with notes 1 and 2.

[20] *Le rôle*, p. 27: "L'attribution en tant qu'attribution ne pose pas autre chose parce qu'elle est un pur rapport de dépendance."

[21] *Disp. metaph.*, disp. XXVIII, sect. iii, no. 16.

very notion of that thing; for from the fact that a thing exists by participation, it *follows* that it is caused by another." [22] Thus it is simply a question of pointing out that being is ontologically prior to relation: things are things before they are *related* things.

To speak of intrinsic attribution is to speak "materially." [23] It is true that this intrinsic *character* is actually found in certain cases: in the so-called cases of "mixed analogy," where there is a "material coincidence" of attribution and proportionality. Being, for example, is intrinsic to accident and substance: they both *are*, intrinsically, though in different ways: they have being *proportionately* to their natures. And being is *attributed* to accident in virtue of its intrinsic relation to substance. But the attribution itself is not "intrinsic." The "intrinsicism" here consists precisely and solely in the common though diverse (proportional) possession of a common "form," namely, the act of being. Accidents are *said* to exist in virtue of their *relation* to substances (attribution), but they *do* exist in virtue of their inherence in substances; and this existence is in every case proportional to the natures of those accidents and of those substances, so that a proportion of proportions, a "proportionality," in *being* is thereby established. Thus, to mention this one instance among innumerable others, in the case of the analogy of accident to substance, there is indeed a kind of "material coincidence" of attribution and proportionality. Nevertheless, as Penido

[22] *S. th.*, I, 44, 1, ad 1: "Licet habitudo ad causam non intret definitionem entis, quod est causatum, tamen consequitur ad ea quae sunt de ejus ratione, quia ex hoc quod aliquid est ens per participationem, sequitur quod sit causatum ab alio."

[23] Cf. Penido, *op. cit.*, p. 37.

justly remarks,[24] to speak "materially" is to risk introducing a fundamental univocity into the very heart of analogy, with the result that between the various modes of analogy there will remain only an accidental difference, thus making all these modes formally the same and only relatively different. In other words, analogy will then be defined in terms of univocity and formally reduced to a species of it. But such a reduction would be profoundly false. For "a diverse mode of existing makes univocal predication impossible." [25] And to make this really self-evident point concretely clear, St. Thomas uses a very simple example: the actually existing house and the idea of it in the builder's mind are formally the same, but the term "house" is not predicated univocally of them both, because the form of the actual house has material being, while in the mind of the builder it exists immaterially. In the last analysis, any diversity in mode of being, of *esse*, rules out univocity.

5. CONSEQUENCES OF THE FALLACY OF INTRINSIC ATTRIBUTION

The "risk" which Penido speaks of does not belong in the category of philosophical rhetoric. Suarez' notion of analogy seems to have enjoyed only a precarious existence in his own mind. His analysis of the concept of being, far from putting analogy on a sound footing, apparently made its status all the more insecure.

Suarez rejects the Scotist doctrine of the univocity of being on the argument that, despite the subtle distinctions

[24] *Ibid.,* pp. 37 f.
[25] *De pot.,* VII, 7, c.: "Diversus modus existendi impedit univocam praedicationem."

of its author,[26] that doctrine implies the reduction of being to a genus, with the result that God and creatures would no longer be differentiated *as beings*.[27] But, as we have seen, Suarez denies that there is any analogy of *proper* proportionality. For him, moreover, the objective concept of being cannot actually and implicitly contain the various modes of being.[28] This implies, however, that the notion of being has an absolute unity; a unity like that of a generic concept; a univocal unity, in other words, not that merely relational unity characteristic of proportionality.

Sensing this difficulty, Suarez goes so far as to admit that "what 'we' have just said concerning the unity of the concept of being seems far clearer and more certain than that being is analogical; to defend analogy, therefore, the unity of that concept is not to be denied; but, if it is necessary to deny one or the other, analogy, *which is uncertain,* should be denied, rather than the unity of the concept of being, which seems to have been demonstrated by conclusive arguments." [29]

Suarez cannot uphold his theory of an analogy of intrin-

---

[26] Cf. Cyril L. Shircel, O.F.M., *The Univocity of the Concept of Being in the Philosophy of John Duns Scotus*. In this study, Father Shircel quotes and refers to numerous texts on this subject from the writings of Scotus. It appears that Scotus held that the concept of being is "univocal" primarily because it is "an essentially indifferent concept," a concept which is therefore "equally applicable to all things" (p. 168). But of course Scotus denies that being is a genus or is predicated after the manner of a genus (p. 169, with references).

[27] Suarez, *op. cit.,* disp. ii, sect. v, nos. 5 and 10; disp. xxviii, sect. iii, no. 7.

[28] Suarez, *op. cit.,* disp. ii, sect. ii, no. 21 ff.

[29] Suarez, *op. cit.* (Vol. XXV), disp. ii, sect. ii, no. 34: "Nunc solum assero, omnis quae diximus de unitate conceptus entis, longe clariora et certiora videri, quam quod ens sit analogum: et ideo non recte propter defendendam analogiam negari unitatem conceptus; sed si alterum negandum esset, potius analogia, quae incerta est, quam unitas conceptus, quae certis rationibus videtur demonstrari, esset neganda."

sic attribution between the creature and God and at the same time maintain the absolute unity of the concept of being. For if the creature is a participated being and God is unparticipated Being, it clearly follows that they differ in their very actuality. In other words, these two beings exist in *essentially diverse* ways. But where there is utter diversity in *essence*, there can be no other likeness than that of a proportional sharing in existence, in the act of being itself.

It seems that Suarez' position logically *leads toward* the doctrine of the univocity of being, thus making him in some sense a continuator of the Scotist tradition.[30] At any rate, to introduce an analogy of "intrinsic" attribution is to mistake the very formal character of attribution and to blur the distinction between attribution and proportionality. Penido notes that, when St. Thomas explains his theory of the *nature* of analogy of attribution, he never speaks of intrinsicism.[31] I know of no text in St. Thomas which can be cited to the contrary. The whole Suarezian thesis, Penido believes, is deduced from Thomistic texts which do not purport to expound the theory of analogy itself but which only exhibit particular applications of this principle to "mixed" cases; for in no text, he says, do we find intrinsic analogy of attribution explicitly affirmed, its extrinsic character being everywhere emphasized.[32] Perhaps no one has submitted the texts of St. Thomas on anal-

30 Cf. Garrigou-Lagrange, *Dieu*, p. 586.
31 *Le rôle*, p. 38.
32 *Ibid.* Penido refers to S. th. I, 15, 6 (cf. I–II, 20, 3 ad 3), and calls attention to the "decisive text" in I *Eth.*, VII, 96, where St. Thomas indicates the radical distinction between attribution and proportionality, the only reason he gives for this opposition being that the one analogy is extrinsic, the other intrinsic.

ogy to a more thorough scrutiny that has Penido. But though his analysis is certainly helpful, one need not have recourse to it to see wherein the Suarezian error lies.

That error stems from the failure to grasp the nature of analogy of attribution formally, to see what it actually is in itself. In a sense, the very effort of some scholastic "analogists" to hew closely to the Thomistic line has been responsible for this error; I mean that a literal, a too literal, fidelity to the texts of St. Thomas on this point renders the Suarezian fallacy well-nigh inevitable. For in many places where St. Thomas gives concrete applications of analogy (and these texts are far more numerous than his doctrinal statements on analogy), he presents analogates which realize intrinsically a perfection common to them all proportionately, and which are at the same time all ordered to a principal term.[33] We need not wonder, then, that some philosophers, and in particular those with a Suarezian background, have concluded to an analogy of *intrinsic* attribution.

In the end, however, this position leads logically to the destruction of all analogy. In the measure that attribution is stressed and proportionality denied, or given a secondary role, analogy will tend to resolve itself into univocity. And if proportionality in the proper sense is excluded and attribution set up as the sole constitutive character of true analogy, then in effect a basic formal univocity will have been substituted for analogy. In the metaphysical order,

---

[33] This also, I believe, accounts for the fact that Sylvester of Ferrara (1474–1528) and those who follow him on this question (e.g., Balthasar, Blanche, van Leeuwen, Laurent) have affirmed that analogy of proportionality necessarily requires a prime analogate. But this problem belongs to the last Part (see chapter 18).

this means that being will have been taken as a generic formality (as if, in the manner of a genus, it were both logically one and physically one), thus reviving the error of Parmenides. Nor will an appeal to "intrinsic attribution" ease one over the difficulty, since it has been clearly shown that attribution, formally considered, is necessarily "extrinsic." In itself attribution posits an extrinsic denomination, and nothing else.

Ultimately there is no middle ground between any species of metaphysical or metaphysicized univocity and philosophical analogy rightly so called. For in the order of being there is either an essential diversity or there is not. If there is not, then there is no real plurality: the "differential modalities" of being themselves will have no being in their own right; in the substantive sense, they will not be things at all. But if the many are not, if being is not essentially diversified, we must finally come round to absolute monism and assert that all multiplicity is illusory. At least this would be the result if the aforesaid doctrine of being were pushed to its ultimate limit. Of course "univocist" philosophers ordinarily stop short of this extreme conclusion, which is implied and demanded by their own principles, and they attempt, inconsistently, to occupy some intermediate position.

All this is necessarily bound up with the real composition of essence and act of existence in creatures, and their identity in God.[34] To deny this composition, even in principle, is to court metaphysical and theological disaster.

[34] Herein lies "the fundamental truth of Christian philosophy," to quote the title of a very important modern book (N. Del Prado, O.P., *De veritate fundamentali philosophiae christianae*, Fribourg, Switzerland, 1911).

Obviously no Christian philosopher could draw out the final implications of that denial and still think as a Christian, or even as a metaphysician. In theological terms, the final result would be either to rob God of His deity or to elevate the creature to the rank of God. In metaphysical terms, the result would be either monism or pantheism or both together; and either of these positions in its pure and absolute form spells the death of metaphysics.

In place of the "real distinction," some kind of accidental composition or distinction of degree may be substituted. In that case, unparticipated being (the Being who alone is pure act) and participated beings (things composed of potency and act, creatures) may be and ought to be put in the same class: the class *being*. But this would be absurd for many reasons. We need mention only one. If unparticipated Being and participated beings were both included in the genus of being, then *being* would be predicated univocally of them. But that is impossible, because diversity in the order of being (*esse*) precludes such predication: "*diversa habitudo ad esse impedit univocam praedicationem entis.*" [35] This principle is absolutely general. Here St. Thomas is concerned only to show how it applies to God and creatures: God *is* in respect of the act of being (*se habet ad esse*) in a way other than any creature, because He is His own act of being; indeed, no predicate applies univocally to God and creatures.[36]

[35] St. Thomas, *De pot.* VII, 7, c. See above note 25.
[36] *Ibid.,* "De Deo et creatura nihil praedicetur univoce."

CHAPTER X

THE REDUCTION OF ANALOGY TO UNIVOCITY

1. The Alleged Primacy of "Proportion" in Theodicy

BETWEEN any effect and the agent which produces it there is necessarily a certain proportion or "analogy." This consists in the relation which links the effect to its cause. Now, creatures are effects of God: He is their efficient cause, the cause of their very being. Hence the relation of creatures to God is one of utter dependence in the order of being. But that relation itself establishes an analogy, a proportion, between the creature and the Creator. It therefore seems reasonable to suppose that this analogy, in the realm of natural theology or theodicy at least, is the absolutely primary and basic one.

Once more, however, it must be pointed out that the very being itself of the creature does not consist in its *relation to* God: the relation itself is ontologically posterior to the being of the creature. Moreover, as we tried to make clear in the preceding chapter, analogy of proportion itself implies a pure relation of dependence, and that alone.

Without entering into a detailed discussion of proportionality here (that problem will be treated fully in Part

Four), it is evident that the proportional possession of being, of *esse,* by the creature and the Creator is prior, absolutely speaking, to the proportion whereby the one is related to the other. The first analogy (technically called analogy of proper proportionality) is the analogy *of* being and *in* being; the second is the analogy, the proportion, between related beings. Clearly, without the first analogy, without the actual proportional possession and exercise of being, the second "analogy"—the proportion between the terms in question—would be impossible. Consequently the knowledge of the second term (in this case the Creator) is rooted in the first analogy, which bears on the relations *within* the very being of the related terms, not on the proportion or relation between the terms themselves. Using mathematical language but giving it a purely metaphysical meaning, the first analogy has been called a "proportionality," a proportion of proportions (the nature of a thing "is to" its act of being as the nature of any other thing "is to" its act of being), whereas the second is merely a proportion, a simple, direct relation between one term and another.

It is true that the knowledge of uncreated being is analogous to the knowledge of created being: there is a proportional likeness between them. But such knowledge is possible only by reason of the intrinsic proportional sharing of both orders of being in the act of being itself. To hold, therefore, that analogy of proportionality exists solely in the order of knowledge is to deprive analogical knowledge of its real and only basis.[1]

1 See below, chapter 20, sect. 5; chap. 22, sect. 4.

This seems to be a good place to deal briefly with a rather prevalent error regarding the nature and function of analogy of proportion in that department of metaphysics sometimes called theodicy.[2] The whole doctrine of the primacy of this analogy has many significant implications, and I will attempt to do little more than scratch the surface here.

A. Biard's statement of this doctrine as applied to natural theology (a statement typical of many others) is instructive because it indicates clearly the ultimate disaster which must befall analogy if the primacy in question is consistently maintained.

For Biard there is a double analogy in theodicy: analogy of proportion, whereby created being is analogous to uncreated being, and analogy of proportionality, whereby the knowledge of uncreated being is analogous to the knowledge of created being. The first analogy is found in the order of being, the second only in the order of knowledge.[3] It is obvious that there is an analogy of direct proportion between the creature and the Creator. Knowledge of the Creator, however, is subject to the mode of knowledge of the creature; thus, Biard argues, since the order of knowledge is based on the order of being, it follows that it is analogy of proportion which lies at the root of all the analogies of proportionality. The analogy of proportion, he says, directly relates the creature to God, whereas anal-

2 As established by Leibnitz in 1710, this term applied (improperly) to that part of theology which was held to be concerned with the "justification" of divine providence through the reconciliation of evil with the goodness and sovereignty of God. Since that time "theodicy" has come to be used quite generally as a synonym for natural theology.

3 A. Biard, *Analogie en Théodicée*, p. 28; cf. pp. 32 ff.

ogy of proportionality relates a certain *knowledge* of God to a certain *knowledge* of the creature; [4] for analogical likeness in the ontological order is the basis of analogical likeness in the order of knowledge.[5] This last proposition is indeed true. But by analogical likeness in the ontological order Biard means analogical likeness according to analogy of *proportion*.

After very properly excluding from the notion of analogy the idea of "indeterminate, superficial resemblance," Biard proceeds to reduce the kinds or modes of analogy to three: analogy of extrinsic attribution, of proportion, and of proportionality.[6] This division is itself revealing; for, apart from plentiful additional evidence, it is clear that for Biard if analogy of proportion is not analogy of extrinsic attribution, then it is the familiar analogy of "intrinsic" attribution; and we are back with Suarez again. If this doctrine is allowed to work out its own conclusions, the result will be the positing of a fundamental univocity in being and, consequently, in knowledge. In that case, "analogy in theodicy" will have been turned into "univocity in theodicy." But univocity in theodicy is impossible.

2. The Quest for a Univocal Basis of Analogy

To maintain the primacy of analogy of attribution indicates a desire to discover a univocal ground for analogy itself. In the order of knowledge, as well as of being, it is

[4] *Ibid.*, p. 33.
[5] *Ibid.*, p. 36.
[6] *Ibid.*, p. 65.

axiomatic that every multiplicity must be reduced to a unity. It is, so to speak, natural to conceive such unity univocally.[7] The conviction arises almost spontaneously that all analogical concepts must finally be reduced to univocal concepts. For human knowing is rooted in the perception of sensible objects; and the concepts of such objects are univocal.

It is always true that the apprehension of a univocal case of an analogical object *precedes* the *understanding* of the analogical object itself, and indeed continues to condition that *understanding*. Consequently, it is true that, *psychologically speaking,* analogical concepts are all somehow "reduced" to univocal concepts. But this statement is not true either from the standpoint of logical or of metaphysical analysis. It is not true that in analyzing analogical concepts logically or in analyzing them metaphysically, the mind is in the end confronted with the univocal. In either case the mind is confronted with the analogical. In the case of logical analysis it is confronted with the proportionately similar significations of the analogical concepts; in the case of metaphysical analysis, with singular realizations having a proportional or an analogical unity, not a univocal unity.[8]

In analogy of attribution the principal term or "prime analogate"[9] is not only a real term which is absolutely one, numerically one in a positive, predicamental sense, but a term which is univocal in itself, formally univocal, and hence conceived univocally.

[7] Cf. above, chap. 7, sect. 1.
[8] Cf. below, chap. 23, sect. 2.
[9] The problem of the Prime Analogate is treated in chap. 18, below.

If there is any metaphysical analogy, however, it is an analogy in the order of *existence*. But in that order, no univocal unity is possible.[10]

3. Attribution Must Be Understood Formally

Moreover, this general point bears emphasis: a logical impasse confronts all those who would attempt to understand the nature of analogy "materially." For example: a "material" interpretation of certain texts on analogy in St. Thomas is in some cases largely responsible for the thesis that the Thomistic analogy par excellence is analogy of attribution. To take this stand is to ignore the fact that that analogy as such (formally considered) imports extrinsic denomination alone. As Cajetan remarks,[11] analogy of attribution does not itself belong to the order of the "formal inherent cause" but has always an extrinsic character. But this statement makes sense only if it is understood formally; for in actual fact it is not the case that *every* term which is analogical by attribution is common to the analogates in such a way that it applies formally only to the first analogate, and to the others merely by extrinsic denomination. This is true in some instances (for example, in the predication of "healthy" or "healthful" of a person and of medicine or food); but it is not universally true, as we see in the case of "being" said of accident and of substance, or of "good" said of this good thing and of that, and in any number of similar cases; in fact, wherever the analogous

10 E.g., see below, chap. 22, sect. 4.
11 *De nom.* II, 14 f.

character is actually inherent in the things to which it is attributed. But the point is that the attribution itself is a matter of extrinsic denomination and simply abstracts from or ignores the inherence or non-inherence of the analogous character in the things of which it is predicated.

Thus, *under the formality of attribution,* all the accident-modes of being are said to *be* by extrinsic denomination from the substance-mode, although under some other formality they can also be said to exist in virtue of the being actually inherent in them. Likewise, under the formality of attribution, all "goods" are said to be good by extrinsic denomination from the First Good, although under some other formality they can also be said to be good in virtue of the goodness actually inherent in them. Attribution as such entails only a relation of dependence with respect to a single term (principle, end, subject) which, therefore, has the role of prime analogate; whereas in metaphysical analogy, considered formally, there are not diverse relations to a *single* term but relations to *diverse* subjects wherein the analogical notion is formally and properly realized. Attribution thus proceeds according to an extrinsic denomination, proportionality according to an intrinsic participation.[12] It is clear that, while they are formally distinct, both analogies may in some sense *exist* together. The "order of specification" is not the "order of exercise." In the field of analogy, it is absolutely necessary to proceed in the light of this distinction. Without it, confusion is inevitable.

[12] Cf. Penido's article, "Cajetan et notre connaissance analogique de Dieu," p. 154.

4. Attribution as Prime Analogate for All Analogies

To make analogy of attribution the analogy par excellence is to make it prime analogate for all other analogies. The term "analogy" would then be attributed antonomastically to this analogy; and if one were really thoroughgoing in the matter he would say that all other analogies merited the name only in virtue of an extrinsic denomination from analogy of attribution. Thus the latter would be considered the genus of which all other analogies (popular analogy, experimental or experiential analogy, mathematical analogy, "analogy" of inequality, symbolic analogy, analogy of proper proportionality) were species. Each species might have an indefinite number of sub-species, and so on. But all these species and subspecies would derive their analogical character from "the supreme analogy"; they would all be proportioned to It. There could be no more effective way of disposing of all analogy. For in that case all the modes of analogy would be reduced univocally to their principle, and analogy itself would be converted into univocity.

It is evident that analogy cannot be divided like a genus into its species; it must be divided in such a manner that each mode of analogy realizes in its own way the common character of analogy as such. Hence the principle of this division cannot be any extrinsic difference; it can only be a diverse mode of sharing the common analogical "form." Thus in his Commentary on the *Sentences,* St. Thomas points out that the equivocal, the analogical, and the univocal are divided in different ways: the equivocal according to things signified, the univocal according to differences, the analogical according to *diverse modes*.[13] This implies that analogy itself must not be regarded univocally, in the manner of a genus or category or class, but analogically. As a matter of fact, analogy itself can be understood only analogically.[14] This is true of analogy in general and would hold even if the analogy which was taken as prime analogate for all other analogies were truly analogical in itself. Such, however, is not the case with respect to analogy of attribution.

5. THE UNIVOCAL CHARACTER OF ANALOGY OF ATTRIBUTION

Perhaps this point can be made clear more easily by considering the logical properties of analogy of attribution, and in particular the type and role of the concept it involves. Maritain's treatment of this matter, though brief, is very precise, and here it will be sufficient to review his analysis.[15] In the first place he remarks that in this sort of analogy, considered formally in its "pure state" apart from any "concomitant" analogy of proper proportionality, we are dealing with a concept which is *univocal* in itself and which the mind merely *uses analogically* by transferring it to other things. For example, "healthy" said of the living organism (concept no. 1) is univocal in itself, but it may be employed "analogically" by being attributed to such objects as climate (concept no. 2), where

13 I *Sent.*, XXII, 1, 3, ad 2. See also *ibid.*, XLII, 1, 3; cf. *De pot.*, IX, 2, ad 6.
14 Cf. Ramirez, *art. cit.*, La Ciencia Tomista, XXV, 29.
15 *Degrés,* p. 822.

it designates something made known solely by its relation to the object signified formally by concept no. 1, namely, the health of the living organism. Thus a climate can be called "healthful" not, of course, because there is any health actually inherent in it, but only because of its relation (of efficient causality, in this instance) to the health of the animal or man. It is evident that by such a procedure we shall never be able to reach a knowledge of any "analogated" quality or form or perfection according to that which the concept of it signifies properly. As John of St. Thomas points out,[16] of itself analogy of attribution merely allows us to attain a form which exists intrinsically only in the prime analogate, and in the others extrinsically and by denomination alone.

Considered formally and absolutely, therefore, analogy of attribution is reduced to univocity, because it entails a concept which is univocal in itself and which is merely employed analogically. So if we inspect this analogy in what Maritain calls its pure state, we easily see that it is not an analogy in its own right at all. It is we who give it its quasi-analogical character; we make this "analogy" ourselves. It is thus an "artistic" production, a production of the art of logic.

6. THE ANALOGICAL INGREDIENT IN THIS ANALOGY

It is therefore clear that if anything existing in the extra-logical or metalogical order is analogical in a proper sense, it is not in virtue of this analogy alone. Nevertheless

16 *Logica*, II, q.13, a.4 (ed. Reiser, p. 486).

it would be a mistake to conclude that analogy of attribution has no place at all in metaphysics or philosophy. For the relations, at once similar and diverse, which unite the secondary analogates to the prime analogate may well be "real" (as distinct from any species of logical or ideal relation) and *are* real if they proceed from a real extrinsic cause.

The relations in all the instances of analogy of attribution given thus far are obviously real ones. There is no doubt that diet, climate, complexion, medicine, are really related to health; and no one would say that the hypodermic and the scalpel, serums, drugs and pills, orderlies and nurses, are irrelevant to the practice of the art of medicine (*analogiae plurium ad unum*). Also, while the logician may say that "man" predicated of the actual man and of his picture is predicated "equivocally," everyone knows that the picture is, or at least is usually intended to be, an actual representation of the man.[17] Whatever may be said of the "reality" of the relation in some cases, there is between John and the photograph or painted picture of him a certain entitative relation, a relation which is said to be real in the measure that the "likeness" obtained is a "good" one. Even the relation between the dog and his namesake in the heavens is not purely "equivocal": some likeness suggested the name. And although the Great Dipper is not a dipper, it looks like one (*analogiae unius ad unum*). Analogies of attribution, one and all.

Such things are actually related to their principal, univocal, terms: there is something really in them which

[17] Cf. Cajetan, *De nom.*, II, 20, with note 4.

makes a common designation possible. But the real object or character signified by that word in fact exists only in the principal term; the others receive the common name only by denomination from that term. The Great Dipper cannot be called a dipper by any "intrinsic," in the sense of proper and formal, denomination. Yet "dipper" said of the heavenly constellation designates something (i.e., likeness of geometrical pattern or shape) made known by its *relation* to that which the word signifies properly and formally, namely, the household utensil. "Dipper" is thus in itself a univocal term. It can be applied to a configuration of celestial bodies only by "extrinsic denomination," because the likeness which is the basis of the common designation, while real, is "extrinsic" in the sense of being extra-essential.

St. Thomas calls analogy of attribution analogy *secundum intentionem et non secundum esse* because in this case the analogous name is not actually and formally common; it is not common "according to being" but only "denominatively" or "according to intention." [18] It is for this reason that Cajetan puts this analogy in the class of analogies improperly so called.[19] And by so doing he invites a false inference. But Cajetan does not mean that analogy of attribution is in no sense a true analogy; he means only that it is an improper analogy as compared with that analogy which is analogical both "according to intention" and "according to being." [20]

Analogy of attribution has a truly analogical character

18 Cf. *ibid.*, p. 21.
19 *Ibid.*, III, 23.
20 *Ibid.*, note 1.

inasmuch as it contains a certain similarity in diversity; for it is based on different relations which are at the same time similar inasmuch as they all refer to a single term. Nevertheless it should be remembered that this type of analogy as such has to do with a formality which is univocal in itself.

CHAPTER XI

THE DEGRADATION OF THE FINITE

1. ECKHART AND THE NOTHINGNESS OF CREATURES

IN MEISTER ECKHART (c. 1250–c. 1328) we find a doctrine which closely approaches analogy of attribution in the "pure state." From the principle that in the beginning God created all things immediately in Himself, Eckhart concludes that all things except God have being from God Himself; yet nothing is so intimate, he says, nothing so primary and proper to creatures, as existence itself.[1] Nevertheless the creature does not possess that existence in itself in the manner of a substance; it does not exist in itself, it exists in God. "It is in God," as Muller-Thym puts it, "not merely as the root or source of existence, but as the place where alone that existence is possessed in a positive sense of the word." [2] Eckhart himself states this point very strongly: "Every created being, therefore, has being, life, knowledge, positively and radically, from God and in God, not in created being itself." [3]

It is clear that Eckhart has identified existence itself

[1] *Exp.* (I) *Gen.*, in Heinrich Denifle, O.P., *Archiv. für Litteratur und Kirchengeschichte* (1886), Archiv II, p. 551, lines 14–16. I am indebted to Dr. B. J. Muller-Thym for this text and for all the texts from Eckhart used in this chapter, except one. See Muller-Thym's *The Establishment of the University of Being in the Doctrine of Meister Eckhart of Hochheim* (New York and London: Sheed & Ward, 1939), p. 7, note 20.

[2] *Op. cit., ibid.*

[3] *Exp. Exodi*, Denifle, Archiv II, p. 588, lines 24–26; in Muller-Thym, *op. cit.*, p. 7, with note 21.

with God. The denial that creatures have any existence in their own right, then follows with logical necessity; for it is already contained in the premise. From all things in the finite or created order, everything that could properly be called their own will have been removed. Quoting a remarkable text, Muller-Thym observes: "Meister Eckhart does not shrink from that conclusion"; on the contrary he proclaims in forceful language that "all creatures are a mere naught." "I say not, they are small . . . they are absolutely naught. A thing without being is not (or is naught). Creatures have no real being, for their being consists in the presence of God." [4] Muller-Thym points out that Eckhart is not speaking only of the non-being of creatures *relatively to God,* but also, and even more emphatically, of their utter nothingness in themselves.[5]

Eckhart indeed held that all creatures are contained virtually in the one *esse* of the universe, namely, in God; but, on the principle that the part adds nothing to the whole, he denied that the creature is part of God. Nevertheless, outside the one existence which is God, the creature is and remains an absolute nonentity. There is only one existence, which, viewed under different aspects, "is the *esse* which is God and the *esse* which the creature as *ens* signifies, according to the dictum *ens significat solum esse.*" [6] A more complete "sublation" of the finite order would seem inconceivable. Yet it is a perfectly "logical" doctrine.

---

[4] *Op. cit.,* p. 9, with note 25.

[5] *Ibid.,* p. 9.

[6] *Ibid.,* p. 111. This conclusion, in accordance with the method of this excellent study as a whole, is based directly on the texts of Eckhart.

2. Eckhart and the Univocity of Being

Even the foregoing scraps of Eckhart's system permit us to see that being (*esse*) is there taken univocally, and an analogy of attribution is set up according to which creatures as secondary analogates do not realize intrinsically and properly the perfection attributed to them, namely, *esse*. This perfection, which is the chief of all, is reserved exclusively for the Prime Analogate: *Esse* resides formally and properly only in God. Creatures (if they can be properly said to "exist" at all) have being solely in virtue of the relation of dependence in which they stand to God and in God. To say that their being is constituted by their relations to God is hardly an exaggeration; at least, it is constituted by the "presence" of God to them.

The assertion of the equivocity of all terms predicated of God, or of the One Reality, generally goes hand-in-hand with such a doctrine, and will do so if that doctrine is thoroughly self-consistent. We should not be surprised, therefore, to find Eckhart following in Plotinus' footsteps in this matter and maintaining the absolute equivocity of the divine names.[7]

3. The Removal of Substantiality from Things

Analogy of attribution is particularly dear to mystics, Penido observes.[8] Mystics throughout the ages have echoed the word of Plotinus: "All is full of signs." [9] In a sense that

[7] Cf. Sermon on *Renewal in the Spirit* (no. 99, Pfeiffer collection, Göttingen, 1914), pp. 317–20.

[8] *Le rôle*, p. 40.

[9] *Enneads*, II, 3, 7.

proposition is true; in mystical theology it is profoundly true. In metaphysics it may be profoundly false. I mean that if an idea proper to the religious or theological or mystical order is made a *principle of explanation* in the philosophical order, the result will be philosophically disastrous. This has happened, as we have seen. If mysticism descends to the purely human level of metaphysical knowledge, assumes the role of philosophy and proceeds to philosophize mystically in accordance with the doctrine of "signs," the whole natural order will finally be turned topsy-turvy. Things will tend progressively to lose their own proper reality and become nothing more than images, reflections, traces of the Highest Being—in Christian terms, of the One and of the Three. Their entire function and their very being will come to be viewed as merely symbolic, and in the end they will be reduced to the status of mere signs of a supra-natural or transcendent Reality. The humblest as well as the sublimest things will exist solely as appearances under which That-Which-Alone-Truly-Is lies concealed.

This tendency is already evident in Plato, who often suggests that objects of the sensible world have no being proper to themselves but are mere fleeting shadows of eternal, never-changing Ideas. This is indeed the only conclusion consistent with the principle that the universal **is** itself the real. For in that case the highest universal must be the most real being, and everything else an appearance, an expression or a sign of It.

A doctrine of this type implies analogy of attribution. In extreme cases, the being, truth, and goodness of things will not be intrinsic to them but will consist in pure relations. All things will be that which they are solely in virtue of their dependence upon a single term, which alone is Being and Goodness and Truth intrinsically and properly and formally. Or, in another manner of speaking, all things of the created universe will be related to God as signs to their ultimate Signification.

The whole Platonic (or Neo-Platonic) tradition has implicitly favored the employment of analogy of attribution. In all philosophies where this tradition is dominant, this analogy, virtually at least, has a central role. I am thinking of the tendency to deny substantial reality to things, to creatures, and to give everything to God. It is He, then, who is regarded as that which alone is truly Being, everything else having the character of being only, as it were, by proxy. The reality of creatures will be primarily and above all representative, their status essentially that of symbols or signs.

4. THE TWOFOLD ANALOGY AT WORK IN "MONISTIC" PHILOSOPHIES

It is difficult to find any cases of pure analogy of attribution in philosophy, though certain cases, like that of Eckhart, come perilously close to being "pure." "Monisms," or systems virtually monistic, ordinarily exemplify a double analogy: analogy of inequality, positing diverse or unequal participation of all things in a single univocal perfection, coupled with analogy of attribution, arising from the relation of dependence of all things upon a single term. That term may be called the One, the Good, Substance or Nature, Pure Being, the Monad of Monads, the Absolute Idea, Will, the Absolute Ego, Matter, and now, currently, Existence. The titles vary; but the point is that all things under the *Unum Princeps* (however its own nature be conceived) will be considered as dependent upon it in such a way and to such an extent that, in the last analysis, It constitutes the sole *essential* reality, everything else having in relation to it the character of an "accident." Or, from another angle, that Term will be a generic perfection or nature, and everything else will have the character of a "difference," that is to say, an extrinsic determination, with respect to It.

As a matter of fact there is an analogy of attribution between accident and substance; for accident is *denominated* being from the being of substance. Yet there is another, a more fundamental, analogy, based on the fact that the accident properly and formally has being, and in an incomplete mode is a being. Under the formality of attribution, however, the accident has being only by extrinsic denomination from the being of substance. So, in a radical monism (which is generally at the same time a "pantheism") things could not be said to have being intrinsically and formally.

In what may be called pan-monism (all-one-ism), therefore, we have analogy of inequality. As we saw in Part One, this analogy consists in the unequal participation of all "things" in a single univocal form, thus positing between them a community of *essence*. Since those things will all share in varying degrees in an identical univocal essence, none of them will have an essence which is properly its own. Each will have only a borrowed essence, an essence formally identical with that of the One Essence. For indeed there is only one Essence or Substance or Form, diffused unequally throughout all being. Thus, according to this doctrine, all things are *in* an Other and *from* an Other and *of* an Other—and that Other is One. Therefore they have the status of "accidents" in relation to that Other.

An extreme intrinsicism in the order of essence is proper to a "metaphysics" of pan-monism. For such a doctrine is of its very nature immanentist: it is immanentist precisely in the measure in which it is consistent with itself. The One is all and in all, and all are One and in One and of One, though not equally. Hence analogy of inequality. But no proper analogy; rather, as we have seen, a fundamental formal univocity. Intrinsicism, yes; but a univocal intrinsicism. The presence of this "element" in all panmonistic ontologies cannot be ascribed to the unwitting employment of analogy of attribution by the authors of such systems, because that kind of analogy, as such, exists only in the order of extrinsic causality. But it can be attributed in some measure, often in large measure, to the hidden operation of analogy of inequality.

Viewed structurally, therefore, monistic or pan-monistic types of philosophy present a double aspect: (1) an accident-inherence aspect, inasmuch as there is only one Substance, conceived as a univocal perfection in which all things "inhere" in the manner of accidents and in which they all share unequally; and (2) a substance-attribution aspect, inasmuch as all those "accidents" exist only by reason of their dependence upon the one Substance, are extrinsically denominated from It, and are related to It in the manner of differences vis-à-vis their Genus. Under the first aspect we have a univocal intrinsicism, the characteristic notes of which are "in-aleity" and "de-aleity"; under the second, an "accidental" extrinsicism whose dominant note is "ab-aleity."

To sum up: Accidents (all things other than the one Substance) have being in It. This being is really in them, but it is not their own being. It is not *essentially* proper to them; on the contrary, it is essentially identical with the being or essence of the one Substance. This is the element of univocal intrinsicism, based on the accident-inherence aspect and made manifest by the logic of "analogy" of inequality. On the other hand, all the accidents of the one Substance have their being or reality from It and from It alone. And although the being of that substance is really and intrinsically in them, they have no being or essence which is proper to them as such, no *inseitas* in the manner of substances. On the contrary, they are essentially though unequally that which the one Substance is and they are therefore said to be that which they are by extrinsic denomination from that one Substance. Thus we have the element of accidental extrinsicism, founded on the substance-attribution aspect and brought to light by the logical procedure called analogy of attribution. In any case—and this is the point—the finite will have been de-graded, stripped of its substantiality, relegated to a modality of the Supreme Essence, the one Substance—it matters not what name it be called. If philosophy is a search for the principles of all being in the finite beings of common experience, and if those beings are merged with and lost in some super-essential Unity, then philosophy, which depends upon the senses and proceeds according to finite human reason, will literally have nothing actual, nothing substantial, to work with. The unwitting misuse of a purely logical analogy, analogy of attribution, will have been largely responsible for this subversive result.

CHAPTER XII

EFFICIENT CAUSALITY AND THINGS

THE term "nature" signifies the essence of a thing so far as that essence is considered the source of the thing's operations.[1] Thus nature is the basis of activity, of function. It is a curious fact that many great thinkers, for various motives (some very noble, some philosophically expedient), have considered it necessary to remove from things their proper essences or natures. But this, you will say, is obviously contrary to common sense. So it is. Yet it has been done, and apparently for excellent reasons. In this chapter I merely wish to introduce some examples, point out the results, and, at the end, indicate the place of analogy of attribution in all this development.

1. "Theologism" in Early Moslem Thought

Gilson has used the term "theologism" to designate "theologies clothed in philosophical garb."[2] It is the doctrine that "God is and does everything, while nature and men are and do nothing";[3] and he cites the case of the doctrine of the Asharites, a Mohammedan sect of the late ninth and early tenth century, founded by one Al Ashari. The great Spanish Jewish theologian Maimonides (1135–1204),

---

[1] Cf. St. Thomas Aquinas, *De ente*, 1.
[2] *The Unity of Philosophical Experience* (New York: Scribner's, 1937), p. 37.
[3] *Ibid.*, p. 38.

it seems, is the primary source of our knowledge of the doctrine of Al Ashari and his school. Basing his analysis on the texts of Maimonides, Gilson states that these Moslem theologians "assumed that it was quite useless to worry about the real nature and order of things, because things have indeed neither nature nor order. Even though its existence be convincingly established, that which actually is proves nothing at all, 'because it is merely one of the various phases of things, the opposite of which is equally admissible to our minds.' " [4]

The doctrine of these theologians may be summed up in such propositions as the following: (1) motion is an "accident created by God" in moving things; (2) "there does not exist any thing [other than God] to which an action could be ascribed"; (3) despite appearances, "the real Agent is God." [5] Overwhelmed by the sense of the omnipresence and especially the omnipotence of God, these men could not see how mere creatures could have any "causal efficacy" in themselves. For if God is indeed all-powerful, how can the things He has made *really* have any power to do anything themselves? They may seem to have such power, but at bottom that is an illusion; it cannot be so.

[4] *Ibid.*, pp. 41 f. The quotation within this quotation is from Maimonides, *The Guide for The Perplexed* (2nd ed.; London and New York, 1928), p. 110.

[5] Maimonides, *op. cit.*, I, lxxiii, prop. 6, pp. 125 f. Gilson cites this text (*op. cit.*, pp. 46 f.), and points out that Malebranche was to teach the same doctrine, and even the puritan divine Cotton Mather: "With a little less zeal for the glory of God, or rather, with a still greater zeal enlightened by common sense, these men would no doubt have realized that the destruction of causality ultimately meant the destruction of nature, and thereby of science as well as of philosophy" (p. 48).

2. THE THEOLOGICAL EPISTEMOLOGY OF ST. BONAVENTURE

The great thirteenth-century Franciscan mystic and theologian, St. Bonaventure, maintained that "God has created all things present and future at the very instant of creation"; so that "any particular thing, taken at any time of world history, should be considered, so to speak, as the seed of all those other beings, or events, that are to flow from it according to the laws of divine providence." Consequently, "If, in the beginning, God created, together with all that was, all that was to be, the end of the world-story was in its beginning, and nothing can really happen to it; in such a system God is the only efficient cause, and this world of ours is a completely barren world, just as in the doctrine of Malebranche and of Al Ashari," and, Gilson continues, "That is exactly what St. Bonaventure wanted it to be. His piety needed a world which, like an infinitely thin and translucid film, would allow the all-pervading power and glory of God to shine forth to the human eye." [6]

Thus, on the epistemological side, we have the doctrine of divine illumination. This doctrine was variously modified by other Franciscans, but it remained substantially the same and entailed the same "destructive consequence" for natural knowledge. This consequence was perfectly consistent with St. Bonaventure's own principles; or rather, with his view of the implications of the true prin-

[6] Gilson, *op. cit.*, pp. 53 f.

ciple that God is Truth. For if God is Truth, He is the One Truth, and there is no other. He is therefore the source of all the truth there is. It follows, then, that the truth of our own judgments comes to us from God alone, not from our own reason: we in no way make it; God gives it to us. Hence a purely human science of human knowledge is clearly impossible; and if philosophy is a human science of things humanly knowable, then obviously epistemology cannot belong to it. Epistemology can belong only to theology.[7]

Theologically speaking, it is true that creatures, being the handiwork of God, in some way represent Him. But, as Gilson points out,[8] where every particular thing in the universe is only a mystical symbol of its Creator—a trace, an image, a shadow cast by the divine Light—the real object of natural knowledge is not the particular thing itself, but its idea in God.[9]

In the field of classical modern philosophy, a number of very interesting "solutions" of the problem of the communication between substances in the finite order have been propounded with great ingenuity and high rhetorical skill. In the two following sections I shall consider the eminent cases of Spinoza and Leibnitz.[10]

[7] Cf. *ibid.*, pp. 56 f.

[8] *Ibid.*, pp. 57 f.

[9] Thus Matthew of Aquasparta held that sensible things need not even exist in order for us to acquire true knowledge; for, as long as the divine Light illuminates our minds, we can know the whole truth about things. (See Gilson, *op. cit.*, p. 58.) Gilson sees in this doctrine an anticipation of Malebranche's famous "Vision in God," and of Berkeley's "radical idealism" as well (*ibid.*).

[10] The facts in Descartes' case are so well known that they need only be mentioned here. If spirit-substance and body-substance exclude each other, it follows of necessity that there can be no interaction, no real communication, between them. (The pineal gland theory was a *deus ex machina*, pure and

3. Causality in Spinoza

"Surely everyone," says Spinoza,[11] "must admit that without God nothing can either be or be conceived. For it is acknowledged by all that God is the sole cause (*unica causa*) of all things, both of their essence and of their existence, that is, God is not only the cause of things, *secundum fieri,* as people say, but also *secundum esse.*" To be sure, "the modes of any attribute have God for their cause only in so far as He is considered under that attribute of which they are modes, and not in so far as He is considered under any other attribute." [12] However, there follows the famous proposition that "the order and connection of ideas is the same as the order and connection of things." [13]

This proposition asserts an ontological and epistemological correlation, not a so-called psycho-physical parallelism, as this phrase is commonly understood. A scholium, following the order-and-connection proposition, makes this clear:

We have already demonstrated that everything which can be perceived by the infinite intellect as constituting the essence of substance pertains entirely to the sole substance alone; and consequently that substance thinking and substance extended are one and the same substance, which is now comprehended under this attribute, now under that. Thus also a mode of extension and the idea of that mode are one and the same thing expressed in two different ways. . . . For instance, the circle existing in nature and

---

simple.) As Gilson puts it, "Descartes' geometry had turned the world into a mosaic of mutually exclusive substances that could neither act nor be acted upon, neither know nor be known" (*op. cit.,* p. 219).

11 *Eth.* II, Prop. X, Schol. ii.
12 *Ibid.,* Prop. VI.
13 Prop. VII.

the idea which is also in God of an existing circle are one and the same thing, which is manifested through different attributes. And therefore, whether we conceive nature under the attribute of extension or under the attribute of thought, or under any other attribute whatever, we shall discover one and the same order or one and the same connection of causes, that is, we shall find the same sequence of things. . . . So that when things are considered as modes of extension, the order of the whole of nature must be explained through the attribute of extension alone, and so with other attributes. Wherefore God is in truth the cause of things as they are in themselves inasmuch as He consists of infinite attributes.[14]

All ideas, then, are in God, and the idea of a thing in God is the same as the thing itself. The idea of a thing and the thing itself are not two different things, but one and the same thing viewed under different attributes. And, as Spinoza states (see chap. 5), both thought and extension are infinite attributes of God, each expressing His infinite and eternal essence. If we ask, What is the cause of the ideas of God's attributes and of individual things? the answer is, God alone. He is their sole efficient cause: "The ideas both of God's attributes and of singular things do not recognize as their efficient cause the objects of the ideas (*ipsa ideata*) or the things which are perceived, but God Himself in so far as He is a thinking thing." [15]

Implausible as this doctrine may seem, it nevertheless fits in the system of Spinoza in a perfectly logical manner. For, he explains, "The idea of a singular thing existing in act has God for its cause, not in so far as He is infinite, but in so far as He is considered to be affected by another idea

14 Prop. VII, Schol.
15 Prop. IV.

of a singular thing existing in act, of which idea also He is the cause in so far as He is affected by a third, and so on *ad infinitum.*" [16] That is to say, every individual idea has for its cause another idea, and that other idea is none other than God Himself so far as He is affected by it; while of this second idea God is again the cause, and so on. This particular theory is merely a special application of Spinoza's doctrine of substance and attributes.

We should always keep in mind that the idea and the thing are the *same* reality viewed under different attributes.[17] If it be objected that confused and inadequate ideas do exist, the answer is that "All ideas are in God (*Eth.*, I, xv), and, in so far as they are related to God, are true (*Eth.*, II, xxxii) and adequate (*ibid.*, vii, Corol.). No ideas, therefore, are inadequate or confused unless in so far as they are related to the individual mind of some person." [18]

Clearly there is no place in this scheme for any actual communication between things, for the exercise of any efficient causality by substances upon one another. There are in fact no substances; there is only one substance.[19] In Spinoza's world there is no room for the operation of real secondary causes. No such causes exist: no causes which are causes in their own right. If it be asserted or assumed

16 Prop. IX.
17 For instance, "The idea of the body and the body, that is (Prop. XIII, Part II), the mind and the body, are one and the same individual, which at one time is considered under the attribute of thought, and at another time under that of extension; the idea of the mind, therefore, and the mind itself are one and the same thing, which is considered under one and the same attribute, that of thought" (*Eth.* II, Prop. XXI, Schol.).
18 *Eth.* II, Prop. XXXVI. See also Part II, Props. XXIV, XXVIII.
19 See above, chap. 5, sect. 2.

that there are efficient causes, even so, they will be ideas in the mind of God, of which He is the sole efficient cause; or, if they be viewed under the attribute of extension, they will be things of which, also, God is the sole efficient cause.

4. THE METAPHYSICAL HARMONIES OF LEIBNITZ

In his *Discourse on Metaphysics,* Baron Gottfried Wilhelm von Leibnitz (1646–1716) states: "A particular substance never acts upon another particular substance, nor is it acted upon by it." [20] To explain the relation between body and soul, Leibnitz had recourse to his celebrated doctrine of "pre-established harmony," according to which body and soul will indeed be "conformed" to each other, but not actually united. As he says in the *Monadology:* "The soul follows its own laws, and the body likewise follows its own laws. They are fitted to each other in virtue of the harmony preëstablished between all substances, since they are all representations of one and the same universe." However, soul and body are not in the same order of causality. Unlike Spinoza, who eliminated final causes altogether, Leibnitz finds room for them: "Souls act in accordance with the laws of final causes through their desires, ends and means. Bodies act in accordance with the laws of efficient causes or of movements. And the two realms, that of efficient and that of final causes, are in harmony with each other." [21] This text is one of the "keys" to Leibnitz' theory of causality.

[20] *Discourse on Metaphysics,* XIV, in *Disc. on Metaph., Corresp. with Arnauld and Monadology* (Eng. tr. by Dr. George R. Montgomery, 2nd. ed., revised; Chicago and London: The Open Court Pub. Co., 1918), p. 25.
[21] *Monadology,* 78, 79; in *Opera philosophica* (ed. Erdmann, 1840), p. 711 b.

Now, in the vocabulary of Leibnitz, the terms "soul" and "body" do not apply *merely* to human beings, or to animals or plants, or any sort of living organism. Every substance other than God consists of both body and soul.[22] It may be asked, Why, then, did Leibnitz not use the apparently more appropriate names "matter" and "form," or some equally inclusive expressions? The answer is that for Leibnitz soul and body are equally as inclusive as form and matter, and, from his point of view, far more appropriate, especially the word "soul." The reason lies in his "ontologized" theory of "perception," according to which the soul is the relatively distinct *perception* of the substance,[23] and, at the same time, its activity.[24] Hence the soul is the final cause of the substance or the end for which it exists. No substance can be adequately explained by mechanical causes; it has no mere static self-identity, but "unfolds itself in the series of its changes." [25]

On the other hand, the body of every substance, that is to say, its matter (its *confused* perception, its passivity) is the physical or mechanical cause of the substance. Considered in itself, body is a sheer abstract possibility. But if body cannot exist by itself, neither can soul. The truth is that the world is made up of Monads, each of which is a concrete unity of soul and body, of entelechy and matter. In reality, therefore, everything in nature is a living entity. Contrary to appearances and vulgar opinion, no

22 *Monad.*, 72; *ed. cit.*, p. 711 a: "God alone is completely without body."

23 For, says Leibnitz, "There is nothing besides perceptions and their changes to be found in the simple substance" (*Monad.*, 17; *ibid.*, p. 706 b).

24 *Monad.*, 18; *loc. cit.*

25 Cf. Robert Latta, *The Monadology and Other Philosophical Writings* (Eng. tr., with introduction and notes; Oxford, 1898), p. 107.

substances are actually "inorganic." [26] "Bodies would doubtless be imaginary and a mere appearance," observes Leibnitz, "if they were composed only of matter and its modifications." [27] For "the substance of a body, if it has one, must be indivisible; whether we call it soul or form makes no difference to me," says Leibnitz.[28] In other words, that which makes a body real is the soul, which is its entelechy.[29]

Nevertheless, besides perceptions and their changes there is nothing to be found in the simple substance, in the Monad. Hence Latta's judgment seems correct, namely, that for Leibnitz, "The body of every created substance is the point of view of its soul"; the body is "like a special lens through which the soul sees the universe." The metaphor is very appropriate in view of the fact that, for Leibnitz, body as such—body in general—is relatively confused perception, since each substance, "from its own point of view," mirrors or re-presents the whole universe. And that point of view, as Latta well says, "is simply the degree of con-

[26] Cf. *Monad.*, 63–69; in Erdmann, p. 710 a-b.
[27] Letter to Arnaud (1686); in Montgomery, p. 161.
"Nevertheless," he goes on, "it is useless to make mention of the unity, the concept, or the substantial forms of bodies when it is a question of explaining the particular phenomena of nature." . . . For, "all the phenomena of bodies can be explained mechanically or by the corpuscular philosophy in accordance with certain postulated mechanical principles without troubling oneself as to whether there are souls or not" (*ibid.*, pp. 161 f.). Thus we may have an abstract science of physics by which the phenomena of matter are explained on purely mechanical principles, or as a system of physical or efficient causes. But we cannot explain the concrete reality even of material substances by mere mechanical principles. For, says Leibnitz (p. 162), "In the ultimate analysis of the principles of physics and mechanics it is found that these assumed principles cannot be explained solely by the modifications of extension, and the very nature of force calls for something else."
[28] Letter to Arnaud (Nov. 28–Dec. 8, 1686); in Montgomery, p. 153.
[29] Cf. *Monad.*, 63.

fusedness (or of distinctness, for they are entirely relative) of its perceptions." [30] In fact, Leibnitz himself says: "Efficient causes are dependent upon final causes, and spiritual things are in their nature prior to material things, as also they are to us prior in knowledge, because we perceive more immediately the mind than the body." [31]

For Leibnitz, the real entities of the universe are simple forces, dynamic units, atoms of activity, "metaphysical points"; in a word, Monads.[32] And they all act together in harmony. Doubtless everything is "causally" related, every state in every Monad following as the effect of the preceding state in that Monad, and acting in unison with the states of all other Monads.[33]

As a matter of fact, however, in this system causation simply means concomitant change, a harmonious action, predetermined by God, of all the parts of the universe.[34] The Monads, which are the really real entities, the actual individual substances, exercise no real causality upon one another, and in this sense do not communicate with one another. In Leibnitz' famous phrase, "The Monads have

[30] Latta, *op. cit.*, p. 112.

[31] Epistola ad Bierlingium (1711); in Erdmann, p. 678; in Latta, p. 108, note.

[32] Cf. *Monad.*, 2, 61; in Erdmann, pp. 705 a, 710 a; cf. also "Epistola ad R. C. Wagnerum" (1710), Erdmann, p. 466 a; and "Réplique aux réflexions de Bayle" (1702), *ibid.*, p. 186 b.

[33] E.g., see Leibnitz' "pin-prick" example in his letter to Arnaud (1687); in Montgomery, pp. 212–14.

[34] See Leibnitz' letter to Arnaud (Hanover, July 14, 1686; in Montgomery, pp. 133–35); letter to Arnaud (Nov. 28–Dec. 8, 1686; *ibid.*, pp. 148–52); letter to Arnaud (Göttingen, Apr. 30, 1687; *ibid.*, pp. 185 f.), containing the famous example of the bands of musicians or choirs which, without seeing or hearing one another, agree perfectly in following their notes. Finally, see the example of the clocks in *Third Explanation of the New System*, in Erdmann, pp. 134 a–135 a.

no windows through which something might either come in or go out." [35] At once the root and the full flowering of this doctrine are revealed in the following text: "In the case of simple substances, the influence which one Monad has upon another is only ideal; it can have its effect only through the intervention of God, inasmuch as in the ideas of God one Monad reasonably demands that God, in ruling the others from the very beginning of things, also have regard for it. For since a created Monad cannot have a physical influence upon the inner being of an other, it is only in this way [i.e., by the primal regulation of God], that one can have dependence upon another." [36]

The connection between cause and effect in different substances, therefore, is a purely ideal relation, a harmony of internal changes and operations, entailing no physical influence whatever of one substance upon another.[37] "Causation" is merely the relation of activity in the one

[35] *Monad.*, 7; in Erdmann, p. 705 a.

[36] *Monad.*, 51; *ibid.*, p. 709 a.

[37] The following text, it seems to me, confirms this statement in an especially emphatic way: "A body is an aggregation of substances and is not a substance properly speaking. Consequently, everywhere in the body there must be indivisible substances, ingenerable and incorruptible, having something corresponding to souls. . . . Each of these substances contains in its own nature a law of the continuation of the series of its operations, and all that has happened to it and will happen to it." (Cf. doctrine of "seminal reasons.") "All its actions," Leibnitz continues, "come from its own inner being, except its dependence on God. Each substance expresses the entire universe, yet one more distinctly than another, and each more especially with regard to certain things and according to its own point of view. The union of the soul with the body, and indeed the operation of one substance upon another consists only in this perfect mutual accord of substances, definitely established through the order of their first creation, in virtue of which each substance, following its own laws, agrees with the rest, meeting their demands; and the operations of the one thus follow or accompany the operation or change of the other" (Letter to Arnaud, 1690; in Erdmann, pp. 107 b–108 a).

to corresponding passivity in the other, that is, the relation of distinct to confused perception. "It is not in the object," says Leibnitz, "but in the modification of the knowledge of the object that the Monads are limited. In a confused way they all strive after the infinite, the whole, but they are limited and differentiated by the degrees of their distinct perception." [38]

Thus each Monad, through its *relations* to all other Monads (and thence to God, the Monad of Monads), is a "perpetual living mirror of the universe." [39] Just as there is an infinite number of monads, so there is an infinite number of universes. But each Monad, and each universe in the infinity of universes, is that which it is only in virtue of its relations to the supreme Monad, of which it is a sort of representative-at-large. The nature of the Monad is *representative*, says Leibnitz.[40] He does not say that the Monad is by nature a causal agent. God alone is properly such: "In the strictly metaphysical sense, no external cause

[38] *Monad.*, 60; in Erdmann, p. 710 a: "And composites in this respect," he says further (*Monad.*, 61), "are symbolic of simple substances" (*symbolisent avec les simples*). That is, what is perceived confusedly in composite substances is a symbol of the real nature of simple substances. This would seem to involve a very far-reaching symbolism, according to which the reality of imperfect things consisted in their symbolic character—which would mean that such things *are* because they are symbolic, and not conversely.

[39] *Monad.*, 56, 57; in Erdmann, p. 709 b: "Now this relationship, or this adaptation of all created things to each particular one, and of each to all the rest, brings it about that every simple substance has relations which express all the others and that it is consequently a perpetual living mirror of the universe. And as the same city regarded from different sides appears entirely different, and is, as it were, multiplied respectively, so, because of the infinite number of simple substances, there are a similar infinite number of universes which are, nevertheless, only the aspects (*perspectives*) of a single one, as seen from the special point of view of each Monad."

[40] *Monad.*, 60; in Erdmann, p. 709 b.

acts upon us excepting God alone. . . . We may say that God is for us the only immediate external object, and that we see things through Him." [41]

What is true of us, is true of all Monads: for them all, God is the only "external cause" and the only "immediate external object." He is the sole efficient cause properly so called, because He alone acts *upon* things. Moreover, He alone is the author of all the concomitant changes, of all that harmonious action, in this universe, and in all others, whereby the "parts" act in unison with one another without acting *upon* one another.

5. CONCLUSION

One may wonder whether, in all this exposition, we have not lost sight of the principle of analogy. On the contrary, with those examples before us (of the early Moslem theologians, of St. Bonaventure, Spinoza, and Leibnitz) it is not difficult to see how this principle, at least implicitly, has been operating all the time. For it is plain that in all those cases, analogy of attribution, in the order of efficient causality, has been at work. It has always been God who, as prime analogate, alone properly and formally possesses the power of efficient causality, finite or created "agents" having a right to the name, if at all, only by extrinsic denomination from the one Agent. [42]

---

[41] *Disc. on Metaph.*, XXVIII; in Montgomery, pp. 46 f.

[42] The doctrine of "occasionalism" (propounded by the Asharite theologians in the late ninth and early tenth and by Malebranche in the seventeenth century), according to which mental and physical processes are not causally related but merely run parallel to one another, an event in the physical order being the "occasional cause" for God's producing a corresponding idea in us, this doctrine was actually not a *solution*, but merely a statement of one prob-

The conclusion of this chapter, therefore, is that where things are stripped of their proper reality; where their own natures are so to speak taken away from them and they are absorbed into God or reduced to the status of images, traces, symbols, modes, imperfect representations, of the one Reality (God, Substance, the supreme Monad, etc.); where, consequently, things are denied any causal efficacy in their own right, an analogy of attribution, of varying degrees of "purity" or absoluteness, has in fact been set up. And, according to this "analogy," efficient causality will pertain properly and formally to one Being alone. It follows that such causality can be attributed to other things, if it be attributed to them at all, solely in virtue of their *relation* to that one Being—a relation of strict and absolute dependence—and not in virtue of their having any causal power of their own through the exercise of which they could communicate directly and efficaciously with one another.

---

lem within the general problem of the "communication of substances" or, more specifically, of the efficacy of secondary causes.

CHAPTER XIII

ATTRIBUTION AND THE *QUINQUE VIAE*

1. NOTE ON WHY THE "FIVE WAYS" ARE SOMETIMES MISUNDERSTOOD

THE purpose of this brief chapter is not to discuss the Five Ways themselves but only to indicate how the principle of analogy applies to them. This is not the place to expound those Ways or to introduce any direct defense of them. Nevertheless it is perhaps not too much to say that this cursory treatment of the problem implicitly contains the elements, at least, of an indirect defense. Even a fragmentary account such as this of the part analogy plays in the demonstration of God's existence may in some measure contribute to a better understanding of what that demonstration actually is and how it actually operates.

There is considerable evidence that the main cause of the failure to grasp the significance of this demonstration is the misapprehension or non-apprehension of its radically analogical character. This applies not only to the Five Ways as formulated by St. Thomas, but to any substantially valid formulation of the proof in question, whether medieval or modern. (I say proof, because there is reductively only one, although it may be presented in an indefinite number of different ways.) However relevant it may be from a logical or grammatical point of view, criticism which is directed solely upon details of terminology and the surface mechanics of the arguments by-passes, so to speak, the very substance of the proof.

Thus many critics of the Five Ways, and of other formulations essentially like them, argue on the assumption—of which they are usually themselves unaware—that the problem at issue is a logical one. They will therefore inevitably find some flaws in the "proofs," because the demonstration of God's existence is not a problem in logic but in metaphysics. Not only will they find some flaws; they will, if they press their criticism to its logical conclusion, find that, far from demonstrating God's existence, the alleged proofs do not demonstrate any existence at all. For, not only is logic incapable of producing a demonstration of God's existence, it is impossible for logic to produce a demonstration of any existence, because logic is solely concerned with second intentions, with essences or intelligible forms so far as they are known; in short, with intellectual determinations.

Whereas logical demonstration is a business of showing necessary connections between second intentions, in a typical metaphysical demonstration the existence of something is inferred from the existence of something else. While univocal terms signify generic or specific concepts ("universals"), metaphysical terms, as such, are analogical, because they signify "transcendental" concepts, that is, concepts which are capable of realization, in *essentially diverse* modes, and which, therefore, are not (as are universals) limited by differentiating characters to univocal genera. Our problem, then, is to show the place of analogy, and particularly of analogy of attribution, in the meta-physical demonstration of God's existence.[1]

2. Via Ascensus and Via Descensus

Under one aspect, this demonstration imports analogy of attribution according to efficient, final, and exemplary causality. For it is necessary to demonstrate or infer an existence before exploring a nature. However, one can arrive at the existence of God without having recourse to analogy *explicitly*.[2] In the analogy of attribution, the sec-

[1] It is well to point out that the middle term in every formulation of that proof is the same, namely, the term *cause*. For, reflexively considered, all the Ways are reduced essentially to the same syllogistic form: The world neces-sarily requires an extrinsic first cause. But that cause exists (as was shown from the existence of finite and contingent things), and the name of that cause is "God"; hence God exists. Only the nominal definition of God is presupposed. But the point is that *cause* is analogical. Does it follow that the syllogism in reality contains four terms and thus exemplifies the fallacy of equivocation? It does not indeed, because, as Cajetan shows in his *De nominum analogia* (cap. X, *ed. cit.*, pp. 80–83), a concept having a unity of proportionality—an analogical unity in the proper sense—may serve as middle term in a syllogism, provided that in both premises the term be understood to have the same extension; that is, it must be understood to signify the *proportional likeness* between the analogates and not to signify (univocally) that which pertains exclusively and properly to only one of the analogates. Thus the term "cause" must in both premises designate not that causality which is proper to created or finite things as such, but solely the proportional likeness which exists be-tween causality of that order and causality of another (and essentially diverse) order. There is no equivocation, therefore, in the use of the term "cause" in demonstrating God's existence. This is not a logical thesis devised to make that demonstration possible; for Aristotle had already laid down the doctrine of the analogical middle term in valid demonstrations. (See *Post. Anal.*, II, c. XIV and XVII, and St. Thomas' commentary, lect. 17 and 19.)

Cajetan's statement on the nature of contradiction is valuable not only as a remedy for skepticism concerning the possibility of demonstrating the existence of God, but as an aid to the understanding of metaphysical demon-stration in general: "Contradiction consists in the affirmation and denial of the same attribute of the same subject, not in the affirmation and denial of the same univocal attribute of the same univocal subject. Both in the order of things and of concepts, identity extends also to proportional identity" (*op. cit.*, p. 84). It is in the latter sort of identity that analogy consists.

[2] Penido, *Le rôle*, p. 85.

ondary analogates subsist as such only in virtue of their dependence on the prime analogate. Thus it is first necessary to show that the latter exists,[3] and that it is an efficient,

[3] Although we are not here concerned with the mechanics of the Five Ways, I think it may be helpful to comment briefly on certain difficulties raised by Mortimer J. Adler in his article, "The Demonstration of God's Existence" (*The Thomist*, Vol. V, January, 1943; New York: Sheed and Ward; pp. 188–218). In a mere note, it would not be practicable to discuss his specific criticisms of the proofs, so I will deal only with his general conclusions and difficulties. (*Op. cit.*, pp. 217 f.)

A. *Conclusions:* (1) No corporeal thing can cause the being of another corporeal thing; (2) There exists a cause of the existence of the whole material world; (3) This *causa essendi* must be spiritual, i.e., an incorporeal thing; (4) If more than one incorporeal, contingent being exists, the number which do must be finite.

B. *Difficulties:* (1) "It would *seem possible* for incorporeal beings, albeit contingent, to cause the existence of corporeal things, since spiritual action can take place without time or local motion." (2) "It would also *seem possible* for one incorporeal, contingent being to cause the being of another." (3) "How can I learn that this is impossible, so that I may know by reason that a necessary being exists—the cause of the being of every contingent thing corporeal and spiritual?" "The answer," he goes on, "would seem to lie in the impossibility of a circle of causation in which, among a *finite* number of contingent beings, each causes the being of another. If such circularity in causation is impossible, then a necessary being is required, for every contingent being must be caused to be." Adler then states that "to see this last impossibility is tantamount to seeing that a contingent being cannot cause being, which makes self-evident the proposition that if anything exists, a necessary being exists. With the self-evidence of this proposition as a major premise, the conclusion 'God exists' can be demonstrated with certitude."

Reply to difficulties (1) and (2): It is true that spiritual action can take place without time or local motion. But no incorporeal being can cause the existence itself of any thing, corporeal or incorporeal. For the "distance" between being and non-being is infinite: a thing either is or it is not; between "is" and "is not" there is no mean; the "ontological gap" is infinite, absolute, in no way relative or subject to degree. Consequently only an infinite being, with infinite power to give being (i.e., to create), can close the gap. (Cf. St. Thomas, *S. th.*, I, 45, 5, ad 3.)

Reply to difficulty (3): From the fact that no finite contingent agent, whether corporeal or incorporeal, can cause the being (*esse*) of another, it follows that, if any such agent exists, it must be caused by an infinite, non-contingent or necessary agent. There can be no "circle of causation" in the sense used above, namely, production of being among contingent beings, because no contingent being can produce *being*, i.e., create. The production of an existence where "previously" there was none is the act of creation. All other sorts of production entail transformation of something already existing. And, as we have seen, only God can give being itself.

final, and "exemplary" cause.[4] For example, having arrived at the terminus of the Five Ways of St. Thomas, we discover a Mover that moves, a Cause that causes, etc., and then and then only do we perceive creatures—finite, contingent things—as secondary analogates in strict dependence upon God, the prime analogate in the order of being. At this point, therefore, there is explicit attribution.[5] We have reached the end of the *via ascensus:* we have attained the *an sit.*

We now enter upon the *via descensus,* the downward path from God to creatures, from the Supreme Analogate to the secondary analogates. And in this *démarche* we see at once that the whole finite (created) order is "like a chain linked to the Supreme Analogate." [6] We are then viewing that order under the aspect of analogy of attribution. But we do not stop there. The relation between those secondary analogates and the *Primum* which, in virtue of that initial simple attribution, seemed purely extrinsic—a mere external linking of creatures to God—this relation is on closer inspection seen to be internal. And we are then confronted with the fact that between the Supreme Analogate and the secondary analogates, between the infinite unparticipated Being and finite participated beings, between God and creatures, there is intrinsic likeness, *com-*

There are numerous Thomistic texts on all these points, and many proofs in addition to the one I have given above. For proofs that only God can create, see, for instance, *S. th.,* I, 45, 5, c and ad 3, and *Contra Gentiles,* II, 21, where nine arguments are advanced. For proofs that no angel (incorporeal finite being) can create, see, for instance, *S. th.,* I, 65, 3, 4; 90, 3, *et alibi passim.*

[4] Penido, *op. cit.,* p. 86.
[5] *Ibid.,* p. 86, note 3.
[6] *Ibid.,* p. 87.

munity of relations, notwithstanding the essential diversity in mode of being proper to these two orders. We are then regarding not the relation itself between the terms of this all-embracing analogy, but the proportional likeness within the very being of the related terms, the interior "harmony" of relations in which these terms stand vis-à-vis their respective acts of being. We are then in the order of analogy of proper proportionality.

3. ON THE ANALOGY BETWEEN EFFECT AND CAUSE

Of course it is possible to arrive at a very certain and sound knowledge of the existence of God without making any reference whatever to the principle of analogy, without any explicit use of this principle or even any explicit knowledge of it.[7] It is a fact, however, that the very reasoning whereby we conclude from the existence of finite, contingent, created things (whether corporeal or incorporeal, temporal or eternal or sempiternal) to the existence of their infinite, non-contingent, or necessary, uncreated Cause, itself implies that the notion of cause is analogical by a proper analogy. Otherwise the four-term fallacy will have been committed, since "cause" would have been used equivocally, that is, in utterly different senses, in the major and the minor premises. (See above, note 1.) This reasoning process implies also that the uncreated Being which is the term and the created being which is the starting-point of the inference are both given the name "being" not only because the first is the *cause* of the second but (more

---

[7] Cf. Maritain, *Degrés,* p. 826; John of St. Thomas, *Logica,* II q. XIII, art. 4; q. XIV, art. 2 (ed. Reiser, pp. 512–14).

significantly) because being is actually present in both beings according to a likeness of proportions, that is, according to analogy of proper proportionality.[8]

4. The "Virtuality" of Attribution

In the order of being, analogy of attribution is only *virtual*. This means that is has no actual status in the nature of things. It is only in *virtue* of the analogy intrinsic to being as be-ing that this analogy (which involves the logical use of a univocal term after the manner of a true analogy) has a place in metaphysical demonstration at all. It is evident that the concept of being is not analogous in the manner of a concept formally univocal which can be applied analogically to a number of different subjects. This would be the case if being were actually and formally analogical by analogy of attribution. But it obviously is not.[9]

It is not the case that being is intrinsic to only one analogate (the "prime"), and that the term "being" is then transferred to all the other analogates because they are somehow related to the Prime. For of course in actual fact being is intrinsic to them all: every thing that is, is. In technical language, the analogy of being in be-ing (*in actu exercito*) contains only virtually analogy of attribution, inasmuch as it has the *virtus* or power of producing an

---

[8] This is not the place to discuss that analogy. But it is impossible not to make mention of it when dealing with analogy of attribution in the metaphysical order, because wherever we find (a virtual) analogy of attribution in that order we find an underlying analogy of proper proportionality, without which the former would be impossible.

[9] Cf. *Degrés*, p. 423.

effect, namely, extrinsic denomination *ex uno*, which analogy of attribution alone produces formally.

A fitting conclusion to this Chapter and this Part is found in the words of Gerald B. Phelan:

To attempt to solve the problems of metaphysics upon such a basis [i.e., of analogy of attribution] would be futile. For, in such conditions, the formal *ratio* of being would be possessed by but one Being and merely *attributed* by the mind to every other thing, but not formally and intrinsically possessed by them. In other words, there would be but one Being, and Parmenides would rejoice. It is only when the analogy of attribution is mingled with an analogy of proper proportionality that it appears to give a firm foundation for metaphysical demonstration. But even in such cases the metaphysical value of the demonstration rests wholly upon the analogy of proportionality involved.[10]

[10] *St. Thomas and Analogy*, pp. 37 f.

Part Three

**SYMBOLIC ANALOGY OR
ANALOGY OF METAPHOR**

CHAPTER XIV

THE MEANING OF METAPHORICAL PROPORTIONALITY

1. PROPORTION, PROPORTIONALITY, AND THE COMMUNICABILITY OF NAMES

"PROPORTIONALITY is nothing other than equality of proportion as when *This* has an equal proportion to *This* and *That* to *That*." [1] And there is a clear distinction between the analogy which consists in two things having different relations to one and the same thing (a case of analogy of proportion or attribution) from that analogy which consists in an equal proportion of two things to two other things; just as tranquillity *is to* the sea, for instance, so serenity *is to* the air, because tranquillity is the quiet of the sea and serenity the quiet of the air. For these quaint terms one may substitute any terms one likes, provided they illustrate the analogy in question, namely, analogy of proportionality. [2]

In other words, there are two classes of analogy which arise from two types of agreement or conformity: the one of proportion, the other of proportionality. [3] The first type consists in a certain concordance among things which have

[1] St. Thomas, V *Eth.*, V, 939.
[2] V *Meta.*, VIII, 879.
[3] *De ver.*, II, 11, c. ("Convenientia enim secundum proportionem potest esse duplex.") See note 39, *Introduction*.

some sort of "proportion" to one another (proportion being understood in the sense of finite, determinate relation), whereas the second type consists in the likeness of two proportions to each other. The term (terminus *ad quem*) of the first type is always one; whereas the second type always involves two or more termini. Thus the fundamental modes of analogy are reducible to two: analogy of one or of several to one, and analogy of several to several.[4]

It will be recalled (Introduction, sect. B. 4) that in its primitive signification, or according to the first imposition of the term, "proportion" applies properly to quantities, and signifies a certain relation of one quantity to another according to a determinate excess or defect or equality: four is the double of two, nine the triple of three, etc. Similarly, "proportionality" in the mathematical sense simply means equality of proportions whose terms are quantities. But we have now abandoned those mathematical meanings; we are considering "proportion" in the broadest sense as signifying any relation whatever of one entity to another,[5] whether that relation entails a finite and determinate "distance" between the terms related, or an indefinite, indeterminate, and even infinite distance.[6] So too, we are here concerned with proportionality in the most extensive sense, as signifying likeness between all sorts of relations.[7]

[4] Cf. Penido, *Le rôle*, p. 34.
[5] Cf. *De ver.*, XXIII, 7, ad 9.
[6] Cf. *S. th.*, I, 12, 1, ad 4; *De ver.*, VIII, 1, ad 6; XIII, 7, ad 9; *De pot.*, VII, 10, ad 9, etc.
[7] Cf. Cajetan, *De nom.*, III, pp. 24 f.

There are, however, two types of proportionality: metaphorical and proper.[8] Now, to speak metaphorically is to speak "by similitude." And a name is communicable in two ways: properly and by similitude.[9] It is communicable properly when its entire meaning is applicable to a plurality of things; it is communicable by similitude when only part of its meaning is applicable to the things of which it is predicated. The word "lion," for instance, is properly communicable to all actual lions, and to nothing else: "lion" said of anything other than a lion is communicable to that thing only by similitude. A man may be called "Achilles" metaphorically because, like Achilles, he is strong or swift, but the name Achilles applies properly only to Achilles himself.

Nevertheless, metaphorical predication is not identical with predication by similitude. The latter has a broader and less precise meaning.[10] Metaphor is not based on merely any sort of likeness but on some real likeness, a likeness really characteristic of the thing or things of which the metaphorical term is predicated. Yet even so the metaphorical term is not communicable properly but only by similitude. Now, in what precisely does the likeness in question consist?

2. EXAMPLES OF METAPHORICAL PROPORTIONALITY

We have seen that analogy in the sense of composite proportion or proportionality has a qualitative as well as a quantitative sense; that it signifies not only identity of

---

8 *De ver.*, II, 11, c. ("Sed tamen hoc dupliciter contingit.")
9 *S. th.*, I, 13, 9, c. ("Respondeo dicendum quod. . . .")
10 *De ver.*, VII, 2, c.; cf. *De ver.*, X, 10, ad 6.

quantitative relationships between two sets of terms but similarity in any kind of relationship between two sets of terms. Human speech is shot through with metaphors. The expression "sweet melody," for example, is merely an abridgment of the analogy: this melody affects the ear in the same pleasing way as sweet things (e.g., candy) affect the palate. It is obvious that this analogy has the form of a metaphorical proportionality: melody : auricular sensation : : candy: palatal sensation (sweetness). Although such analogies are conveniently expressed in this mathematical form, it is important to realize that they are in no respect mathematical. This *caveat* is relevant to all cases of non-mathematical proportion and proportionality, and especially relevant to metaphysical, that is to say, proper proportionalities, which would be completely unintelligible if the quasi-mathematical form in which they are commonly presented should invite the assumption that after all they are in some sense only mathematical analogies.

Metaphorical analogies are ubiquitous in every language. They are to be seen in almost every page of print and are used in all our common talk. It is interesting to note that inventions are often given names based on "analogy" of this sort. Thus airships are machines which do in the air what ships do on water.[11] Wings used in reference to a building, an airplane, hockey players, an army; caterpillar said of a certain type of tractor; bomber said of a celebrated contemporary boxer; black horse said of a political candidate; fox, wolf, lion, lamb, goose, snake,

11 Cf. article entitled "Analogy" by A. Wolf in *Encyclo. Brit.* (14th ed.), I, 864.

pig, rat, donkey, ass, star, rock, said of men: all such expressions are of course pure metaphors.

Now, it may be objected that the *proportion* between, say, the cunning fox and the cunning man, the courageous soldier and the courageous lion, is not itself metaphorical but is real, inasmuch as the man, like the fox, is really cunning, and the soldier, like the lion, really courageous. Obviously, when one calls a man a fox one means that he is really and truly wily or cunning; and when one says that Shipwreck Kelly is a lion one affirms that he is really and truly courageous. Such expressions, however, are nonetheless metaphorical, because the metaphor bears not on the word "cunning" nor on the word "courageous" but on "fox" and on "lion" respectively. So long as we limit ourselves to saying: the man is cunning, the fox is cunning; the lion is courageous, the soldier is courageous, there is no question of metaphor; we simply have analogical concepts of cunning and of courage, abstracting from the cunning man and the fox, the soldier and the lion. The metaphor arises only when we call the one a fox and the other a lion. For the nature of a lion or of a fox, of course, is not found intrinsically or integrally in a man. What is common is only a *likeness in the dynamic order*, in the order of effects produced or actions done.[12]

When our Lord said to the apostles: "I am the vine, you are the branches" (John 15:5), He indicated that, as there is a vital circulation between the vine and its branches, so likewise between the Master and His disciples. And when we profess that "Christ is the Head of the

[12] Cf. Penido, *Le rôle*, pp. 52 f.

entire Church" (Eph. 1:22; I Cor. 11:3), we mean that the "active supereminence" of the head in relation to the rest of the body is found proportionately, in a spiritual manner, in Christ in relation to the Church: head : body, in natural order : : Head (Christ) : Church, in supernatural order ("threefold supereminence").[13] Evidently, therefore, metaphor is truly an analogy of proportionality because it involves at least two relations in which, in a certain way, the common analogical notion is realized.

3. Metaphor an Improper Mode of Analogy

Although metaphor is a type of proportionality, things can receive a metaphorical predication not because they share integrally and properly a perfection or form which is common to them proportionately, but only because there is some dynamic likeness between them—a likeness consisting in the production of similar effects. A thing is said metaphorically because of a certain "likeness of operation" or "similar effect." [14] Thus the effect of water in washing away corporeal stains is similar to the effect of grace in effacing spiritual stains.[15]

The metaphorical analogies which abound in Holy Scripture are instructive philosophically as well as morally and theologically. St. Thomas has illuminated, for philosopher and theologian alike, a large part of this immensely rich field of knowledge. And he has done so by applying a very simple principle or rule. With characteristic lucidity

13 Cf. St. Thomas, *S. th.*, III, 8, 1, c.
14 Cf. St. Thomas, *De malo*, XVI, 1, ad 3; *De ver.*, II, 1, c, ("Et ideo alii dixerunt, quod scientia. . . . ")
15 IV *Sent.*, I, 1, 1, qcl. 5, ad 3; cf. *De pot.*, IX, 3, ad 1.

he sets forth the mechanism of symbolic reference in Holy Writ. There is, he points out,[16] a mode of agreement or likeness "through a certain *proportionality,* according to which in the Scriptures metaphors of corporeal things are transferred to spiritual things, God [for example] being called the sun because He is the principle of spiritual life, as is the sun of corporeal life." [17] It is this principle of metaphorical proportionality which alone makes intelligible a great many biblical texts, casting light upon truths obscured sometimes by the very grandeur and beauty of the poetical imagery in which they are, and in which they can only appropriately be, expressed.

Maritain observes [18] that every metaphorical or symbolic analogy has to do with a concept *univocal in itself* ("eagle" said of the bird, concept no. 1), which the mind *uses analogically* by transferring it to other things ("eagle" said of an orator, concept no. 2), where it designates something made known by the *likeness of relations* in which, respectively, this subject (the orator) stands to a certain term (sublime eloquence) and in which likewise the object signified by concept no. 1 (the bird) stands to another term (elevated flight). So, in the common formula: orator : sublime eloquence : : eagle : elevated flight (sublimity or elevation). It is therefore clear, as Maritain points out, that metaphorical analogy (analogy of *improper* proportionality) never, by itself, permits us to attain the thing analogically known according to that which the concept *properly* signifies.

16 IV *Sent.,* XLV, 1, 1, qcl. 1, ad 2; cf. Penido, *op. cit.,* pp. 42 f.
17 Cf. I *Sent.,* VIII, 2, 3, ad 2; *De ver.,* II, 11, *et alibi.*
18 *Degrés,* p. 823.

It is plain, then, that metaphorical analogy is a proportionality because it posits a likeness of relations or proportions between several terms, and it is equally plain that it is an improper proportionality because, as in analogy of attribution, it operates with a concept which is univocal in itself and which is merely employed analogically. Thus, in the example of the word "sun" said of God, it is evident that we have to do with a concept univocal in itself ("sun" said of the heavenly body, concept no. 1), which the mind uses analogically in transferring it to another subject ("sun" said of God, concept no. 2), where it designates something made known by the likeness of relations in which this subject (God) stands to a certain term (spiritual life) and the object signified properly by concept no. 1 (the heavenly body called the sun) to another term (corporeal life). Thus, God, the divine Sun : spiritual life : : the natural sun : corporeal life (principle).[19] So it is clear that in metaphorical proportionality the character signified by the common name is found formally in one term and denominatively in the other, just as the act of smiling pertains formally to human beings alone, and to a meadow only in a metaphorical sense.[20] Similarly, to liken Christ to a lion is to say that His actions, like those of a lion, are powerful in their effects.[21]

Since whatever is denominated metaphorically from some other thing is not said to *be* that thing but to be *like* it, it is clear that things said metaphorically do not retain

[19] Cf. I *Sent.*, XXXIV, 3, 1, ad 2; II *Sent.* XVI, 1, 2, ad 5; III *Sent.*, II, 1, qcl. 1, ad 3; IV *Sent.*, I, 1 1 qcl. 5, ad 3.
[20] Cf. John of St. Thomas, *Logica*, II, 13, 3 (ed. Reiser, p. 485).
[21] Cf. *S. th.*, I, 13, 6, c.

the same concept at all (not even in the sense of proportionately the same), but only the same name. For the terms
used in metaphorical analogies are not intrinsically analogical but are merely given an analogical reference by
the mind.

4. Metaphor and Attribution Compared

All the modes of analogy are themselves mutually analogous. It is not difficult to see wherein metaphorical analogy
is analogous to analogy of attribution. In neither type do
we find one common concept; we find many concepts,
having a unity only of comparison or connotation. Since
such "analogicals" are not, formally considered, analogical
at all, the unity of the analogates will not, in either case,
be based on any intrinsic possession of a common analogical character. Thus the terms healthy, smiling, lion, are
univocal in themselves because properly and directly they
signify the health which is in the living organism, the smile
on a human face, and the actual lion of the jungle or the
zoo. By reason of some sort of likeness or connotation such
terms may be applied to other things, yet they do not even
indirectly signify those things themselves; they merely
serve as terms of comparison or relation. So, observing that
medicine and food are conducive to health, we call them
healthy or healthful; because a meadow covered with
flowers occasions a feeling of joy, we say that it is a smiling
meadow, and so on. The concepts of health or of smiling
are obviously univocal in themselves and neither directly
nor indirectly signify the nature of food or medicine nor
of a beautiful meadow and are applied to such objects only

by metaphorical transference. This is why analogicals of this kind can in no sense be reduced to one concept, but require as many concepts as there are analogates.[22] That these two types of analogy may in no way be confused, however, we will indicate more precisely their points of similarity and of difference.[23]

Attribution and metaphor are similar in three respects: (1) in both analogies, the common term (the *analogon*) is formally present in only one analogate, and (2) only contingently and improperly present in the other analogates; finally (3), in both analogies knowledge of the proper analogate is prior to the knowledge of the improper analogate or analogates: to know what is meant by healthy or healthful said of medicine, one must first know what is meant by healthy said of the living organism; to know what is meant by "smiling" said of a meadow, one must first know what smiling said of a human face connotes. It is of course impossible to know the meaning of any term in its metaphorical signification without prior knowledge of what it means in its proper signification.

Between analogy of attribution and metaphorical analogy there are likewise three main points of difference: (1) attribution is a simple proportion, metaphor a proportionality; (2) attribution, as such, is limited to the order of extrinsic relations and of logical intentions, whereas metaphor, being eminently dynamic, bears on the real order of efficient causality; (3) attribution has only a "virtual" role

---

[22] Cf. John of St. Thomas, *Logica*, II, 13, 3 (*ed. cit.*, pp. 491 f.); Cajetan, *De nom.*, VII, pp. 60 f.

[23] Cf. G. M. Manser, "Die Arten der Analogie," *Divus Thomas*, VII (Fribourg, 1929), 339 f.

in metaphysical demonstration; metaphorical analogy is capable of providing a basis for rhetorical and therefore only probable demonstrations.

Point (1) requires no explanation. As for point (2), attribution, formally considered, is a purely logical analogy and, as such, it is limited to the realm of logical intentions; moreover, in attribution the minor analogates are named and receive their character as analogates from a principal term or prime analogate, and for this reason attribution is wholly in the order of extrinsic relations. (See chap. 12.) Metaphorical analogy, on the other hand, consists in the similarity in activity or mode of operation of two or more agents which are diverse in nature; so that the analogated character or form is actually present in each of the analogates: in one of them properly and formally, in the other or others only virtually and therefore improperly. In regard to point (3), the fact should be kept in mind that the mode of participation of the analogates in the common analogous form is the basis of the value of every analogical demonstration. But since, in the case of metaphorical analogy, the mode of participation is improper, the demonstration founded on it will also be improper. At best such demonstrations will be only probable. Thus we read [24] that no argument based on symbolical expressions can be demonstrative; that symbolic theology is not "argumentative." [25] What is true of symbolic theology is also true of symbolic analogy in all fields: it is not probative, demonstrative, argumentative. The reason is close at hand.

24 St. Thomas, I *Sent*, prol. I, 5, c.; cf. Manser, *art. cit.*, pp. 340 f.
25 St. Thomas, I *Sent.*, prol., I, 5, c.

Every metaphor is indeed based on some actual dynamic likeness between the things compared; [26] yet this likeness will necessarily be only partial [27] and accidental, although it must be founded on a characteristic quality of the terms involved.[28] Nevertheless metaphor is based on a likeness which touches not the *natures* of things but only their actions or operations. Consequently metaphor is capable of revealing only accidental aspects of things (taking accident in the strict sense as including properties or proper accidents). Hence the possibility, in fact the wide prevalence, of forced and unreal metaphors. Hence, too, the inevitable element of subjectivism in the choice of points of comparison.[29] Demonstration reaches down to the essence of a thing. Metaphor can never attain to the essence but only the mode of operation.[30]

Although metaphors include a purely subjective element and have no place in philosophical demonstration, they are not mere linguistic artifices having no truth-value at all. Names of that sort are not metaphors properly speaking; for, as we have pointed out, not everything that is said by similitude is said metaphorically. In the philosophical and proper sense, metaphor is one of the modes of analogy of proportionality and as such it imports a certain intrinsic realization and thus a measure of objectivity. This results from the fact that metaphor is in the order of

---

[26] Cf. *S. th.*, I, 13, 9; I, 33, 3.
[27] Cf. *De ver.*, VII, 2, ad 5.
[28] Cf. *ibid.*, 2, c.
[29] Cf. Penido, *Le rôle*, pp. 106 f.
[30] Cf. *S. th.*, I, 13, 6 c.; I *Sent.*, XVI, 1, 3, ad 3; *De pot.*, IX, 3, ad 1.

efficient causality since it posits a functional or dynamic equivalence.[31]

It is clear, then, that the objective value of metaphor does not depend on any actual comparison between natures but only on a certain likeness between causalities. Thus, in theology, it is through metaphor that we acquire knowledge of the attributes of action, of the different modes of divine causality.[32] There is no doubt that metaphorical analogies are perfectly legitimate so long as one does not try to make them "say" more than they actually do. Of course the *via metaphorae* will never lead us into the order of demonstrative knowledge. But no such claim need ever be made: "To speak metaphorically is not to speak falsely; for by such speech one does not intend to express the *natures* of the things which are signified by the [metaphorical] words one uses, but rather those characters which have a certain likeness to those things." [33] Metaphor always essentially affirms some sort of likeness in the effects produced by different agents; and it is from this real likeness that it derives its truth-value. To characterize Joe Louis as a "bomber" is not to speak falsely.[34]

Since metaphorical terms have no intrinsically analogical meaning, it follows that metaphorical or symbolic analogy is not a proper mode of analogy. Metaphor, in fact, constitutes an analogy of *improper* proportionality. Metaphor, like attribution, implies some sort of causality,

31 Cf. I *Sent.*, XLV, 1, 4, c.
32 Cf. Penido, *Le rôle*, p. 103, with note 7.
33 I *Sent.*, XVI, 1, 3, ad 3.
34 Cf. *S. th.*, I, 13, 9; I *Sent.*, III, 2, 1, ad 2.

and in both types of analogy one of the relations defines the other or others. For it is impossible to grasp the metaphorical meaning of any term except through its proper meaning. Being expressed in the form of a proportionality, however, metaphor is a type of analogy of several to several, and not, like attribution, an analogy of several to one; and metaphor is more intrinsic than attribution: it strikes deeper, because the order of operation, wherein metaphor lies, is closer to essence than is *relation*.[35] The first act of an essence is being (*esse*), its second act, operation. Operation, therefore, follows upon the being of things.[36] While there is no health *in* climate, there *is* "something leonine" in Achilles.[37] Analogy of metaphor is a kind of "mean" between analogy of attribution and analogy of proper proportionality.

5. ANALOGY REDUCED TO METAPHOR: AN INGENIOUS THEORY

If it cannot be truly said that the fundamental mode of analogy is analogy of attribution, neither can this be truly said of analogy of metaphor. Proper analogy does not consist in any sort of dynamic likeness or equivalence. Nevertheless this is the upshot of a theory which would make of analogy an essentially dynamic thing, requiring a total diversity of natures coupled with a certain "functional" equivalence.

It is held that the basic elements of analogy are two: diversity in nature and equivalence in function. By the

35 Cf. Penido, *op. cit.*, p. 44.
36 Cf. *C. G.*, III, 69 ("Item, si agere . . . "); *S. th.*, III, 34, 2, ad 1, *et alibi*.
37 Penido, *loc. cit.*

latter is meant Being itself so far as it is related to a certain effect.[38] This "theory of analogy" is thus intended to be metaphysical and absolutely comprehensive. But to conceive analogy in this way is to identify it with metaphor; and metaphor constitutes an analogy of *improper* proportionality. It is stated that "The role of proportion is essentially to relate two different natures, of which only one is known directly, to an identical *effect*."[39] Clearly, it is a question of *metaphorical* analogy.[40]

But metaphorical analogy employs a concept which is univocal in itself and which is merely used by the intellect in an analogical manner. This fact is strikingly confirmed in the theory referred to above. For its author holds that there must not be more than three terms in any analogy and that what one might call the "denominator" must be strictly common, i.e., *univocal* in the two members.[41] The logic of this doctrine is simply working itself out to its own logical conclusion, namely, the reduction of analogy to univocity: "Analogy loses nothing in attaching itself to the univocal by multiple intermediaries."[42] On the contrary, analogy thereby loses its very analogical character.

Such is the net result of this doctrine of analogy; yet it contains subtleties which should not be ignored: the concept of Nothing is "univocal"; it is from this concept that thought returns to Being; thanks to the relation perceived

[38] Auguste Valensin, "Une théorie de l'analogie," p. 324.

[39] *Ibid.*, p. 328: "Le rôle de la proportion est essentiellement de rapporter deux natures différentes, dont une seule est directement connue, *à un effet identique*."

[40] Cf. *ibid.*, p. 327.

[41] *Ibid.*

[42] *Ibid.*, p. 328: "L'analogie ne perd rien à s'accrocher à l'univoque par de multiples intermédiaires."

between these two concepts, a third concept is obtained, the concept of existence, namely, of *that-by-which-Being-is-not-Nothing;* a concept very poor and very abstract, but for that very reason of universal application.[43]

There is an element of truth in this theory, but the error outweighs the truth. Here we have what has been appropriately called a "psychological expedient"; for "The metaphysical nothing of all possible beings is necessarily analogical, as are the beings to which it refers." [44] As for the proposed reduction of analogy to metaphor (which constitutes the essence of the theory), it is sufficient to point out that in order to enter the realm of analogy "It is necessary to quit the dynamic order for the order of being, and functional likeness for entitative likeness." [45]

---

[43] P. 333.

[44] N. Balthasar, *L'abstraction métaphysique* . . . , p. 65; "Le néant métaphysique de tous les êtres possibles, est nécessairement analogique, tout comme les êtres auxquels il se rapporte."

[45] Penido, *Le rôle*, p. 45: "Il faut quitter l'ordre dynamique pour l'ordre d'être, et la similitude fonctionnelle pour la similitude entitative." Cf. Le Rohellec, "Cognitio Nostra Analogica de Deo" in *Problèmes philosophiques*, p. 154, note.

It cannot be said that Desbuts has grasped the notion of proper analogy, for he claims that analogical knowledge results from a likeness in the *functions* of different beings. ("La notion d'analogie d'après St. Thomas d'Aquin," p. 381.) Like Valensin, he would reduce analogy to metaphor, and thereby, inevitably to univocity.

CHAPTER XV

SYMBOL AND SYMBOLISM

1. WHAT IS A SYMBOL?

SINCE analogy of metaphor is "symbolic" analogy, the question immediately arises: What is a symbol? Σύμβολον is defined as a "sign or token by which one knows or infers a thing"; it is used of omens, badges, ensigns, of the ivy wreath, of standards, of the insignia of the deities, etc.[1] The English word "symbol" is defined as "something that stands for, or represents, or denotes something else (not by exact resemblance, but by vague suggestion, or by some accidental or conventional relation); esp. a material object representing or taken to represent something immaterial or abstract (A.D. 1590)."[2] It is pointed out also that "symbol" may be said of "a written character or mark used to represent something; a letter, figure or sign conventionally standing for some object, process, etc. (A.D. 1620)."[3]

From these definitions we see that a sign or symbol implies relation to a cognitive faculty, and that it is something which represents something other than itself. These are important points, no doubt, but the lexicographers are concerned with usage and not with exact definition. Some logicians are of more help in this matter.

[1] Liddell-Scott, *A Greek-English Lexicon* (Oxford, 1901), p. 1458 b.
[2] *Shorter Oxford Dictionary*, s. v., no. 2.
[3] *Ibid.*, no. 3.

A sign has been defined in a general way as "that which represents to a cognitive faculty something other than itself." [4] This definition includes all signs. It does not tell us anything specific about symbols, which, as common usage indicates, are not merely any sort of signs. But the verb "to represent" has a very broad meaning, because everything that is made present to a faculty is in a sense "represented." [5] This may happen in three ways: objectively, formally, instrumentally. Thus, as objects of knowledge, things are representative "objectively"; knowledge itself is representative formally; a footprint, mark, trace, track, etc., are representative instrumentally.

The verb "to signify," on the other hand, is less broad in meaning, being said only of that by which something *distinct from itself* is made present to a *cognitive* faculty. Fundamentally, therefore, this verb is used in only two senses: the one formal, the other instrumental. Consequently signs are subject to a twofold division: 1. considered in their relation to the cognitive faculty, they are either *formal* or *instrumental;* 2. considered in relation to the thing signified, they fall into three classes: natural, arbitrary, conventional. [6]

Now a *formal* sign is a formal "knowledge," which is itself re-presentative without the mediation of anything else.

---

[4] John of St. Thomas, *Logica,* I, 1, 2 (ed. Reiser, p. 9, col. 1).

[5] Except the act of being itself. There is no representative concept of the act of being, because this act is unique and individual and diverse in every case and therefore offers no basis, as do essences or natures or substances, for a universal, that is to say, a re-presentative concept. John of St. Thomas does not note this exception. But he is writing a logical treatise, and in that context the problem does not arise. It belongs solely to metaphysics.

[6] Cf. John of St. Thomas, *Logica,* I, 1, 2 (ed. cit. pp. 9 f.).

Thus that which is signified by a formal sign is known at the same time as the "sign" is itself known; it is known *in* the sign itself. Such a sign is the concept, the formal concept, or *verbum mentis*.[7] An *instrumental* sign, on the other hand, is that which, from prior knowledge, represents something other than itself.[8] For example, the olive branch, representing peace, is an instrumental sign; and of course it must be known as an olive branch before being known as a symbol of peace. I say *symbol*, because the symbol is an instrumental rather than a formal sign. Nor is the symbol a purely natural sign; for the latter, apart from any conventional imposition, is representative by its very nature, as smoke is of fire, whereas the symbol is a product of custom or convention.[9]

The symbol is not a clear-cut type of sign, then, but a mixed variety, so to speak; since at one and the same time it may be both instrumental, arbitrary, and conventional. This is evident, for instance, in the case of patriotic insignia of all sorts, as well as of mathematical and chemical symbols. But symbols may also contain an admixture of the *natural* type of sign. This element, along with the conventional, is apparent in allegories and religious symbols; for, in this order, only those things are chosen to symbolize other things which by their very nature prefigure in some way the realities they are intended to represent.[10] Thus the symbol is neither a purely arbitrary nor a purely conven-

[7] The "formal concept" is that *in which* we know. The "objective concept" is *that which* we know formally.
[8] Cf. John of St. Thomas, *ed. cit.*, p. 10, col. 1.
[9] Cf. Penido, *Le rôle*, p. 68, and John of St. Thomas, *loc. cit.*
[10] Cf. Penido, *op. cit.*, p. 68; St. Thomas, *S. th.*, I–II, q. 102.

tional sign, having a merely subjective, practical or pragmatic value. Nor, on the other hand, is the symbol a purely
natural sign; and, properly speaking, it is not a formal
sign at all. It is primarily an instrumental sign. And it is
a sign which does not necessarily resemble the object signified.

If the symbol is considered a purely arbitrary and conventional sign, we will find that symbolism, or symbolic
analogy, is denied all "objective" value. But if symbols
are viewed as purely or essentially natural signs, there may
appear the remarkable theory that everything is, of its
very nature, really symbolic. In such a system symbolic
analogy becomes the master key of all knowledge.

It has been shown that modernist symbolism in theology
has very often erred in the first direction, taking "symbol"
in the sense of purely arbitrary sign.[11] But notable ex-

---

[11] "Modernist symbolism . . . too often corresponds to pure equivocity"
(Penido, Le rôle, p. 69). Certain modernists, he points out, hold that our dogmatic concepts are merely affective or moral or pragmatic or prophetic symbols, and that all religious knowledge is essentially subjective. Thus Sabatier
"decrees" that religious knowledge is conditioned by a triple necessity: it is
essentially subjective, it is theological, and finally, it is symbolic (in Sabatier,
Esquisse d'une phil. de la rel., p. 390; quoted by Penido, op. cit., p. 70, with
note 2). "The true content of the symbol," Sabatier says (op. cit.; in Penido,
p. 70), "is entirely subjective; it is the relation in which the subject is con-
scious of being with God, or, better still, the way in which he feels himself
affected by God." Apart from this experience, the symbol is devoid of all significance: "When every metaphorical element is eliminated from it, our general
ideas regarding the object of religion become simply negative, contradictory,
and lose all real content" (ibid.). For Sabatier, dogmatic theology is only a
kind of higher symbolism, because dogmas themselves are only intellectual
transcriptions, continually subject to amendment, of subjective experience.
(Sabatier, op. cit., p. 300; in Penido, p. 70.)

The many forms of modernist symbolism in theology seem to have this in
common: denial of the objective value of dogmatic or theological formulas:
"All, in different ways, refuse to abandon the darkness of equivocity for the
light, flickering indeed but none the less luminous, of analogy" (Penido, p.
70). If this is so, it follows that modernist theological symbolism tends to take
the symbol as a purely arbitrary and conventional sign. If that is done, sooner

amples of this species of symbolism are to be found in philosophy as well as in theology. I will next consider an extreme case, not because it is philosophically significant in itself, but because it illustrates pointedly how a mistake about symbolism can be one important contributing cause of philosophical failure.

2. THE FICTIONALISM OF HANS VAIHINGER

More than most titles, the title of Vaihinger's chief work actually tells what it is about: *The Philosophy of "As If": a System of the Theoretical, Practical and Religious Fictions of Mankind.*[12]

The author says he is a "critical positivist." [13] But it is clear that this whole doctrine of *als ob* is substantially only a variant of an ancient theme: nominalistic empiricism or sensationalism. On this he bases his elaborate theory of "fictions".

From the standpoint of Critical Positivism, then, there is no Absolute, no Thing-in-itself, no Subject, no Object. All that remains is sensations, which exist, and are given, and out of which the whole subjective world is constructed with its division into physical and psychical complexes. Critical Positivism asserts that any other, any further claim is fictional, subjective and unsubstantiated. For it, only the observed sequence and co-existence of phenomena exist,

---

or later there will come the flat, dogmatic denial that theological knowledge is knowledge at all, in the sense of being properly and formally expressive of the being, nature, and attributes of God: it may be conceded indeed that theological formulas do teach us a great deal about religious experience but, since they are only symbolical transcriptions of that experience, it is evident that they really cannot teach us anything about God.

12 Eng. tr. by C. K. Ogden (London, New York, 1924). All references in this chapter to the *Philosophy of "As If"* are found in this edition.

13 Vaihinger, *The Philosophy of "As if"* . . . , p. 77, *et alibi*. (Since notes 14–37, below, all refer to this work, the title will not be repeated.)

and upon these alone it takes its stand. Any explanation going beyond this can only do so by using the accessories of discursive
thought, i.e. through fictions. The only fictionless doctrine in the
world is that of Critical Positivism. Any more detailed or elaborate
claim about existence, as such, is fictional.[14]

This passage is a résumé of the System of Fictions. Evidently the author is moving in the orbit of Hume and of
Kant. (But I am not here concerned with historical parallels or "reductions.") The line of thought is simple and
clear. As soon as we pass from the order of immediate sense
experience to the conceptual or "ideal" order, we are at
once in the realm of fictions. The attempt to understand
experience takes us outside experience, and thereby outside the order of the real. We have landed in a world not of
"is" but of "as if," and that world is purely "subjective."
Nevertheless, fictions are not negligible notions; they have
a certain pragmatic value.

As distinguished from hypotheses, fictions are ideas or
"constructs" consciously recognized to be false in the sense
of having no "objective" correlates in "reality," but
which, for practical reasons, must be used in the physical
sciences, in ethics, in religion and theology, in the arts,
and even in logic.[15] For it must be remembered that all

[14] P. 77.

[15] Cf. pp. 85–90, 266–70. Vaihinger states (p. 268): "Whereas every hypothesis seeks to be an adequate expression of some reality still unknown and to
mirror this objective reality correctly, the fiction is advanced with the consciousness that it is an inadequate, subjective and pictorial manner of conception, whose coincidence with reality is, from the start, excluded and which
cannot, therefore, be afterwards verified, as we hope to be able to verify an
hypothesis. For that reason a fiction can never be expressed in the form of a
problematical judgment but must claim as its proper form of expression the
fictive judgment." However, in view of Vaihinger's own conception of ideas as
subjective intellectual tools, his contention that hypotheses are *essentially distinct* from fictions (e.g., p. 266) is untenable. As concepts, they must be a

our ideas about phenomenal reality have a fictional aspect. Truth, for example, is merely "the most expedient error." [16] Truth is the fiction that "works," that enables us to explain, predict, and control. The proper definition of fiction, then, is "legitimized error." [17] It is "error" because our ideas, which are the content of truth, are subjective and therefore inapplicable to anything real; it is "legitimized" because, though false, our ideas facilitate action in this world.

The central thesis of the system thus follows from a nominalistic assumption, an assumption having in this instance the inflexibility and the force of a dogma. It is the unshakable conviction that our ideas have no "objective" value, that they do not put us in contact with the real world. Given this assumption, coupled with the assumption that truth consists in the agreement of the conceptual world with the world of sense-phenomena, and, finally, the colossal assumption that "the sequence of sensations constitutes ultimate reality," [18] it is not difficult to follow the logic of the denial "that the world as conceived by us has value as knowledge." [19] Nor is it difficult to see why it should be held that "only the practical test is the final guarantee" but that "even here we can only conclude that combina-

---

species of "fiction," regardless of their distinctive role in "scientific knowledge"; for they fall within the general class of "ideational constructs." It is to be noted that by "reality" or "objective reality" Vaihinger does not mean actual things or qualities or operations or events themselves, but only our perceptions or apperceptions of them; for these experiential phenomena are the only "things" we actually know. Cf. pp. xlvii, 4–6, 67–77, et alibi passim.

[16] P. 108.
[17] P. 106.
[18] P. 76.
[19] P. 66.

tions of ideas fulfil their purpose and have been rightly formed." It is then indeed an easy step to the conclusion: "From the standpoint of modern epistemology we can therefore no longer talk about truth at all, in the usual sense of the term." [20] Since, then, truth is "merely the most expedient error" and the conceptual world is through and through subjective, we arrive at the formula: "Subjective is fictional; fictional is false; falsehood is error." [21]

All our ideas, scientific, social, ethical, philosophical, religious, all are subjective, fictional, false. Nothing concerning the "truth" (i.e., "expedient error") of our conceptual world can be inferred from the fact of its "utility." [22] Not even our "elementary sensations" can introduce us into a realm of real *things*.[23] Indeed "reality," in the commonly accepted sense of a world of actual self-existent beings or things, is itself a fiction.[24] Philosophy's final end has been finally reached. But not only does the anti-philosophy of *als ob* undermine the foundations of all philosophical science, it undermines the foundations of every conceivable science. Any possible science would be nothing more than an organized body of fictions.

One may wonder what all this has to do with analogy. The preceding sketch of the System of Fictions seemed necessary as groundwork for the author's doctrine of "analogical fictions." In that system it is a far-reaching doctrine indeed, and much stress is laid upon it. For analogy is

[20] P. 4.
[21] P. 108.
[22] Cf. pp. 108, 15.
[23] Cf. p. 16.
[24] Cf. pp. 76 f.

equated with symbolism, and conceptual knowledge is made "analogical."

In a chapter entitled "Symbolic (analogical) Fictions," it is written: "There is another variety of fictions important for science which I call *tropic* fictions; they may also be called *symbolic* or *analogical*. They are closely related to poetic similes as well as to myth." [25] Instances in point are Locke's "illustrative fiction" of the *tabula rasa* and Plato's myths. "Symbolic" is thus synonymous with "analogical." But that is not all. "The analogical method is natural to metaphysics no less than to theology. . . . In the theory of knowledge categories are examples of such analogies. They are simply analogical fictions. . . . Reality is, and must be thought of, on the analogy of human and subjective relations. All knowledge, if it goes beyond simple succession and co-existence, can only be *analogical*." [26] So metaphysics is aptly characterized as "metabolic" or "metaphoric"; which is obvious, because metaphysics certainly goes beyond "simple succession and co-existence." We have, then, the equation: analogy = symbolism = metaphor.

"Anyone acquainted with the mechanism of thought knows that all conception and cognition are based upon analogical apperceptions." [27] And if all conceptual knowledge is symbolic (or "analogical") because by its very nature it goes beyond simple succession and co-existence, it follows that "All discursive thinking is symbolic" (or

[25] P. 27, with note 1.
[26] P. 29.
[27] *Ibid.*

"analogical").[28] It is symbolic in two respects: "First, in so far as it operates with symbols in the mathematical sense; and secondly, in so far as all knowledge gained thereby forms but a kind of simile, image, or counterpart of reality, but does not enable us to obtain knowledge of reality itself, or at least not in any adequate form." It is now quite apparent what kind of signs concepts are in the philosophy of As If.

The categories are analogical fictions which are at the same time instrumental and essentially arbitrary signs. They are not formal signs properly speaking, because they are not representative formally, they do not re-present the forms of *things*. They are instrumental because they are useful tools, even in the practical order.[29]

They are arbitrary because they are constructed largely "at will" and have in themselves a purely subjective value. It is only too true, therefore, that "When the categories are regarded as *analogical fictions,* the whole theory of knowledge takes on a different complexion. They are then recognized as simple representational constructions for the purpose of apperceiving what is given."[30] And what is given, of course, is not things themselves but "experiences," "apperceptions." For indeed we have no contact whatever with external existent things as such.

If this is so, the conclusion is perfectly correct, that "Objects possessing attributes, causes that work, are all mythical," and that "We can only say that objective phe-

28 P. 30.
29 In Part One, see chap. 39, "The Practical Utility of the Fiction of Categories."
30 P. 31.

nomena can be regarded *as if* they behaved in such and such a way." [31] It is clear that under such conditions "there is absolutely no justification for assuming any dogmatic attitude and changing the 'as if' into a 'that' "; for "As soon as these analogies are interpreted as hypotheses we get all those systems of theology and philosophy whose object is the explanation of the resultant contradictions." [32]

A distinction is drawn between "real analogies" and "fictional analogies." The former are based on likenesses which we actually observe and hence can found valid inferences having a high degree of probability, whereas the latter are "due merely to subjective method." [33] But in the System of Fictions there is really no room for this distinction. It is canceled out at once by the thesis that all discursive knowledge is symbolic or "analogical." For if it is analogical, it is fictional; and it is fictional precisely because it is conceptual: the so-called "real analogies," built

[31] *Ibid.*

[32] "We have only to recall," says Vaihinger (p. 31), "the time and trouble spent in elucidating the father-relationship of God to Christ; and the simplicity of Schleiermacher's solution! Of still greater interest are the endless attempts to determine the nature of substance and its relations to its attributes, of cause and its relation to effect, etc." All such ideas, along wih those of the possible, the necessary, the potential, the actual, etc., are mere fictions.

Concerning Schleiermacher's "solution," Vaihinger says (p. 28): "The remarkable thing is that Schleiermacher and his school regard most dogmas as analogical fictions, provisional auxiliary constructions, because the actual metaphysical relationship remains incomprehensible to us. Thus, for instance, the relationship of God to the world, which for the *philosopher* Schleiermacher is completely unknowable, is conceived of by the *theologian* Schleiermacher on the analogy of the father-son relationship; and so on. This is not a rationalistic reinterpretation of dogma, but a subtle epistemological maneuver by means of which Schleiermacher held thousands of people to Christianity. 'God' is not the 'father' of men but he is to be treated *as if* he were. Such an interpretation is of tremendous importance for the practice of religion and worship, and by means of it Schleiermacher similarly transformed all dogmas from hypotheses into fictions."

[33] *Op. cit.*, p. 32.

up by "induction" and "hypothesis" are themselves only conceptual constructs. Moreover, even in the order of sensible experiences we do not observe any real likenesses between things; we observe only certain likenesses between our sense-experiences. There are no real analogies in the sense of real likenesses between things which are immediately accessible to us, nor are there any real analogies in the sense of real likenesses between the *relations* of real things. There are only various sorts of fictional analogies or analogical fictions.[34]

It is in the philosophy of Kant, more than in any other philosophy, that Vaihinger finds confirmation for his own theory of fictions.[35] He argues at length that the *As If* is fundamental to the whole Kantian system, and he cites many texts where Kant uses this very expression. Only students of Kant are qualified to judge whether Vaihinger's case is well taken or not. But aside from the specific historical point, which is here irrelevant, it may be argued with apparent plausibility that if our conceptual knowledge is not knowledge of the real, and if our theoretical knowledge, with its a priori categories, laws, and rules, is after all only conceptual knowledge, then we may take the latter *as*

---

[34] For Vaihinger knowledge is always in the form of categories, and categories are only "analogical apperceptions," that is, a type of analogical fiction. Categories are "ideational" symbols, arbitrary and conventional and subjective signs. They may also be called "primitive analogies" (p. 103). The categories are not "innate possessions of the psyche but analogies which have been selected and applied in the course of time, and according to which events have been interpreted." "How the analogies arose," Vaihinger goes on, "it is not difficult to guess; from inner experience. The Thing and its attribute is the abstract expression of the most primitive type of proprietary relationship; the relations of reality are regarded *as if* they were things which had as their 'property' certain 'attributes' " (pp. 172 f.). Cf. J. Jastrow's "primitive analogies" in his *Fact and Fable in Psychology* (Boston, New York, 1900), pp. 236–39.

[35] Cf. *The Philosophy of 'As if,'* pp. 271–318.

if it were based on the real and as if it applied to the real.

But if we do this, we shall be faced with the question whether on those grounds there actually is any intrinsic, intellectual necessity for positing such an "as if." Hume apparently saw no such necessity; and certainly Vaihinger has not advanced beyond Hume in any speculatively significant respect. Both adopt essentially the same starting point and both make essentially the same basic assumptions; and in consequence the philosophy of *als ob* is no less destructive of knowledge than the critique of "abstract ideas."

As a matter of fact, the whole System of Fictions is itself a fiction. According to the doctrine of its author, it could be nothing else. But to deny knowledge is to claim that one's denial is itself knowledge. This simple datum alone should cause the denier to suspect that there may be something wrong with his presuppositions, with his starting point. If, whether professedly or not, he is actually in the *als ob* position, the position of nominalistic sensationalism, and does not go back and make a fresh start (a start from *things* sensed and not from sheer sensations–without-things), the most he can get out of "knowledge" is fictions. The real value for philosophy of the extreme case of the philosophy of "As If" is that it provides a clear demonstration of that very point. It does not, however, contain even a suggestion of this further point: that anyone who fundamentally follows the line of "critical positivism" or of "positivist idealism," in the sense exemplified in the doctrine of "As If," cannot in the end avoid moving from fiction to fiction in an infinite regress of nonsense. For there is no rational stopping-point anywhere along this line. Any possible system of "As Ifs" must, logically, lead to the positing of another, and so on indefinitely in a logical series of actual absurdities.

The relevance of all this discussion to the theory of analogy lies in the fact that fictionalism is only a form of symbolism; it is a symbolism posing as an analogism. But it is a spurious symbolism, because it has absolutely no contact with the order of objective dynamic likeness in which all genuine symbolism is found. It is a symbolism purely subjective, at best merely "pragmatic," and for that very reason radically arbitrary. It is "nominalistic": it tends of its very nature toward sheer equivocity and the destruction of all science. There exists, however, a totally different type of symbolism. It is the contrary of the fictionalist species.

3. "Naturalist" or Ontological Symbolism

"It is evident that the symbol is not a purely natural sign, but is willed by custom or convention." [36] If this is so, it is by no means evident in the kind of symbolism with which we are presently concerned; for symbols are here considered as natural and even formal signs. A contemporary French philosopher gives an excellent characterization of the highest level of this type of symbolism:

The totality of the universe has a unique principle, and a common end. Everything originates in the creative fecundity of the Infinite; and the absolute Being assuredly cannot have any other end than Itself. Everything springs from God in order to return to

[36] Penido, Le rôle, p. 68. "Il est évident que le symbole n'est point un signe purement naturel, mais qu'il est voulu par la coutume ou la convention."

God; that is indeed the metaphysical meaning of being and of the evolution of the world. But God is one and simple. Hence, despite the sage arguments which are advanced in order to establish the plurality of the divine ideas, all the immense reality of the universe seems to correspond to a thought sovereignly one. Then must there not be correspondences between the different levels of the real? Are not the relations and activities we observe in nature indicative of profounder tendencies and superior events which escape us? Is not matter itself just a veil which hides and reveals the world of minds? This tendency to seek out the hidden meaning of things, to see in nature the projected shadow of a spiritual and moral world, is nothing but "symbolism." [37]

For philosophers or theologians who think along those lines symbols are not mere comparisons, still less are they merely conventional or arbitrary signs, nor are they merely instrumental signs, selected as such because of their natural appropriateness to represent spiritual and transcendent realities. On the contrary, they tend to become natural and formal signs of those realities. On the highest level, symbolism of this type will declare, in effect, that all things of the finite order are to God as signs to their ultimate signification; that creatures are to be considered not only as things but as signs at once natural, inasmuch as they have being in the nature of things, and formal, inasmuch as they have the character of forms in and through which the objects they signify are known. In theology especially, this symbolism has had a long and splendid history.[38] In

[37] M. de Munnynck, "L'analogie métaphysique," p. 135.

[38] From the early days of the Church there have always been theologians who have discovered "symbols" of the Trinity in nature and in the human soul. St. Augustine, for example, held that there is in the soul a certain "trinity" of memory, understanding, and will, which represents truly, though of course very imperfectly, the Trinity of the Divine Persons; and there is also the "trinity" of mode, species, and order, which all created things exhibit. In

that whole development there are immense problems which cannot even be touched on here. But it may be pointed out that in the West the great tradition of meta-physical and theological symbolism has always been essentially and in its roots Platonic.[39]

4. The Neo-Platonist Symbolism of Nicholas Berdyaev

In our day, one of the best-known representatives of this perennial school of theological thought is Nicholas Berdyaev. As in Vaihinger's case, I am here concerned with certain aspects of his doctrine, not at all because that doctrine is intrinsically important but because it aptly illustrates some fairly common misapplications of symbolic analogy.

A symbol, Berdyaev says,[40] is "the visible image of invisible and mysterious things." It is, then, a natural sign of

---

Aristotle there is found the natural "trinity" of matter, form, and composition; in the Bible the "trinity" of number, weight, and measure, according to which God has disposed all things (Book of Wisdom, 21); in Dionysius the "trinity" of substance, power, and operation; in philosophy the classical "trinity" of unity, truth, and goodness. Also, between certain of these trinities, correspondences have been noted. Thus St. Bonaventure states that "*Unity* corresponds to *mode,* which considers God as efficient cause; *truth to species,* which considers Him as exemplar; *goodness* to *order,* which considers God as end." In the first case, we have God as Father, in the second, God as Son, in the third, God as Holy Ghost. See R. McKeon, *Selections from Mediaeval Philosophers,* I, 193–200; II, 146–48, for textual material and references on all these points.

I merely mention these facts. It is for the theologian to test and determine the true value of such "analogies." Rightly interpreted, they may contain or suggest important theological truths. But they are obviously not philosophical analogies.

[39] This adjective is used in a broad sense; it refers not only to the authentic Platonism of Plato but also to the variously modified "Platonism" of all the Neo-Platonists, pagan and Christian.

[40] *Freedom and the Spirit* (Eng. tr. by O. F. Clark. New York: Scribner's, 1935), p. 60.

things above nature. Consequently we have the familiar doctrine that "God can only be perceived symbolically, for it is only by means of symbols that it is possible to penetrate the mystery of His Being"; and again, "symbolism . . . is the only means through which men can attain divine knowledge and wisdom." [41]

Assuming that the only way we can attain any "rational" knowledge of God is through "logical concepts," that is, univocal ideas, Berdyaev launches a vigorous attack against "rational theology," "metaphysics," and "scholasticism," which he accuses of attempting to "determine" rationally the nature of Divinity: [42]

> Religious knowledge has always been symbolical in contradistinction to all rational theology and metaphysics and to scholasticism. The knowledge of God has never been and could never have been a rational, abstract, intellectual form of knowledge, for it has always had its origin elsewhere.
> All systems of scholastic theology and rational metaphysics have but a limited character, being adapted to this world and to the natural man, so that they possess only a pragmatical and juridical value. Only the facts of mysticism within Christianity are absolute, and our thought about them is always relative. [43]

This is a univocist theology of a radical type. The affirmative attributes of God are "logically contradictory"; [44] "the mystery of divinity can only be approached by way of negations"; and the whole of this negative theology is "symbolic" and "mystical." [45] The works of Dionysius the

[41] *Ibid.*, p. 64.
[42] Cf. pp. 63–65.
[43] P. 65.
[44] P. 66.
[45] P. 67.

Areopagite and of Nicholas of Cusa confirm this doctrine: [46] "God is nothing that is; He is non-being. The greatest thinkers have expounded the negative theology, whether pagans like Plotinus, or Christians like Nicholas of Cusa. Negative theology demonstrates precisely that the Divine Being is *not* being in the sense in which that word is used with regard to the natural world, where everything is positively and limitatively determinable." [47] And so on.

Evidently Berdyaev has seen that univocal ideas, like the idea of *being* considered univocally as a logical concept, simply do not work in theology. He then joins hands with the ancient and medieval Neo-Platonist theologians and, in slightly modernized form repeats some of their worst errors. The brilliance and the vigor of Berdyaev's thought have apparently concealed from many the nihilistic consequences of his position. For what is at stake is nothing less than theology itself as a science—the whole of theology, natural as well as revealed.

A symbolism of the sort advocated by Berdyaev completely destroys the scientific basis of theology. Natural theology is a metaphysical science built up by human reason on the basis of naturally knowable facts; dogmatic or revealed theology is the science of Divinity built up by

---

[46] Cf. p. 67, *et alibi*. Nicholas of Cusa, scholar, philosopher, churchman (cardinal), was one of the greatest figures of the fifteenth century. As a boy he was educated under the Brethren of the Common Life at Deventer in Holland, whither the author of *The Imitation of Christ* had preceded him some twenty years earlier. His "negative theology" shows the influence of Dionysius the Areopagite and of St. Augustine. In his celebrated treatise, *De docta ignorantia* (in *Opera omnia*, Lipsiae, Meiner, 1932), he teaches the doctrine of the equivocity of the divine names. (Cf. Lib. I, cap. XXIV, XXVI.)

[47] Berdyaev, *op. cit.*, p. 67.

human reason on the basis of revealed truths. Human reason is the instrumental cause of both sciences. But the function of human reason is to know things as they are. If it cannot, in some way, know God as He is, then theology as a science is impossible. It is true that "Divinity cannot be rationally determined and remains outside the scope of logical concepts." [48] But this means only that we cannot know God through the univocal ideas which we form of classes or categories of things or of other ideas. We can acquire some knowledge of God through metaphysical ideas. All such ideas are analogical, that is, they apply to God and to finite things only in a proportional sense. It is only through the analogical idea of "cause," for example, that we can know, demonstratively, that God exists. A univocal idea of cause can apply only to finite causes, and God is not a cause in that sense. But if we say, as Berdyaev does,[49] that it is impossible to have any intellectual knowledge of God because all such knowledge is "rational" and "abstract" and applicable only to finite objects existing in the natural world, then there is clearly no basis in human reason for any science of theology. The same, of course, is true of metaphysics.

In place of that science, Berdyaev would substitute a "mysticism" whose terms are "symbols." But he cannot have a mystical theology properly speaking, since that presupposes a theology, a science of divine truth, arrived at by human reason. There still remain the facts of religious experience. But for Berdyaev it is impossible to know with

[48] *Ibid.*, p. 64.
[49] P. 65, *et alibi passim.*

intellectual certainty the object of that experience if it transcends the natural order. Consequently it could never be known whether the experience was purely subjective or actually derived from a divine source.

Berdyaev states [50] that "all the dogmas of Christianity giving expression to the facts and events of spiritual experience have a supra-logical and supra-rational character and are above the law of identity and contradiction." It is true that those dogmas are "supra-logical" and "supra-rational"; but if they are so far beyond human reason that they transcend and even contradict [51] basic laws of thought (the law of identity is also a basic law of *things*), then they cannot be known rationally or intellectually in any sense or to any degree.

To say that they can be known only "mystically," through "spiritual experience," is to fall back on a psychological relativism which offers no basis whatever for any judgment of absolute truth. Where religious experience, even Christian mystical experience, is the measure and criterion of theological truth, "theology" becomes a species of empirical psychology, a purely descriptive study of mental and emotional states. Of course a study of that kind is quite legitimate, and may be highly significant; but it is not theology, either natural or revealed.

Historical evidence warrants the statement that within the main stream of Platonism there has always been a tendency to reduce things to symbols. This has in turn

[50] P. 65.
[51] Cf. p. 66.

given rise to an identification, at least implicit, of symbolism with analogy and, in the extreme instance, the conversion of all knowledge, theological and metaphysical as well as moral, social, and scientific, into an "analogical" mode. The "Platonist" will then speak of the natural world, the shadowy world of sensible form, as being "analogous" to the "higher world," the real world of intelligible form. And, if he carries his "analogy" into the moral and theological order, he will assert that observable objects and events teach us "by analogy" the hidden sense of spiritual things. But he will be speaking incorrectly; for his "analogy" is only a kind of symbolism, and an extreme and improper kind at that. It is not analogy.[52]

There is in the mind a power or an aptitude, normally very active, which may be called the symbolizing faculty. In persons of superior intelligence and keen sensibility this faculty sometimes operates on the high level of the "creative imagination" and is then a fruitful source of artistic insight and a powerful aid to speculative and scientific thought. But if it breaks away from the rule of reason, this "power" may generate all manner of egregious notions. Thus if symbolism is allowed to inundate the field [53] of knowledge, philosophy will be swallowed up in poetry, drowned in a flood of "analogies," metaphors, similes, myths. The abuse of symbols is not something unknown in poetry itself, as will be evident from the following example.

[52] Cf. M. de Munnynck, "L'analogie métaphysique," pp. 136–38.
[53] I take this figure from E. Gilson, *Unity of Philosophical Experience* (New York, 1937), p. 37.

5. THE SYMBOLISM OF THE FRENCH "SYMBOLIST" POETS

There is nothing in the world which may not express, signify, or suggest something other than itself, and in this sense there is nothing which cannot in some respect become a symbol. A single symbol may, in fact, express many things. Beatrice is a real person whom Dante really loved; yet she is also his inspiration and his muse. In addition she is Science and Philosophy. The Diana of Euripedes is the goddess of the woods and the mountains; but she is also the protectress of Hippolytus and the irreconcilable foe of Venus. Finally she is that "chastity which makes hearts cold, minds lucid, and wills firm." In these multiple significations lie the symbol's beauty, power, and depth. Symbolism thus understood is the very essence of poetry; it is as old as poetry itself, and permanently contemporary. Poetic symbolism of course was no invention of the nineteenth-century French symbolists. It was for this principle that they all stood; and it was because of their common championship, in however various ways, of "symbolism" in poetry that they have been grouped under a single name. Far from inventing that principle, they (or at least some of them) actually abused it.

In opposition to the naturalist, Zolaesque theory of art as mere imitation of the external appearances of life and of things, the symbolists taught that things have an "inner soul," of which the senses grasp only the outer covering or mask. Between nature and ourselves, they held, there are "correspondences," "affinities," mysterious identities;

and it is only so far as we apprehend them that, penetrating to the interior of things, we truly approach their "soul." This doctrine or this attitude is especially evident in Baudelaire, who believed that there are relations, correspondences, affinities, between sounds, colors, and states of soul; and some, like Rimbaud, even went so far as to identify certain vowels with colors, instruments, feelings; and they were all apparently obsessed with the idea of a musical poetry. Mallarmé thought that by imitating sounds the poet could arouse "musical" emotions; and for Verlaine, in poetry music should come "before all things —music ever and always." [54]

The symbolists were right in insisting that nature has certain internal characters of which the mere naturalist can never express more than the most superficial appearance. They therefore held that the true artist's aim is to grasp the inner essence whose manifestations play about on the surface of things. And herein they fell into a great error. For they—I am thinking especially of Rimbaud— attempted to make poetry fill the role of philosophy and even of religion, demanding that poetry become a means of knowledge. They failed to see or would not see that poetry, being non-conceptual, non-scientific in its mode of knowing and "operating," can never rationally be transformed into or substituted for a conception of the world or of life. Being unable to realize itself in a concpet from within, poetry must realize itself in a work *ad extra*. Thus

[54] Though a considerable amount of the poetry of the symbolists is of a high order and doubtless possesses qualities of lasting significance, some of it is so fantastically "symbolist" that, the authors being dead, it is probably no longer intelligible to anyone, and is therefore perhaps already irrevocably dated.

in knowledge of the artistic operative type, "it is the work made, the poem, the picture, the symphony, which plays the role of the mental word and of the judgment, in speculative knowledge." [55] Obviously, if poetry is not philosophy, neither is poetic symbolism, whether extravagant or sane, analogy in the philosophical sense. The symbolic analogies of poetry are incapable of yielding any properly philosophic or speculative knowledge of the real. But as suggestive material for speculative discovery and research they may have for the aesthetically gifted a great indirect philosophical value.

The main points of this chapter may be set down as follows.

6. Recapitulation

(1) The symbol is a hybrid species of sign, partaking of the arbitrary and the conventional, the instrumental and the natural. But it is primarily an instrumental sign.

(2) If the symbol is considered a purely arbitrary and conventional sign, the resultant symbolism (or symbolic analogy) will be devoid of "objective" value. This was found to be the case not only in theology but also in philosophy, as Vaihinger's system of fictions shows. And this judgment applies to any possible variant of that system which is based on the same presuppositions.

(3) If the symbol is considered as a purely, or an essentially, natural sign, there arises the tendency (sometimes,

[55] Maritain, "De la Connaissance Poétique," *La Revue Thomiste* (January, 1938), p. 94. "C'est l'objet créé, *l'œuvre faite,* le poème, le tableau, la symphonie, qui joue le rôle du verbe mental et du *jugement* dans la connaissance spéculative."

as in Berdyaev, assuming the form of a radical anti-intellectualism) to *reduce* things to symbols. This has in fact happened in the great Platonic tradition, both in theology and in philosophy, and in other spheres of knowledge as well. It has happened in poetry—in nineteenth century French symbolism, for example.

(4) The moral of the chapter is that, if symbolic analogy is removed from its proper order (that of real dynamic likeness, likeness in the order of efficient causality) and transposed to the order of play or imagination or of nature, etc., the most curious vagaries sometimes result, and even absolute nonsense. In any event knowledge of the real is not advanced by such maneuvers. This is true even of the highest and best types of misplaced symbolism, although it is not just to call them maneuvers.

CHAPTER XVI

THE SYMBOLISM OF MAIMONIDES

FAR deeper than most, if not all, modern symbolism and far more significant for the understanding of metaphorical analogy is the doctrine of Maimonides, the greatest Jewish theologian of the Middle Ages.[1] The symbolism of Maimonides is the consequence of a profound grappling with real theological difficulties. It was a grappling with problems relevant not merely to one age or even to one system or type of theology but to every age and to every effort, theological or philosophical, to make symbolism serve as a principle of true analogy in the search for knowledge of ultimate being. For, although in this chapter we shall be dealing specifically and primarily with theological symbolism, the philosophical implications are present throughout, and I trust they will become increasingly apparent in the course of the discussion.

1. "NEGATIVE THEOLOGY" AND THE ATTRIBUTES OF GOD

An attribute is an "accident" distinct from and super-added to the essence of a thing. But God is pure act; He is

---

[1] Cf. Penido, *Le rôle*, p. 126. Maimonides, perhaps more than anyone else, represents the Jewish faith seeking to understand itself. For St. Thomas, "Rabbi Moyses" was a thinker of the first order, a man whose opinions were always to be respectfully considered. Perhaps no theory of the divine names, with the exception of that of "Dionysius the Areopagite," engaged St. Thomas' attention more than did the doctrine of the great Spanish rabbi. (See, for instance, *S. th.*, I, 13, 2; *De pot.*, VII, 4–7; I *Sent.*, II, 1, 3, ad 3, and XXXVI, 1, 1).

one and absolutely simple. It follows that nothing can be attributed to Him essentially; that no name can be said of Him substantially, properly, and formally. Those who posit essential attributes in God are thus faced with no mere rhetorical dilemma but with a real and inescapable one. For those "attributes" are either distinct from His essence or they are not. If they are distinct, they are in reality accidents which are superadded to His essence and which, therefore, would introduce plurality into His very being. But God is One God, and there is no other. If the alleged attributes are not distinct, then they are vain; they are barren tautologies, empty names. Essential attributes in God, then, must be rejected. This is the position of Maimonides.[2]

2 Maimonides, *Guide for the Perplexed;* Eng. tr. by M. Friedländer (2nd ed. revised. London: George Routledge & Sons Ltd.; New York: E. P. Dutton & Co., 1936), Part I, chap. 51. In the doctrine of Maimonides the theory of the real distinction between "attribute" and essence is absolutely fundamental. He emphasizes this distinction time and again, e.g., in Part I, chaps. 20, 47, 50–53, 59–61, 75. One especially clear and pointed statement is found in chap. 51, pp. 68 f.: "For it is a self-evident truth that the attribute is not inherent in the object to which it is ascribed, but it is superadded to its essence, and is consequently an *accident;* if the attribute denotes the essence . . . of the object, it would be either mere tautology, as if, e.g., one would say 'man is man,' or the explanation of a name, as, e.g., 'man is a speaking animal'; for the words 'speaking animal' include the true essence of man. . . . It will now be clear that the attribute must be one of the two things, either the essence of the object described—in that case it is a mere explanation of a name . . . or the attribute is something different from the object described, some extraneous superadded element; in that case the attribute would be an accident, and he who merely rejects the appellation 'accidents' in reference to the attributes of God, does not thereby alter their character; for everything superadded to the essence of an object joins it without forming part of its essential properties, and that constitutes an accident. Add to this the logical consequence of admitting many attributes, viz., the existence of many eternal beings. There cannot be any belief in the unity of God except by admitting that He is one simple substance, without any composition or plurality of elements; one from whatever side you view it, and by whatever test you examine it; not divisible into two parts in any way and by any cause, nor capable of any form of plurality

If "attribute" is merely another name for accident, then to apply attributes to God is to destroy His unity and simplicity and thus to fall into polytheism. Moreover, to introduce attributes in God is to introduce composition in Him; hence multiplicity, hence divisibility, hence corporeality. For where there is multiplicity there is matter, and "there is no real unity without incorporeality." [3] Maimonides appeals repeatedly to the *way of negation* or *remotion* in order that everything which implies corporeality, passivity, change, assimilation to creatures, may be banished completely from the One God.[4] For Maimonides, God can have absolutely no "affirmative" or positive attributes.

All such attributes fall into five classes: (1) attributes of definition (inapplicable to God because at best they would be mere tautologies, i.e., "explanations of a name"); (2) attributes designating a part of the definition (likewise inapplicable because God has no parts); (3) attributes of quality (inapplicable as qualities are accidents, and there are no accidents in God); (4) attributes of relation (inapplicable because relation is an accident implying similarity in kind, and God has "nothing in common with any other being"); (5) attributes of action, which alone are

---

either objectively or subjectively." (All references to Maimonides in this chapter are to the above-cited edition of *The Guide*.)

[3] *Guide*, I, chap. 1, p. 13. See Maimonides' extensive proofs (based on Aristotle) of the unity and incorporeality of God. (Part III, chap. 1, pp. 145–54.)

Many Jews of the time believed that God had a body (cf. I, chap. 1, pp. 13 f.), and Maimonides spares no pains to show them that to materialize God is to destroy Him and to deny that very monotheism which is the glory of their race (I, chap. 26, pp. 34 f.; chap. 35, pp. 49 f.; chap. 36, pp. 51 f.)

[4] Cf., I, chap. 50, pp. 78 f., *et alibi passim*.

"appropriate to be employed in describing the Creator."
For "God is one in every respect, containing no plurality
or any element superadded to His essence"; so that "The
many attributes of different significations applied in Scripture to God, originate in the multitude of His actions, not
in a plurality existing in His essence." [5]

Attributes of this sort, in contradistinction to the alleged affirmative and essential ones, are quite intelligible
because, from the fact that an agent produces different actions, it does not follow that in the substance of that agent
there are a corresponding number of separate and different
"elements" which are the roots of those actions. This is
true of God, as of other agents: all His actions "emanate
from His essence, not from any extraneous thing superadded to His essence," and the attributes of action "do not
refer to the *essence* of God." [6] "All attributes ascribed to
God are attributes of His acts and do not imply that God
has any qualities." [7]

Moreover, there is, properly speaking, no relation between God and His creatures because relation is an accident, and God is not at all subject to any accident.[8] But
"if between two things no relation can be found, there
is no similarity between them." Hence "Those who are
familiar with the meaning of similarity will certainly understand that the term *existence*, when applied to God and
to other beings, is perfectly *homonymous*. In like manner,
the terms Wisdom, Power, Will, and Life are applied to

[5] I, chap. 52, pp. 69–72.
[6] I, pp. 72, 74.
[7] I, chap. 54, p. 78.
[8] I, chap. 52, pp. 71 f.

God and to other beings by way of *perfect homonymity*, admitting of no comparison whatever." God exists without possessing the attribute of existence," and "He is One without possessing the attribute of unity." [9]

This is a straightforward position; there is no mistaking what Maimonides means. Whatever is said about the being of God has a purely negative meaning. Only the "negative attributes" are the "true attributes," because "they do not include any incorrect notions or any deficiency whatever in reference to God, while positive attributes imply polytheism." Consequently we have the following equations: God is *incorporeal* = God is not-corporeal; God is *one* = God is not-many or there are not many gods, etc.[10]

To sum up: "Every attribute predicated of God either denotes the quality of an *action*, or—when the attribute is intended to convey some idea of the Divine Being itself, and not of His actions—the *negation* of the opposite." [11] The "agnosticism" that this implies is radical:

You must bear in mind that by affirming anything of God, you are removed from Him in two respects; first, whatever you affirm is only a perfection in relation to us; secondly, He does not possess anything superadded to His essence; His essence includes all His perfections. . . . Since it is a well-known fact that even that knowledge of God which is accessible to man cannot be obtained except by negations, and that negations do not convey a true idea of the being to which they refer, all people, both of past and present generations, declared that God cannot be an object of human comprehension, that none but Himself comprehends what He is, and that

[9] I, chaps. 56–57, pp. 79–81. Italics mine.
[10] I chap. 58, pp. 81 ff.
[11] *Ibid.*, p. 83. Italics mine.

our knowledge consists in knowing that we are unable truly to comprehend Him.[12]

2. MAIMONIDES THE "SYMBOLIST"

What does it mean, then, to say that Maimonides is a symbolist? Having asserted the homonymity or absolute equivocity of the "names of God" so far as they are held to apply to Him formally and properly,[13] Maimonides went on to say that if those names have any positive content at all it consists essentially in a certain likeness between the effects of our actions and of God's. And, as we have shown, metaphorical or symbolic analogy is always based on some kind of dynamic likeness, or relation in the order of efficient causality. But the doctrine of Maimonides is not so simple on this point as it may at first appear, because he implicitly recognizes a second type of analogy. A name said of God may have at once three distinct meanings: to say that God is "wise," for instance, means (1) that He *acts like* a wise person (analogy of metaphor); (2) that He is the *cause* of wisdom (analogy of attribution); (3) that He is not non-wise (remotion). The same is true of such names as existence, justice, goodness, life.[14]

Maimonides makes no mention of "analogy" when he

12 I, chap. 59, pp. 84 f. Italics mine.

13 Maimonides makes an exception in the case of the Tetragrammaton (the group of four letters representing the ineffably holy name [Yahveh, Jehovah] of the Supreme Being in Hebrew texts, consisting of the four consonants JHVH, JHWH, YHVH, or YHWH): "All the names of God occurring in Scripture are derived from His actions, except one, namely, the Tetragrammaton. . . . It is the distinct and exclusive designation of the Divine Being" (*Guide*, chap. 61, p. 89). But this appeal to tradition is inconsistent with Maimonides' own doctrine. He cannot consistently admit this name and exclude names such as good, wise, just, except in a purely negative or metaphorical sense, or both.

14 Cf. I, chaps. 57–58, pp. 80–83.

is speaking of the divine names, yet he does actually admit both symbolic analogy and analogy of attribution. The latter arises from the fact that according to Maimonides it is permissible to attribute "qualities" like wisdom to God, not as proper predicates, of course, but as attributive analogies based on the truth that God is the *cause* of all things.

However, St. Thomas points out [15] that one who asserts that God is the cause of wisdom must admit also that He is formally and intrinsically wise, because He could not cause a "simple" or pure perfection like wisdom unless He Himself actually possessed it. Therefore "God is not said to be wise because He causes wisdom; but because He *is* wise, He causes wisdom. Hence Augustine says (Book II, *De Doctr. Christ.*, c. XXXII) that because God is good, we *are*; and in so far as we *are*, we are good." St. Thomas observes further that according to the Maimonidean doctrine, it would follow that names such as good, wise, just, would apply by priority to creatures rather than to the Creator. And this, in turn, has a very damaging consequence, for it would then follow that any and every effect caused by God could be predicated of Him. For example, we could say that God is the physical universe inasmuch as it is He who causes it, or, for the same reason, that He is matter, or humanity, and so on.

In this whole problem, the principle which should be kept firmly in mind is that the effect is contained virtually in its efficient and effective cause. This simply means that the cause has within it the *virtus* or power of producing a certain effect. This principle is self-evident; it is merely

[15] *De pot.* VII, 6, c. ("Et ideo dicunt quidam . . .")

an explanation of what an efficient cause is, namely, a cause which is able, which has the power, to effect something. The effect is therefore said to "pre-exist virtually" in its effective cause. Since God is the first efficient cause of all things, it follows that the perfections of all things must pre-exist in Him, in virtue of that very causal power by which He produces them, "effects" them, causes them to be. But in the finite or created order certain "simple perfections" are found, perfections which do not of themselves imply materiality or any sort of limitation. Such, for instance, are being, goodness, unity, truth, wisdom, justice. Perfections of this kind do not exist in God only virtually; they exist in Him formally and must therefore be attributed to Him formally.[16]

The error of symbolist theologians like Maimonides lies in their conviction that to attribute simple or pure or essential perfections to God is to destroy His very essence, to introduce division, plurality, and consequently imperfection into a Being who is absolutely one and undivided and perfect. There is no difficulty in attributing those perfections to men; for all men *are* and each man is one, and there are some "good men and true" and some even wise and just; at least we know what these qualities are when we attribute them to men; we are quite certain that we have good clear univocal ideas of them. But if we try to apply them to God, we are lost; we do not know what they mean in Him and we can never know; indeed, all such perfections are created and they cannot exist in Him because He is One and they are many. So we must be content to speak

16 Cf. St. Thomas, *S. th.*, I, 4, 2, c.; *C.G.*, I, 28.

symbolically, saying that God is "wise" only in the sense that He is the cause, the ultimate cause, of whatever wisdom there is in His creatures.

It is true that if the names of God be understood univocally (as Maimonides does understand them), then they cannot be said of Him in any proper sense at all. The peculiar force of the famous negative theology of Maimonides consists in his logical, clear, and absolutely uncompromising insistence upon this point. To say that God is wise or good or just is to posit in Him univocal perfections, and that is utterly impossible. And as St. Thomas states time and again, nothing is said univocally of God and of creatures. Maimonides well knew that created perfections represent only a very pale reflection of the divine essence, that His effects can in no way represent Him adequately. But what Maimonides failed to see is that God is not a univocal but an analogical cause, some of whose effects can be attributed to him truly, since, in a supereminent mode, He *is* that which they are.[17]

3. "Modus Significandi" and "Res Significata"

Maimonides fails to distinguish between "pure" perfections (such as being, unity, justice, wisdom, goodness, life) and "mixed" perfections, implying limitation. Conceiving all perfections univocally, he cannot see how they can exist according to essentially diverse modes while at the same time remaining proportionately the same. All

[17] Cf. St. Thomas, *S. th.*, I, 12, 12; *C.G.*, I, 31; *De Trin.*, I, 2; *De pot.*, VII, 1, ad 3; I *Sent.*, II, 1, 2.

our names, he holds, are "imposed" from creatures; they are derived from finite things within the sphere of our own experience. That is true; but from this fact he infers that they all apply properly only to creatures; that is not true. For he is not aware of the capital distinction between *mode of signifying* and *thing signified*. Consequently he holds that if any divine attribute has any content other than a purely negative one, it is only because the "attribute" stands in some kind of causal relationship with God. Thus it is quite proper to say that God is the cause of wisdom, justice, goodness, life, etc., but it is not proper to say that He is, actually and formally, wise, just, good, living, etc.

According to Maimonides, moreover, if the so-called attribute is said to be identical with the very essence of the subject of which it is predicated, then predication in that case is purely tautological.[18] But, as regards the divine names, this is not at all the case; for from the fact that the attributes of God are identical with His essence and that we affirm them to be so, it does not follow that *for us* these concepts all have the same meaning.

Synonymity entails a merely verbal distinction, a mere difference in the words used, their meaning being absolutely identical.[19] But the names of God are not synonymous. We do not designate *justice* in God when we say that He is *good;* we affirm that what we call goodness in the creature pre-exists in God in a supereminent mode.[20]

---

[18] *Guide,* I, chap. 51, pp. 68 f.
[19] Cf. Cajetan, *In "De ente et essentia,"* chap. VI, q. 13 *ad quintum* (Turin: Marietti, 1934), p. 183.
[20] Cf. St. Thomas, *S. th.,* I, 13, 2; *C.G.,* I, 35.

We mean that God is really and truly good, but good in a way that transcends infinitely all created goodness yet is at the same time really and truly (though only proportionately) related to and unified with that goodness.

To attribute pure perfections to God, therefore, is not to lapse into anthropomorphism. The anthropomorphism resides only in the *modus significandi*. As regards the objects, the realities, which they are intended to signify and which they actually do signify, some terms do not imply any sort of imperfection or defect. This is evident in the case of such terms as being, one, good, true, wise, just, etc. But as regards the actual manner in which they signify their objects, their *modus significandi,* every term is defective or deficient. The terms we use signify or express things in that very mode in which we conceive them. But our intellect is rooted in the knowledge of things existing in the world of sense. All our knowledge, however abstract, originates in and develops from things sensed.

This is no antiquated, "dogmatic" theory; it is but a factual statement of the evident condition of the human mind. Our intellect is not a pure intelligence; it is an intelligence organically united to a material body and one which, therefore, cannot (in this life, at least) dispense with the services of that body; an intelligence, that is to say, which cannot function without the bodily senses, even though its higher activities are radically distinct from those of the senses. This proposition is backed up by an immense amount of evidence. Apart from philosophical and scientific considerations respecting the constitution and nature of man and of his faculties, human language itself provides evidence enough. All words in all languages are *ultimately* based on and derived from *some* contact of the human mind with sensible things, however far removed from that source many words apparently are.

If, then, our intellect, taking rise in the knowledge of sensible things, does not transcend that imperfect mode of signifying corresponding to the imperfect (composite) mode of being proper to those things, it follows that every name said of God entails some kind or measure of imperfection as to the actual mode of its signification.[21] But it does not follow that no word applies properly to God. As St. Thomas puts it: "In every word we use, as to the mode of signifying, there is found imperfection which does not appertain to God; but the reality signified belongs to Him in a certain eminent mode, as is evident in the terms goodness and good. . . . Hence names of this sort can be both affirmed and denied: affirmed by reason of that which the names signify formally, denied by reason of their [imperfect] mode of signifying."[22]

The cause of the diversity and multiplicity of the divine names is to be sought in our own intellect, which cannot in this life attain to the vision of the divine essence as such, cannot know God "quidditatively," but can "see" Him

21 Although names which apply properly only to finite, created things, their qualities, properties or operations, can be attributed to God only metaphorically, there are some names which import no sort of limitation or defect, and these can be said of God properly and formally. Yet even they do not signify the divine essence according to its subsistent and absolutely simple mode of being. For example, "goodness" is an "abstract" term which, therefore, signifies in an abstract or non-subsistent mode, whereas "good" is a "concrete" term which signifies in a concrete and hence composite or non-simple mode. This radical imperfection in "mode of signifying" is found in every metaphysical or transcendental term we use.

22 *C.G.*, I, 30.

only very imperfectly through deficient similitudes "reflected in creatures as in a mirror." "Thus, if our intellect saw the Essence itself," St. Thomas says, "it would not require many names nor many conceptions. And for this reason, the Word of God, which is the perfect Conception of Him, is only One." [23]

The answer to Maimonides' problem is therefore plain. Names such as good, wise, living, just, said of God, are not synonymous; judgments about God in which such terms occur are not tautological. For while all the divine names signify the same reality, namely, God Himself, they signify Him according to diverse *reasons* or under diverse "aspects"; they signify Him in those different modes in which He presents Himself to the human intelligence.

Thus it is simply a question of applying the distinction between the thing signified and the mode of signifying it. In "divine predication" the former is always the same, the latter always different: all the names of God signify God, but they all signify Him in different ways. God is one, but we see Him under different aspects and we therefore use different names.

4. Conclusion

All our ideas of created perfections signify imperfect likenesses of the divine essence. Between creatures and God there is no common measure, no community of essence. But where there is no such community, univocal predication is impossible. It follows that there can be no univocal correspondence between our conceptions of God

[23] *De pot.*, VII, 6, c (*ad finem*). Cf. *C.G.*, I, 31, *in fine;* I *Sent.*, II, 1, 3.

and that which He actually is. But it has been shown that God is susceptible of a plurality of attributions to which something in Him really corresponds. What, then, is the nature of this agreement?

It is not merely equivocal. Names such as good, wise, just, signify something which is really in God and which He Himself really is. For this reason the divine names are not, as Maimonides held, merely symbolic or attributive. It remains that the agreement in question is analogical.

St. Thomas has shown [24] that names of simple or pure or immaterial perfections are predicated of God substantially (yet imperfectly), since they signify the divine substance itself. Such names are said of God absolutely and affirmatively, properly and formally; in other words, by analogy of proper proportionality; for the perfections found in creatures exist properly in God, yet according to a mode of being essentially diverse from any created mode. Analogy of attribution is also at least virtually in effect, because the names which signify the simple perfections are predicated of creatures through dependence upon God as Cause. Hence this relation of dependence provides a basis for attributive "analogies." However, since the perfections predicated of creatures and of God exist formally and intrinsically in both, though in absolutely diverse modes, analogy of proper proportionality has the fundamental role.

Maimonides does not admit this latter analogy. Indeed, he seems entirely unaware of its presence or even of its possibility. He is willing to allow analogy of metaphor—of

24 Cf. De pot., VII, 5; S. th., I, 13, 2.

improper proportionality—and say, for instance, that the proposition "God is wise" means only that God acts like a wise person or that the effects of His actions are like those of a wise person. But this concession is actually valueless. For in that case, as St. Thomas points out,[25] "there would be no [essential] difference in saying that God is wise and that He is angry, or that God is fire; for [according to this theory] He is called angry because He acts in the manner of an angry man when He punishes. . . . And He is called fire because He operates in the manner of fire when He purges, which in its own way fire also does." In fact any of God's effects could be attributed to Him, and none would have any proper meaning. A metaphorism of this sort thus lends itself readily to a *reductio ad absurdum*.

Nevertheless the doctrine of Maimonides is characterized primarily by the emphasis placed on the "way of negation." He insists that in the final analysis only the "negative attributes" are the true ones. Thus, when we say that God "lives" we do not mean that there is actually any *life* in Him but only that He is not non-living, that He does not exist in the manner of inanimate things. Likewise, if we say that God is intelligent, we do not mean that He really *is* intelligent; we intend thereby only to remove from Him that mode of being which is proper to irrational creatures. Even if we say that God is "one," we do not mean that He is one in the proper sense, that is, in the sense that created individuals are one; for their oneness is essentially composite, divided, non-simple. To say that "God is one" is to say that He is not many, in no way many;

[25] *De pot.*, VII, 5, c.

that there is no other God but God and in Him there is no manyness.[26] But this position is no less untenable than the first.

Predications of God cannot be made simply and solely in order to remove from Him all defects; they cannot be *purely* negative. If the only reason for saying that God is "living" is because He does not exist in the manner of inanimate things, then why could one not say, with equal propriety that God is a lion because He does not exist in the manner of a sheep? [27] Absolute negations are as unintelligible and incongruous as univocal affirmations.

Negation presupposes affirmation. Every negation is based on some affirmation, else the negation itself would be meaningless. Negative and positive terms are distinct but correlative: it is impossible to know what the negative means without prior knowledge of the positive. (Consider these words "negative" and "positive," for example.) Unless the human intellect could know something "affirmatively" of God, it could not deny anything of Him. But if nothing we say about God truly and positively signifies that which He is, then we would have absolutely no positive or affirmative knowledge of Him. Consequently there would be no grounds for any negative attribution, for saying that He is *not* this, that, or the other. Therefore it necessarily follows that some names (of simple perfections such as good, wise, just) do positively, even though deficiently and imperfectly, signify that which God is.[28]

But, for Maimonides (as in our day for the brilliant

[26] Cf. *Guide*, chap. 58, pp. 82 f.
[27] Cf. St. Thomas, *De pot.*, VII, 5 (*Si ergo* . . .).
[28] *Ibid.*

Dominican philosopher, Father A. D. Sertillanges [29]), God remains ineffable and unknowable. "Praised be He!" Maimonides exclaims,[30] "In the contemplation of His essence, our comprehension and knowledge prove insufficient; in the examination of His works, how they necessarily result from His will, our knowledge proves to be ignorance, and in the endeavor to extol Him in words, all our efforts are mere weakness and failure." But Maimonides himself insists that propositions to the effect that God is wise because He causes wisdom (attribution),

[29] In his *Agnosticisme ou Anthropomorphisme*, Father Sertillanges states (p. 60; cf. p. 59) that his position is essentially the same as that of Maimonides and of Avicenna. Not even "being" is said properly of God, Sertillanges holds (p. 26). He rightly points out that all the words we use reflect the composition of essence and existence, but he wrongly infers that any term which could be predicated of God would necessarily be improper (cf. p. 22). Thus God is absolutely unnameable, ineffable (p. 26; cf. p. 31). Thus, to say that God is good is to say that He is not non-good (p. 58), which is precisely what Maimonides said.

In short, all the names of God have only a negative and relative value (p. 32). This was also Maimonides' conclusion. But the doctrine behind it is not the great Rabbi's theory of the real distinction between "attribute" and essence; it is the theory that our knowledge is limited to the "categories". Father Sertillanges therefore argues that, since God is outside the categories, it follows that He is "indefinable, inexpressible, unthinkable, and unknowable" (pp. 40 f.).

Father Sertillanges holds that for St. Thomas God is not, even in Himself, properly an "intelligible"; but only the *Principle* of the intelligibles, and that, if we can know Him and speak of Him in a certain manner, *balbutiendo ut possumus*, it is not because He is Himself intelligible, but because His effects are; so after every effort has been made to know Him, we must finally say: *Deo non conjungimur nisi quasi ignoto* (St. Thomas, *De Trin.*, I, 2, ad 4). Properly speaking, in fact, we have of God neither notion, definition, nor concept (pp. 42, 44).

Unquestionably there is a powerful "negative theology" in St. Thomas. Father Sertillanges excellently expounds the doctrine that we have no positive knowledge whatever of the "divine mode of Being itself." But, having insufficiently applied St. Thomas' distinction between mode of signifying and thing signified, he has failed to note that the "agnosticism" of St. Thomas is radically distinct from the extreme agnosticism of Maimonides. (Cf. Penido, *Le rôle*, pp. 170–75.)

[30] *Guide*, I, chap. 58, p. 83; cf. chap. 60, pp. 87–89.

acts like a wise person (metaphor), or is not non-wise (remotion), give us no positive knowledge whatever of the formal perfections of God. We remain, under such conditions, "in the limbo of symbolism." [31]

Now symbolism goes hand-in-hand with agnosticism, and its principal source is a latent anthropomorphism or univocity. In Maimonides (as in many modern thinkers) we find an anthropomorphic confusion between mode of signifying and thing signified. Since our ideas about God are multiple, the symbolist rushes to the conclusion that to attribute anything to God is to impose upon Him the weakness and imperfection of our own intelligence.[32] Consequently, in order to preserve at all costs the divine transcendence, the symbolist will simply negate every-thing. In so doing he will be more nearly right than the professed anthropomorphist who, being equally ignorant of the principle of analogy, would destroy the divine transcendence by positing univocal perfections in God, thus reducing theology to the status of a purely human, purely anthropomorphic, science.[33]

The attempt to apply univocal concepts to realities out-side the created order will always result in absurdities and contradictions. Hence the symbolist philosopher or theo-logian will inevitably find "antinomies" at the end of his speculations. Man's "metaphysical instinct" and especially

[31] Penido, *Le rôle,* p. 131.

[32] Cf., *op. cit.,* p. 163.

[33] Far from deploring such a reduction, certain "modernist" theologians ap-parently welcome it: "Instead of attempting to evade the reproach of anthro-pomorphism by conceding to the agnostic the inscrutability of the Divine Na-ture, the modern apologist is not afraid to avow the anthropomorphic character of theology, while he insists that in this respect theology is in the same position as every other department of thought" (G. C. Joyce, *Analogy,* p. 419, no. 8).

his natural desire to know God will thus finally be frustrated. His entire philosophical effort will issue in a sweeping agnosticism, in an agnosticism which consists not in the admission that he cannot know ultimate reality in itself, according to its own unique mode of existence (such an agnosticism being a true and necessary one), but in the absolute denial that he can have any positive knowledge whatever of that reality. This is the last word of symbolism; it is the last word because symbolism moves in the order of univocal concepts, concepts which are merely given an "analogical" reference by the mind; and through univocal concepts one can never acquire any proper and formal knowledge of reality as such, because reality is as such analogical. Follow the *via symbolica* as far as you like; follow it as far as it goes; it will never lead beyond agnosticism, either in metaphysics or in theology.

Part Four

ANALOGY OF PROPER
PROPORTIONALITY

CHAPTER XVII

ST. THOMAS AND PROPER
PROPORTIONALITY

1. STATUS OF THE QUESTION

HAVING considered those types of analogy which are of
their very nature improperly analogical in the sense that
they are formally univocal, we arrive finally at that type
which alone, it is claimed, is analogical in the strictly philosophical and proper sense. Essentially the object of this
whole Part is to examine that claim.

Analogy of attribution and of metaphor, we found, are
operative only in the order of univocal concepts. Formally,
therefore, they are both reduced to modes of univocity, yet
they are rightly considered to be modes of analogy inasmuch as they have certain analogical or quasi-analogical
uses; moreover, they do, in divers ways, participate in
analogy. Metaphor, indeed, was seen to be more deeply,
or more nearly, analogical than analogy of attribution as
such. For, while attribution is in the order of extrinsic
relation, metaphor is in the order of operation; and operation is certainly "closer" to being than relation.[1] Nevertheless metaphor is an improper mode of analogy precisely
because it has to do with a concept that is univocal in itself,
since it is realized formally and properly in only one of the

[1] Proportionality is in the "order of relation," too, though not of extrinsic
relation; it is in the order of intrinsic relation to and within being, *esse*.

terms of the proportionality. In analogy of proper proportionality, on the other hand, the common concept is intrinsically analogical because it is realized formally and properly in each and every one of the terms of the proportionality. However, the object of this chapter is not to explore the philosophical significance claimed for this analogy but to expound St. Thomas' doctrine of the nature of it.

2. THE ANALOGY OF THE GOOD

In all the works of St. Thomas one of the most important texts on analogy is found in his Commentary on the First Book of Aristotle's *Nichomachean Ethics*. In this text [2] St. Thomas points out that, according to Aristotle, *good* is predicated of many things, not in a purely equivocal sense but in an analogical sense. But since analogy means *proportion,* to be predicated "analogically" is to be predicated according to proportion. This may happen in two ways, as we see in the case of the term *good:* (1) All things may be said to be good in virtue of their dependence upon the one first principle of goodness from which they are all derived, or so far as they are ordered to that principle as their ultimate end; (2) all things may be said to be *good* proportionately, not in virtue of this relation

---

[2] I *Eth.*, VII, 96: "Sic ergo dicit [Aristotle], quod bonus dicitur de multis, non secundum rationes penitus differentes, sicut accidit in his quae sunt a casu aequivoca, sed magis secundum analogiam, idest proportionem eamdem, inquantum omnia bona dependent ab uno primo bonitatis principio, vel inquantum ordinantur ad unum finem. . . . Vel etiam dicuntur omnia bona magis secundum analogiam, idest proportionem eamdem, sicut visus est bonum corporis, et intellectus est bonum animae. Ideo hunc tertium modum praefert, quia accipitur secundum bonitatem inhaerentem rebus. Primi autem duo modi secundum bonitatem separatam, a qua non ita proprie aliquid denominatur."

of dependence upon their first principle, but in virtue of the goodness actually inherent in them. For instance, just as sight is a "good" of the body, so intelligence is a "good" of the soul. [Sight : body : : intelligence : soul (good)]. "This mode," St. Thomas says, "is the one which Aristotle prefers, because it is based on the goodness inherent in things," whereas the other is based on goodness considered as a principle *separate* from things.

Although St. Thomas does not use the words "analogy of attribution" and "analogy of proper proportionality," actually we have here a formal comparison of these two modes of analogy, attribution being the first, and proper proportionality the second. They are distinguished formally in two ways: (1) analogy of attribution is based on a relation of dependence of several things with respect to a single term (principle, end, subject), which then has the role of extrinsic prime analogate; whereas in analogy of proper proportionality, as such, there are not diverse relations to a single term, but relations to diverse subjects; [3] (2) analogy of attribution, as such, entails an extrinsic denomination from one term, e.g., "the one first principle of goodness," *considered as* separate from things; whereas analogy of proper proportionality involves an intrinsic participation, the proportional sharing of diverse things in a common perfection; so that vision, for instance, is a good which is proportionately common to the bodily eye and to the intelligence. [4] Thus, without in any way forcing the text, we clearly see that for St. Thomas it is these two

---

[3] Cf. *ibid.*, 95; V *Meta.*, VIII, 879.
[4] Cf. *De ver.*, II, 11, c.

characteristics which essentially and formally distinguish the types of analogy in question.

Nevertheless the analogy of the good does in fact participate in both analogies. From the angle of analogy of attribution we have at once a relation of dependence of all *goods* upon a single principle (considered as separate from them) and an extrinsic denomination from that principle. From the angle of analogy of proper proportionality we have an intrinsic participation—no relation of dependence and consequently no extrinsic prime analogate, but only similar relations or proportions. Thus the relation of corporeal vision to the eye is similar to the *relation* of intellectual vision to the intelligence, and the goodness of the one is proportionately similar to the goodness of the other.

3. On Misunderstanding Analogy in St. Thomas

We have already indicated (chap. 10) the importance, for the understanding of analogy, of the distinction between the order of specification, according to which analogy is considered formally (*in actu signato*), and the order of exercise, according to which analogy is considered materially (*in actu exercito*), as actually existing in the nature of things, as *exercised*. Moreover it has been shown (chaps. 9, 10) that certain interpreters of St. Thomas have misunderstood him because they have failed to apply Cajetan's "formal method" to the problem of analogy, and as a result have confused the order of specification and the order of exercise.

In the works of St. Thomas there are many concrete

applications of the principle of analogy. We often find "analogates" which all share intrinsically in a perfection that is proportionately common to them, while at the same time they are all ordered to a principal term on which they depend. Observing such cases (far more numerous than St. Thomas' doctrinal statements on the formal character of analogy), Suarezians, having reduced analogy of proper proportionality to metaphor, have proceeded to set up in its stead an analogy of "intrinsic attribution," while Sylvester of Ferrara and his school have maintained that analogy of proper proportionality always requires an extrinsic prime analogate. Failing to consider analogy formally, these expositors have all in one way or another misused or confused or neglected the great distinction aforementioned, and they have thereby fallen away from St. Thomas himself, who set great store by it. But not only is that distinction proper to the Thomism of St. Thomas, it is proper to philosophy itself; all sound speculative analysis requires it, whether it be explicitly used or not. It is especially necessary in the exegesis of philosophical texts.

The pitfalls here are many and great. But in the case of any group of speculative texts on a single definite problem, it is both a good and a necessary rule to look for that formal principle which orders those texts and makes them mutually intelligible. Of course contradictions may be found, but in first-rate thinkers real contradictions are extremely rare, and no thinker should be charged with contradiction until a very thorough *formal* analysis of his doctrine has been made. By juxtaposing verbally incompatible statements, removed from their context, it should not be very difficult to draw up a list of selected "contradictions" from the works of almost any philosopher.

There is no need here to apply the formal analytical method, in any exhaustive or minutely searching way, to the exegesis of the texts of St. Thomas on analogy. That difficult and subtle task, I am happy to record, has already been done in masterly fashion by such eminent Thomists as John of St. Thomas, Ramirez, Le Rohellec, and Penido.[5] However, we believe that the reader ought to find it useful if at this point we at least indicate the first steps in such an analysis.

Thus in the *Summa theologica* (I, 6, 4), it is asked "whether all things are good by the Divine Goodness?" and St. Thomas concludes his reply with the statement that "everything is called good from the Divine Goodness, as from the first exemplary, effective, and final principle of all goodness." (The "attributive" element.) "Nevertheless," he goes on, "everything is called good by reason of the likeness of the Divine Goodness inherent in it, which is formally its own goodness, denominating itself." (Analogy of proper proportionality.) "And so of all things there is one Goodness, and yet many goodnesses." As in the previously cited text from the Commentary on the *Ethics*, it is evident here that in the analogy of the good there is a certain "participation" of analogy of attribution. Then in the doctrine of St. Thomas, which is the more fundamental, analogy of attribution or analogy of proper proportionality?

[5] See bibliography.

4. The Problem of the So-called Twofold Analogy in St. Thomas

In analogy of attribution (as well as in metaphorical analogy) the analogated character or form exists intrinsically in only one of the analogates and is merely attributed or is transferred to the others. But in the case of transcendental objects, such as goodness, truth, unity, being, the "intrinsic denominating form" exists in all the analogates; for every thing in some way *is*, is one, and, in a certain respect, is true and good. In analogies bearing on terms of this sort, there is no question of any extrinsic denomination, because the analogates will all be denominated by that very analogous perfection or form which they themselves actually are or possess. No extrinsic attribution would be required, or even possible.

But if, in these circumstances, extrinsic attribution is eliminated, then analogy of attribution as such is eliminated; that is, it would not be actually and formally present. If the analogated character is absolutely diverse in respect of all the analogates, then, of course, you have pure equivocity; if it is absolutely the same, you have univocity; but if it is one in a proportional way and exists intrinsically in all the analogates, then you have analogy of proper proportionality. But, formally speaking, you do not have analogy of attribution, because that analogy requires denomination through a form which is present intrinsically in only one analogate.[6]

In this whole problem the test case, the one which has

[6] Cf. John of St. Thomas, *Logica*, II, q. 13, a. 4 (ed. Reiser, pp. 486–91).

caused the real difficulties and misunderstandings, is that of the analogy of creatures to God. Of course the analogy of the good, which has already been discussed, is simply one formulation of this problem; but some additional observations may prove helpful.

The intrinsic necessity and real presence of this analogy are brought to light by an impossible assumption. Thus even if "creatures" did not owe their existence to God, no univocal term could be predicated of them and of God because of the diverse acts of being of these two orders of being. There would still be no basis for univocation. For, as St. Thomas repeatedly says, diversity in act of being makes impossible any univocal predication of being. (This applies equally to the term "good," since being and good are convertible.) Indeed, "God is related to *esse* in a way other than any creature, because, unlike any creature, He *is* His own *Esse*"; consequently "nothing is predicated univocally of the creature and God." [7] Therefore, if you eliminate attribution, if you exclude all extrinsic denomination, metaphorical as well as attributive, there is still place for analogy. Analogy is necessarily present, univocity having been ruled out by the very fact of the diverse mode of exercising the act of being in God and in creatures.

In his Commentary on the First Book of the *Sentences*, St. Thomas points out [8] that in analogy *according to being and intention* (analogy of proper proportionality), the common analogous character must exist intrinsically in each of the analogates, just as being exists intrinsically in

[7] *De pot.*, VII, 7, c.
[8] I *Sent.*, XIX, 5, 2, ad 1.

substances and accidents. Truth, goodness, and all things of this sort, he says (that is, all simple perfections), are predicated of God and of creatures by this kind of analogy. And in his Commentary on the Third Book of the *Metaphysics* he shows [9] that being and unity are not genera and therefore are in no case predicable univocally. The same is true of all metaphysical objects as such.

In the metaphysical order, formally speaking, there is neither analogy of attribution nor metaphor,[10] because there is here no unity or likeness of *things* or of natures, but only of *proportions*. For analogy of attribution and metaphorical analogy as such are found only in the categorial order, the order of univocal concepts. And univocity is not avoided simply because it is possible to establish a comparison of proportions between things of the same category, genus, or class. Where there is only a unity of proportions, however, and no basic univocal likeness, there can be no univocity; there can be only analogy—proper analogy, analogy of proper proportionality. In this order, through a unity of proportions or relations alone, analogy rightly so called is found. The analogous term "principle," predicated of the heart and of the foundation of a house, affords a simple example; both are principles, really and truly and not metaphorically, yet one is a principle of life, the other a principle of art.[11]

We have seen that there is an "element" of analogy of

[9] III *Meta.,* VIII, 432 f.

[10] This means that a metaphysician, as a metaphysician, never uses a term in an analogy of attribution, properly and formally so called; for, in its "pure state," that analogy is in the order of logic, not of metaphysics. (Cf. above, chap. 10, esp. sect. 5.)

[11] Cf. John of St. Thomas, *op. cit.,* p. 489.

attribution in the analogy of the good. But absolutely speaking, good is nothing other than being itself *qua* appetible or desirable.[12] Hence this attributive character will be found also in the analogy of being. Yet how is this possible if analogy of proper proportionality is alone properly analogical? The point is that analogy of attribution is not present formally but only virtually.[13] Although proper proportionality is the only metaphysical analogy, logically speaking, there is a basis in the structure of being for analogy of attribution, since there is a multiplicity of analogates (creatures) all dependent upon a Prime Analogate (God). The presence of being in *all* these "terms" makes an actual analogy of attribution impossible; but there could be such an analogy in the formal sense if the Prime Analogate alone possessed being intrinsically. Thus, from the standpoint of logic, it is said that being contains a *virtual* analogy of attribution.

However, St. Thomas sometimes speaks as if he considered analogy of attribution a proper mode of analogy. In a text in the *Summa theologica*,[14] for example, he seems to recognize an analogy of attribution in respect of created and uncreated truth, while in the Disputed Question *On Truth* [15] he explicitly rejects as improper every mode of

12 Cf. *De ver.*, I, 1, c.

13 Cf. John of St. Thomas, *op. cit.*, p. 490, with q. 14, a. 3, pp. 512–14.

14 I, 16, 6, c.: "Licet plures sint essentiae vel formae rerum, tamen una est veritas divini intellectus, secundum quam omnes res denominantur verae."

15 II, 11, c.: "Quia ergo in his quae primo modo [convenientia *proportionis*] analogice dicuntur, oportet esse aliquam determinatam habitudinem inter ea quibus est aliquid per analogiam commune, impossibile est aliquid per hunc modum analogiae dici de Deo et creatura; quia nulla creatura habet talem habitudinem ad Deum per quam possit divina perfectio determinari. Sed in alio modo analogiae [convenientia *proportionalitatis*] nulla determinata habitudo attenditur inter ea quibus est aliquid per analogiam commune; et ideo

analogy except proper proportionality. There is no contradiction here, because, in the first case, analogy of proper proportionality is not excluded; it is implied. St. Thomas was well aware of the fact that being is intrinsically analogical and that analogy of proper proportionality is the only metaphysical analogy. Things are utterly diverse from one another as regards their acts of being, yet, through their proportional sharing in those acts, they are all brought together in a unity of similar relations. This, according to St. Thomas, is the analogy of being; it is the way things actually are. For St. Thomas, then, unless there were this inner analogical structure in the very being of things, analogy of attribution (or for that matter, any sort of attribution or predication) would be impossible. Attribution can be made only through or on the basis of proportionality. Logically it is conceivable that, if intrinsic participation in being were lacking, there would still be a basis for analogy of attribution; but this is an actual impossibility.

Analogy of attribution, the logical analogy par excel-

---

secundum illum modum nihil prohibet aliquod nomen analogice dici de Deo et creatura. Sed tamen hoc dupliciter contingit: quandoque enim illud nomen importat aliquid ex principali significatione, in quo non potest attendi convenientia inter Deum et creaturam, etiam modo praedicto; sicut est in omnibus quae *symbolice* de Deo dicuntur . . . quae Deo attribui non potest: quandoque vero nomen quod de Deo et creatura dicitur, nihil importat ex principali significato secundum quod non possit attendi praedictus convenientiae modus [proper proportionality] inter creaturam et Deum; sicut omnia in quorum definitione non clauditur defectus, nec dependent a materia secundum esse, ut ens, bonum, et alia hujusmodi."

Although St. Thomas does not use the expressions *improper* and *proper* proportionality, it is perfectly clear that he has here excluded not only analogy of proportion or attribution but also symbolic analogy or analogy of improper proportionality as legitimate modes of "divine predication," recognizing proper proportionality alone as valid. Moreover, in this text (and in many others) it is clearly implied that, for St. Thomas, proper proportionality alone has a metaphysical basis.

lence, has many uses, and St. Thomas often avails himself of its services; but in his formal analyses of the principle of analogy (as in the text referred to from the Disputed Question *On Truth*), he invariably points out, in one way or another, that there is only one analogy which is properly analogical in the sense that it is rooted in "ipsum *esse* commune omnibus."

There remains a problem of considerable importance; it is the question, frequently debated by modern Thomists, whether analogy of proper proportionality has, like analogy of attribution, a prime analogate. This is no "scholastic riddle," but a real problem vitally significant for the whole theory of philosophical analogy.

CHAPTER XVIII

THE PRINCEPS ANALOGATUM

1. Statement and Analysis of the Problem

Some able thinkers hold that analogy of proper proportionality necessarily and formally requires a prime analogate or principal term.[1] Others, although accepting this doctrine, argue ably that it should not be interpreted in such a way as to reduce analogy to an underlying univocity.[2] Without entering into the details of this debate, let us grant that being is *never univocal,* that, considered in relation with beings, it is *analogical,* and apart from that relation, *unique.*[3] But does it follow that every metaphysical analogy necessarily posits a principal analogate, not accidentally, but formally?[4] It does not;[5] because in analogy of proper proportionality the common analogous "character" is not, formally considered, numerically one, but proportionately one, all the analogates sharing proportionately in that "character." So that, understood

---

[1] Cf. F. A. Blanche, "La notion de l'analogie" . . . , pp. 169–93. Cf. "L'Analogie," pp. 248–70. Father Blanche follows Sylvester of Ferrara on this point.

[2] Cf. N. Balthasar, *L'abstraction métaphysique* . . . , pp. 51 ff., who sees this consequence in the treatment of the Prime Analogate given by Blanche and Sylvester.

[3] *Ibid.,* p. 61; cf. pp. 66 f.

[4] As Father Balthasar maintains, *ibid.,* p. 51. See pp. 49–59.

[5] Cf. J. Ramirez, "De analogia" . . . , Part III, *La Ciencia Tomista,* XXV (1922), 27–36.

formally and properly, there is not, as in analogy of attribution, a prime analogate which is placed in the definition of the other analogates. That there be such an analogate, is not a general property of all true analogy,[6] but on the contrary, this is a special property of analogy of attribution alone.

It is true that analogy of proper proportionality always involves priority and posteriority. Because this analogy imports an essential inequality in the realization of the common analogous character, it implies an order and consequently a *principle* of that order. Yet it does not, as in attribution, imply or require a principle that is numerically one, but a principle that is one in proportion, proportionately one alone.

The concept of *first principle* is itself analogical, and there is a vast difference between a principle that is numerically one and a principle proportionately one. A principle numerically one is not included in its inferiors: it does not actually enter into the being of the things which, in different ways, depend upon or follow from it. But those things are, at least virtually, included in that principle. A principle proportionately one, on the other hand, both essentially includes its inferiors, and its inferiors essentially include it: it enters into their very being, and they in turn are intrinsically related to it. Such a principle, therefore, does not define or explicate its inferiors, nor do they define or explicate it. Goodness, for example, is a principle that is proportionately common to all good

---

[6] As Sylvester of Ferrara, Balthasar and Blanche hold, in opposition to Cajetan (*De nom.* II, 61–65).

things; it enters into their very being and they are intrinsically "related" to it. But goodness does not signify any particular sort of goodness; it does not specify any given type or class of good things and hence does not itself enter into their definition. If it did, it would have to be a univocal idea, a genus or species.

The point is that analogy of proper proportionality itself does not require nor does it admit a prime analogate of the sort which must enter into the definition of the others, in the manner of a univocal term. An additional example may help to make this clear. *Accident* is predicated according to proper proportionality of all accidents, corporeal as well as spiritual; yet in this case there is no prime analogate which is placed in the definition of the others, because *accident* itself does not signify by priority any particular species of accident in any particular species of substance. Accidentality is common to all the diverse sorts of accident; it is not univocally common, of course, but analogically or proportionately common. The character designated by the word "accident" is not numerically one in all those different kinds of accidents; it is only proportionately one. For instance, corporeal accident : corporeal substance : : spiritual accident : spiritual substance. Here there is no community of things or of natures, but only of proportions or relations.[7]

In a sense, all analogy depends upon and involves reference to a principal term. That term is being, which is common (proportionately or analogically and not univocally)

[7] Cf. J. LeRohellec, "De fundamento . . . ," *Divus Thomas* (Placentiae), XXIX (1926), 96–98.

to everything that *is,* in any way whatever. For, ultimately all predications, analogical or non-analogical, and all judgments are reduced to being because they are all somehow expressive of being: in one form or another, whether positive or negative, they all "say" or imply *is.*[8]

Nothing can be said analogically without reference to being. This is especially evident in the case of analogy of proper proportionality. It is no less evident, however, that the reference in question is not to an *extrinsic* principal term or prime analogate. Such a term is essential to analogy of attribution. It does not belong to analogy of proper proportionality. Being is an intrinsic principle, present in every conceivable analogate. Analogically speaking, being is the ultimate principal term or prime analogate in every genuine analogy, but, univocally speaking, being is in no case a principal term or prime analogate. Herein lies the main source of confusion in the controversy over the "prime analogate." In analogy of proper proportionality as well as in analogy of attribution, there is always reference, whether explicit or implicit, to *one term.* But in the first case that term is proportionately one and it is intrinsic, whereas in the second case it is both numerically one and extrinsic.

In analogy of attribution the analogated character, the *analogon,*[9] is present in only one analogate which, therefore, has the role of (extrinsic) principal term or prime analogate, and all the other analogates receive their entire being *as analogates* extrinsically from it. The very opposite

[8] Cf. G. M. Manser, "Das Wesen des Thomismus," *Divus Thomas* (Fribourg), VII (1929), 343 f.

[9] Cf. G. M. Manser, *art. cit.,* pp. 343–45.

is true in the case of analogy of proper proportionality, where the *analogon* is formally and intrinsically present in all the analogates. Thus it is obvious that there is no place in this analogy for an extrinsic prime analogate of the kind proper to analogy of attribution. This holds in the case of the celebrated "analogy of attribution" between creatures and God. God is not an extrinsic prime analogate wherein alone the common analogous perfection is formally and intrinsically present. Eliminate the "not" from that sentence and for the phrase, "the common analogous perfection," substitute the word "being." The absurdity of the resultant proposition is patent.

The analogy of creatures to God is often cited as an example of analogy of attribution. Formally speaking, it is not an analogy of attribution; it is an attribution founded on analogy, that is to say, on analogy of proper proportionality, which is the only metaphysical analogy because it is the only analogy that is intrinsically analogical. Analogy of inequality is in fact a pseudo-analogy. But analogy of attribution and of metaphor are said to be "modes of analogy" since, in various ways, they participate in true analogy. In the preceding chapter [10] was discussed the doctrine that metaphysical analogies virtually contain attributive analogies. The analogy of beings to the First Being is of course a metaphysical analogy. Consequently there is formally no analogy of attribution here. But there is a basis for it, since there is an extrinsic principal Term which is numerically one and to which all those beings are referred. However, an essential condition

[10] See also chap. 13, sect. 4.

of attribution is lacking, namely, extrinsic relation to a principal term wherein alone the analogated character is properly realized. All beings are intrinsically related to their ultimate Term, and the common analogous concept, being, is properly "realized" in every member of this all-inclusive Analogy. This is why analogy of attribution is said to be present virtually but not formally. In the analogy of being—the Analogy which embraces all beings—there is not only a basis for analogy of attribution, there is a certain participation of it; for the First Being is that transcendent Prime Analogate upon which all beings depend and to which they are all so intimately related that apart from It they would in no way be. In the analogy of being, God is the ultimate Prime Analogate. But being is analogical in virtue of analogy of proper proportionality alone, and that analogy, it was claimed, does not entail reference to any extrinsic prime analogate. Is this statement of the case not contradictory? In the following section we will try to clarify that problem, and in the final section, formulate a correct solution.

2. Steps toward a Solution

An accident can exist only in a substance. It is the substance that gives to the accident its entire existential reality. Substance, therefore, is prime analogate for the being of all accidents. But both substance and accident are beings intrinsically. Consequently there is a basis here for analogy of attribution; but there is no formal analogy of attribution. This is the case with respect to all transcendental or metaphysical objects when considered from the standpoint of efficient causality. For the effect derives its existential being from its cause; hence the cause is the principal term of this relation. It is an extrinsic term in the sense that it is not contained within the definitive essence of the effect,[11] and it is numerically one. But it is not, as in analogy of attribution, an extrinsic principal term which is foreign to its effects in the sense that it has nothing properly in common with them, even in a proportionate or analogical sense. Nevertheless, since an extrinsic principal term is, as such, a property of analogy of attribution, it follows that, wherever a term of this kind is found, there is a certain participation of this analogy: an element of it, so to speak, is present. It does not follow that analogy of attribution is formally present; it cannot be, since not a single one of its essential conditions is properly fulfilled.

It is sometimes said that metaphysical terms are predicated by a "double analogy": analogy of attribution and analogy of proper proportionality. This is not strictly accurate. Such terms are predicated by and on the basis of analogy of proper proportionality alone; yet, in virtue of that analogy, they may also be said attributively. For instance, being is predicated of the creature and of God by analogy of proper proportionality, since both, proportionately to their natures, are beings. This may be expressed in the form: creature : its (finite, participated) being : : God : His (infinite, unparticipated) being. But being is also *attributed* to the creature in virtue of its relation to God, who then has the role of extrinsic Prime Analogate. Likewise, unity is predicated of the material individual

11 Cf. St. Thomas, *S. th.*, I, 44, 1, ad 1; *C.G.*, II, 52.

and of the immaterial individual by analogy of proper proportionality, since, in different ways, both are actually (yet proportionately) real units. But unity is also attributed to such units in virtue of their relation to the one first principle of unity. It is obvious, however, that all attributions of that kind are made *through* the analogies of proper proportionality on which they are founded and without which they would be impossible. It is also obvious that those attributions are not *analogies* of attribution; they are simply attributions based on analogy.

Replying to the question "Whether names predicated of God are predicated primarily of creatures?" St. Thomas states: [12] "Names predicated analogically of a number of things must all be predicated by reference to some one thing; and this one thing must be placed in the definition of them all." But elsewhere [13] he says, in effect, that this requirement holds only in the case of that type of "analogical community" which is based on a determinate relation between the members of the analogy, that is, in the case of analogy of proportion or attribution in the strict sense. These positions are not contradictory; for in the first case, St. Thomas is speaking of analogy from the standpoint of the *order of exercise:* he is pointing out a general fact about analogy as we actually find it. In the second case, he is simply explaining one of the formal properties of analogy of attribution; he is looking at this analogy from the stand-

[12] *S. th.*, I, 13, 6, c. "In omnibus nominibus quae de pluribus analogice dicuntur, necesse est quod omnia dicantur per respectum ad unum; et ideo illud unum oportet quod ponatur in definitione omnium." Cf. C.G., I, 34.
[13] *Der ver.*, II, 11, obj. 6 and ad 6.

point of the *order of specification;* he is considering what
it is in itself—its nature, not its being-in-act.

Moreover, St. Thomas asserts [14] that the analogy of the
creature to the Creator is such that the former "does not
have being (*esse*) except according as it descends from the
First Being, nor is it said to be except so far as it imitates
the First Being." On the other hand, we find this apparently incompatible statement: "Although relation to its
cause does not enter the definition of the thing caused,
nevertheless that relation is implied in the very notion of
the thing; for, from the fact that a thing is a participated
being, it follows that it is caused by something else. . . .
But, absolutely speaking, to be caused does not pertain to
the notion of being itself." [15] These texts do not imply any
conflicting points of view. In the first text, St. Thomas is
concerned with actual analogy of the creature to the Creator, which, of course, involves dependence, in the order of
being itself (of *esse*), of all things upon that Principal Term
which causes them to be. Consequently there is here a basis
for attribution, though not for any formal analogy of attribution. In the second text, St. Thomas is pointing out
what is involved in the formal concept of *thing caused.* He
is considering that thing from the standpoint of the order
of specification; he is concerned with its definitive essence.

14 I *Sent.,* Prol., I, 2, ad 2: "Creatura enim non habet esse nisi secundum
quod a primo ente descendit, nec nominatur ens nisi inquantum ens primum
imitatur."
15 *S. th.,* I, 44, 1, ad 1: "Licet habitudo ad causam non intret definitionem
entis, quod est causatum, tamen consequitur ad ea quae sunt de ejus ratione,
quia ex hoc quod aliquid est ens per participationen, sequitur quod sit causatum ab alio. . . . Sed . . . esse causatum non est de ratione entis simpliciter."

The distinction involved is a simple one. St. Thomas is saying that, although we can and do know *what* created things are without referring them to their Creator, we cannot know them *as created beings,* actually existing, without referring them. to their Creator. As he himself puts it: [16] "Although the First Cause, which is God, does not enter the *essence* of created things, nevertheless being itself (*esse*), present in created things, cannot be grasped unless it is understood to be derived from the Divine Being (*Esse*), just as the proper effect of a cause can be known only through its relation to the cause from which it proceeds." Being itself, then, does not enter into the concept or definition of created essence. But essence essentially denotes order to being (*esse*). Hence created essence is being-by-participation, into the very notion of which there enters the relation it has to unparticipated Being. Since it is not its own being, created essence falls in the order of participated being. Therefore essence is itself participated along with being (*esse*): "From the very fact that being is attributed to quiddity, not only being but quiddity itself is said to be created." [17] So it is clear that in the order of natural theology all analogies actually imply reference to that ultimate Prime Analogate which is God—*Ipsum Esse Subsistens.* But it does not follow, as Father Blanche holds,[18] that the definition of the other analogates from a prime

----

[16] *De pot.,* III, 5, ad 1: "Licet causa prima, quae Deus est, non intret essentiam rerum creatarum; tamen esse, quod rebus creatis inest, non potest intelligi nisi ut deductum ab esse divino; sicut nec proprius effectus potest intelligi nisi ut deductus a causa propria."

[17] *De pot.,* III, 5, ad 2: "Ex hoc ipso quod quidditati esse attribuitur, non solum esse, sed ipsa quidditas creari dicitur."

[18] "La notion de l'analogie . . . ," p. 186.

analogate is a general property of analogy as such. This property does not result from the formal character of analogy (whose essential note is proportionality), but from the actual conditions of its exercise.

3. CONCLUSION

Now let us refer back to the problem as stated at the end of section 1. God is the ultimate Prime Analogate in the analogy of being. That is the primitive fact upon which everything hinges. It is the next statement that contains the difficulty: Being is analogical in virtue of analogy of proper proportionality alone, and this analogy does not involve reference to any extrinsic prime analogate. As it stands, that statement is not true. For the phrase "any extrinsic prime analogate" there should be substituted the phrase "an extrinsic prime analogate such as is had in analogy of attribution." With this qualification, the proposition is correct. But if, in the original statement, the phrase "formally considered" is inserted between the word "analogy" and the word "does," the proposition will also be correct without further qualification. Thus we have the two correct formulations: (1) this analogy does not entail reference to any extrinsic prime analogate such as is had in analogy of attribution; (2) this analogy, *formally considered,* does not entail reference to any prime analogate numerically one and extrinsic to the secondary analogates.

It is important to bear in mind the fact that *principal term* may be (and in this chapter has been) used in three different senses: (A) as a term proportionately one, which is intrinsic to all the analogates (e.g., being as common to all beings); (B) as a prime analogate [19] numerically one, extrinsic to all the analogates, and the sole term in which the analogated character is properly realized (e.g., *healthy* said of the living organism and attributed to diet, complexion, climate, etc.); (C) as a prime analogate numerically one, extrinsic to all the secondary analogates, but realizing in a proportionate way the analogous character common to them all (God as First Being, First Cause, First Principle of Unity, Goodness, Truth, etc.).

Type A is that principal term which, *formally* and *actually*, belongs to every analogy of proper proportionality. Type B belongs *formally* and *actually* to analogy of attribution. Type C belongs *actually*, but not *formally*, to every analogy of proper proportionality which, under some aspect, includes the First Being.

Respecting type A, it is sufficient to point out that in every analogy of proper proportionality there is a principal term which is proportionately common to all the members of the analogy. For instance, *living*, said of man and of the amoeba, is such a term, as is *cause*, said of a finite efficient cause and of the infinite efficient Cause. In the first analogy, however, there is no reference to an extrinsic prime analogate, i.e., to the First Principle of Life—prime analogate in sense C. But in the second analogy, while cause is a type A principal term, there is explicit reference to that extrinsic prime analogate which is God, considered as First efficient Cause (type C).

It is important to note that the famous attribution in

[19] "Prime analogate" is commonly used to designate only an *extrinsic* principal term.

respect of creatures and God is a "special" case of attribution, distinct from *analogy* of attribution, which is always as such in the order of predicamental being. Analogy of attribution is a purely logical analogy; proper proportionality alone is metaphysical. And it is only in a logical sense that analogy of attribution is said to be "virtually" contained in the analogy of being. It is analogy of proper proportionality which alone makes possible any human conceptual knowledge of God; although it is possible to know many things about God without explicit recourse to this principle, or even without being aware of its existence. But nothing can be known of God—nothing can be attributed to Him truly—except *through* proportionality.[20]

[20] In order to avoid pure equivocation in natural theology it is necessary to fall back on that relation which links every effect to its cause, the only bond which allows us to ascend from the creature to the Creator. This relation, in the language of St. Thomas, is an "analogy," that is, a proportion. It founds a virtual analogy of attribution.

In any event it is essential to recognize that attribution is not the only, nor the most fundamental, type of analogy in the doctrine of St. Thomas. If he repeatedly points to the fact of the "proportion" of every creature to its Creator, he is no less well aware of the fact that this very proportion would not even be possible if the analogy of be-ing were not already in effect, if analogy of proper proportionality in the order of *esse* (the proportional sharing of all beings in their respective acts of being) were not already actually *there*.

It is analogy which alone makes it possible for us to conclude to the existence of a transcendent God by taking our point of departure from sensible things, and it is analogy which alone makes it possible to explain the fact that the universe derives its existence from a transcendent Principle without being confused with that Principle or adding itself to It. The likeness of the created analogue can be explained only by reference to Him whom the analogue imitates. Cf. *C.G.*, II, 15; and Gilson, *Le Thomisme* (5th ed.; Paris, Vrin, 1944), p. 501.

Nevertheless the very existence of this likeness, and hence of this imitation, entails analogy of proper proportionality in the order of *esse*. This absolutely fundamental character of analogy of proportionality is elucidated in Gilson, *The Spirit of Mediaeval Philosophy*, Eng. tr. by A. H. C. Downes (New York: Scribner's, 1936), pp. 447–49, note 14 to chap. 5, a text which supplements the treatment of analogy given in *Le Thomisme*, 5th ed., esp. pp. 154 ff., and 501.

To sum up: Although, in the analogy of being, there is, logically speaking, a virtual analogy of attribution, actually there is but a single analogy, analogy of proper proportionality. Considered formally, this analogy does not contain an extrinsic prime analogate, but where the analogy includes God, under one aspect or another, it always entails reference to Him as prime analogate. In the comprehensive analogy of being—the analogy of creatures to God—divine causality establishes a relation of dependence of the entire created order upon a Principal Term. A basis for attribution is thereby provided, for all participated beings can now be "reduced" to the one Unparticipated Being. But there is no actual basis for any formal analogy of attribution: there is no place in being, which is intrinsically and properly analogical, for that which of its very nature is extrinsically and improperly analogical.

CHAPTER XIX

THE ANALOGICAL CONCEPT

1. No Common Concept in Attributive and Metaphorical Analogies

IN THESE types of analogy the unity of the analogates is not based on the intrinsic possession of a common form: the analogates have a merely external unity of comparison or connotation, hinging on some kind of relation of one or of several terms to a single term wherein alone the analogated concept is realized formally. Hence, in these analogies, there is no single concept that is in any sense common to all the terms. To express the comparisons, connotations, or relations involved, several concepts are required. This is evident from the fact that such analogies are not essentially analogical at all, being rendered "analogical" only by some sort of transference, whether by extrinsic denomination or attribution, or by symbolic reference. As we have seen,[1] terms such as healthy, smiling, lion, are univocal in their primary and proper meanings, and even when transferred to other objects they merely designate certain qualities, operations, or things to which those terms can be compared by reason of some accidental and extrinsic or at best purely dynamic likeness. Simply because names of this sort can serve as terms of comparison or relation with

[1] Chap. 14, sect. 4.

respect to other things, it does not follow that they either directly or indirectly signify those secondary objects in any proper or formal way. In short, such analogicals can in no sense be reduced to *one* concept because a mere unity of comparison or connotation requires as many concepts as there are objects connoted or compared.[2]

2. THE UNITY OF THE ANALOGICAL CONCEPT

Things analogous by analogy of proper proportionality, on the other hand, can and do have a concept which is really, even though only proportionately, one in relation to all its inferiors. It is, indeed, a concept that is inadequate and imperfect, not abstracting from its inferiors so as to include them potentially while excluding them actually, in the manner of univocal concepts, but abstracting from them imperfectly, so as to include them actually and implicitly—not actually and explicitly, as in the case of univocal ideas.[3] That is to say, the analogical concept does not prescind from its inferiors in such a way as to remain in potency to them, being therefore limitable by the addition of a differential concept. This is true only of the univocal concept. *Living organism,* for instance (we need not be concerned with the precise definition of this difficult term) is univocal with respect to all species of living organism; it includes dividing differences only potentially and is divisible extrinsically by them. The analogical concept is radically different: it has only a relative or proportional unity, and it does not include the diversity of its inferiors

---

[2] Cf. John of St. Thomas, *Logica*, II, q. 13, a. 5 (ed. Reiser, pp. 491 f.).
[3] Cf. Cajetan, *De nom.,* IV, where this point is lucidly developed.

potentially. If that were the case, it would be actually one in the absolute sense and only potentially multiple or diverse. In order that it may not be univocal in any degree, therefore, the analogical concept must include diversity actually, without in any way rendering that diversity explicit.

Thus analogical perfections, and especially the transcendentals, are included in all their differences or inferiors, enter into them all actually and formally, and are not, like univocals, limitable by the application of differences which lie outside their essence. The analogical concept has in relation to its inferiors only a proportional unity. So the question arises: How can such a concept only implicitly contain its inferiors, yet at the same time include them actually?

3. The "Confused" Character of the Concept of Being

John of St. Thomas points out [4] that when an abstract concept is not limitable by any extraneous differences but only by things of which it is itself predicated, the abstractive operation whereby it is formed does not involve the exclusion of such differences but merely their *non-explication;* they are not extracted or in any way singled out; they are simply left there in a "latent" state. The concept thus attained will therefore include its differences or inferiors actually yet confusedly. This is evident in the case of the concept of being. Being is "limited" to substance

[4] *Op. cit.,* q.13, a.5 (ed. Reiser, pp. 494 f.). Cf. Cajetan, *In De Ente et Essentia,* prooemium, q.1.

and to accident, to matter, form, spirit, body, etc.; being is predicated of all those things because they are all beings or modes of being, and is not limited by the addition of any extraneous differences, since in the order of being there are no extraneous differences. This means that the abstraction of the concept of being is not effected by the exclusion but merely by the non-explication of its inferiors, which it includes actually and confusedly. St. Thomas, in fact, clearly teaches [5] that being cannot be limited or determined by addition but only by modes which express something not expressed by the word being alone. Such are the transcendentals.[6]

The "confused" character of the concept of being may be illustrated in this wise: [7] When we observe a great mass

[5] *De ver.*, I, 1; cf. I *Sent.*, XXII, 1, 3, ad 2.

[6] Dorothy M. Emmet, in a recent book (*The Nature of Metaphysical Thinking;* London: Macmillan, 1945; p. 187) states: "The 'Transcendentals,' unity, distinction, good, truth, which purport to say something about the universal character of Being, in effect tell us no more than that, 'It is what is.' And since we do not know how the divine attributes are realized in the divine existence, the Analogy of Proportionality in effect tells us no more."

As a matter of fact all the transcendentals signify the same object, viz., being—but under different aspects not expressed by the term being itself. They do not add any determinations to being, yet, for us, they help explain the meaning of "being"; for they signify general modes of being as such, of all being. (There are many Thomistic texts on this point; e.g., see *De ver.*, I, 1.) Hence the transcendentals are not merely synonymous. And they can in no case be predicated univocally. Miss Emmet holds that they can (*op. cit.*, p. 175). The root of her difficulties lies in the search for some solid univocal basis for Thomistic analogy, which she apparently considers too weak to bear the weight of sound metaphysical argument. The very title of the chapter on this subject betrays that quest: *Analogia Entis* (chap. 8). Strictly speaking, there is no "analogia entis" in the metaphysical sense, for *ens* designates being *qua* essence, and metaphysical analogy bears on *esse*, act of being, not on essence. The "analogy of being" is an *analogia entium in actu essendi*. The unfruitful approach to the problem of analogy implied by the phrase *analogia entis*, however, is not to be attributed to non-Scholastics but to certain Scholastics who have misconceived that problem.

[7] Cf. John of St. Thomas, *loc. cit.* (in Reiser, p. 498).

of people in the distance and are unable to discern them individually, we have a single confused vision of them all; we see that whole multitude as one, though it is actually, and not potentially, many. Such is the concept of being in relation to its inferiors, that is, all beings: it represents immediately all things under the "confusion" of *having being*. Since the concept of being embraces all beings in this way, it has only a unity of con-fusion, not of explication. But a unity of confusion requires an actual plurality of those things which it embraces confusedly. For instance, being, predicated of man, merely expresses that common character in which all beings, even those which are absolutely diverse in essence, share proportionately. Thus the "confused" unity of the concept of being is only a proportional, an analogical, unity. But the unity of being is real: all beings are proportionately or analogically one in be-ing.

In analogy of proper proportionality each of the analogates, so to speak, denominates itself, for each possesses in itself the analogous character from which it is formally denominated. Hence the common analogous name does not apply determinately to any given one of the analogates; it stands for one no more than for another, but for all indifferently, indistinctly, proportionately; just as the term "principle" does not as such stand for the principle whence a line or a motion or a life or a house, or anything else, "begins," but for that from which anything *begins* in any way whatever. Likewise the term "being" does not signify any particular being or mode of being; confusedly and proportionately, it stands for all beings.

4. The Analogical Mean

To say that in the case of analogy of proper proportionality the analogon is only proportionately one is not to say that it is not truly one. As Cajetan takes pains to show,[8] proportional identity is a real species of identity, and hence the fallacy of equivocation is not incurred where the predicates are the same proportionately. Not only is the analogical mean in metaphysical and theological demonstration a valid type of mean, it is the only possible type of mean through which demonstrations can be made in those sciences.[9]

The analogical mean alone allows a common predicate to be asserted of creatures and God; for the likeness between creatures and God is radically analogical; between them there is no conceivable basis of univocal community either in the order of existence or in the order of essence. Consider the following syllogism: Every simple perfection is in God; wisdom is a simple perfection; hence wisdom is in God. If "wisdom" is used here in two different senses, then the syllogism contains four terms and consequently is invalid. But "wisdom" is used in only one sense, designating that wisdom which is analogically common to all intelligent beings that possess it; it stands for a perfection that is proportionately one in all beings that share it formally and properly. The same is true of all the divine names which signify God formally and properly.

---

[8] *De nom.*, VI, pp. 52–56; X, pp. 79–81.
[9] See above, chap. 13, note 1, and sect. 3.

This brief chapter may be considered an introductory note to the next one, which treats of certain philosophical errors that are due largely to ignorance or to misunderstanding of the nature of the analogical concept and indeed of the doctrine of analogy as a whole.

CHAPTER XX

EQUIVOCITY, UNIVOCITY, ANALOGY

1. CONCERNING SOME MEDIEVAL "EQUIVOCISTS"

SPECULATIVELY speaking, the main source of the doctrine of the equivocity of being in medieval thought is to be found in Plotinus. The greatest of the early (third century) Neo-Platonists, Plotinus stands at the head of a long line, still unbroken, of philosophical and theological agnostics. He held that nothing can be truly or formally predicated of the ultimate Reality (The One)—not even being, essence, goodness, life—indeed, not even the term "one" itself.[1] Although this is not an essay in intellectual genealogy, understanding of the real significance of the principle of analogy may be furthered by indicating the pervasive influence, both direct and indirect, of this archetypal idea.

Plotinian agnosticism found its way into pagan and Christian thought prior to the Middle Ages (generally reckoned from the downfall of Rome in A.D. 476), continued through the latter period, and persists to this day. It exercised considerable influence on early Scholasticism. Scotus Erigena (c. 810–877), for instance, held that, since God (or the Divine Goodness) is totally incomprehensible,

[1] Cf. chap. 4, sect. 3.

it is proper to call Him "the nothing par excellence." [2] Erigena, in fact, maintained that whatever is said of God affirmatively has only a metaphorical meaning. For him, this is true of terms such as essence, goodness, wisdom, justice, truth, as well as of the names Father, Son, and Holy Ghost.[3]

Through ignorance of the principle of analogy, Maimonides (1135–1204) fell headlong into equivocity, excluding all positive or affirmative attributes from God. In fact, he even denied that existence, unity, or eternity could be properly attributed to Him.[4] And, as we have also seen,[5] Meister Eckhart (c. 1260–1327), following in the same tradition of Neo-Platonic agnosticism, likewise succumbed to equivocity. In the fourteenth century we find William of Ockham propounding the doctrine that the existence, unity, and infinity of God, and the immediate creation of the universe by Him, are among the truths which human reason cannot demonstrate strictly and with certitude.[6]

Ockham's philosophical agnosticism was the necessary consequence of his famous theory of "nominalism" or "terminism" according to which universal ideas do not

[2] *De divisione naturae*, III, 19; in Migne, *Patrologia latina*, CXXII, 681 A: "Dum ergo incomprehensibilis intelligitur, per excellentiam nihilum non immerito vocitatur." Cf. col. 681 D.

[3] *Ibid.*, I, 13; in Migne, *P. L.*, CCXXII, 458 C: " . . . considerandum . . . cur praedicta nomina, essentiam, dico, bonitatem, veritatem, justitiam, sapientiam, ceteraque ejus genus, quae videntur non solum divina, sed etiam divinissima . . . metaphorica fieri, id est, a creatura a Creatorem translata." Cf. col. 457 C for denial of the *proper* predication of the terms Father, Son, and Holy Ghost.

[4] Cf. chap. 16, sect. 1.

[5] Cf. chap. 11, sects. 1 and 2.

[6] *Quodl.*, II, 1; *In I Sent.*, d.3, q.2, F. Cf. Ueberweg, *Geschichte der Phil.* (der patristischen und scholastichen Zeit); Berlin, 1915, p. 605; cf. also Ockham, *Centil. theol.*, concl. I ff.

signify anything actually existing in entities outside the mind.[7] Thus being (which is the very root and basis of true analogy) does not really exist in things because it is only a universal idea: "Unity and being are of the number of universal things which do not have existence outside the soul." [8] Moreover the ten categories themselves are not really based on things: "This division (i.e., of the predicaments or categories) is not a division of things outside the soul, because things outside the soul are not predicated of a plurality of things; for that which is predicated is nothing but a word (*vox*) or concept or some sign introduced arbitrarily; and this division [of the categories] is a division of words (*vocum*), whether of concepts or of intentions in the soul." [9] It is evident that for Ockham "being," in the true ontological sense, is equivocal.

The doctrine of the equivocity of the divine names is epitomized in Eckhart's sermon on Renewal in the Spirit: [10]

If I say God is good, it is not true: I am good, God is not good. I say more: I am better than God is, for what is good can be better and what is better can be best. But God is not good, therefore He cannot be better, therefore He cannot be best. These three: good, better, best, are remote from God Who is above all. And if, again I

[7] Of course it is true that "nullum universale est extra animam existens realiter in substantiis individuis"; but it is not true that the universal is not "*de* substantia vel esse earum" (Ockham, *Expositio aurea super artem veterem*, II (on the *Categoriae*), Proöem.

[8] Ockham, *In I Sent.*, d.2, q.4; "Unum et ens sunt ex rebus universalibus, quae non habent esse extra animam."

[9] Ockham, *Expositio aurea*, II, c. 4, n. 7: "Ista non est divisio rerum extra animam, quia res extra animam non praedicantur de pluribus; non enim praedicatur nisi vox, vel conceptus vel aliquid signum ad placitum institutum; sed ista est divisio vocum sive conceptuum sive intentionum in anima."

[10] No. 99 in the Pfeiffer collection. Eng. tr. by C. de B. Evans of F. Pfeiffer's *Meister Eckhart;* London, 1924.

say that God is wise, it is not true: I am wiser than He. Or if I say, God is a being, it is not true: He is a transcendental essence, a super-essential nothing. St. Augustine says, "the finest thing a man can say about God is that He is silent through consciousness of interior fullness." Wherefore hold thy peace and prate not about God, for prating of Him thou does lie, committing sin. If thou wouldst be free from sin and perfect, babble not of God. Neither know anything of God, for God is beyond knowing.

2. DR. R. L. PATTERSON AND THE KNOWLEDGE OF GOD IN ST. THOMAS

When R. L. Patterson approvingly quotes the text above cited [11] he is simply reviving the ancient Plotinian error it manifests, an error which was passed on to Erigena, Maimonides, Eckhart, to many other medievals, to Spinoza and to numerous moderns. It is the radical mistake of conceiving the simple perfections (such as goodness, wisdom, being itself) univocally. Since no univocal concept can apply to God, the next step is the assertion that all the divine names are purely homonymous or equivocal.

In his study of the natural theology of St. Thomas, Patterson has failed to grasp the principle of Thomistic analogy. He wants a univocal knowledge of God, which is the only type of knowledge he recognizes to be genuine. Little wonder, then, that he finds "contradictions" in St. Thomas. He would revive the position of Maimonides. "When St. Thomas asserts, in contradiction to Maimonides, that we are justified in affirming that God is good because goodness exists in God in some higher mode than it does in us, and then refuses to admit, upon precisely the

[11] See Patterson's *The Conception of God in the Philosophy of Aquinas* (London, Allen & Unwin, 1933), p. 104.

same ground, that our knowledge that this statement is true constitutes knowledge of the divine essence, it is clear that he is trying to occupy two diametrically opposite positions at the same time." [12]

This is not at all clear; indeed it is simply not true. For St. Thomas clearly distinguishes between knowing a thing quidditatively, that is, knowing its definitive essence (knowledge *quid est*), and having quidditative knowledge of it. Any knowledge that we have of a thing is quidditative knowledge; it is, so far, knowledge of what that thing is. Thus everything short of knowledge of a thing's definitive essence falls within knowledge *quia est*—knowledge of the thing's existence and everything else that can be known about it, short of knowing its essence as it is in itself.[13]

---

[12] *Ibid.*, p. 257.

[13] For instance, in his Commentary on Boethius' *De Trinitate* (q.6, a.3) St. Thomas says: "Sciendum, quod de nulla re potest sciri an est, nisi quoquo modo de ea sciatur quid est . . . Sic ergo de Deo et de aliis substantiis immaterialibus non possumus scire an est nisi sciremus quodammodo de eis quid est sub quadam confusione." That for St. Thomas we do have some "quidditative" knowledge of God yet do not know Him quidditatively, is seen in the following: *S. th.*, I, 13, 3; *De pot.*, VII, 5 and 7; *De ver.*, II, 1 and 11; I *Sent.*, VIII, 1, 1. Our positive knowledge of God, then, is not false even though it is in the highest degree imperfect (*De ver.*, II, 1, ad 10), the divine mode of being, the mode proper to God as God, completely escaping the grasp of our intelligence (*De pot.*, VII, 5, ad 2; *S. th.*, I, 13, 3, ad 2; *C.G.*, I, 30). It is therefore true, as Dionysius maintains, that the "negative attributes" are less imperfect than the positive (I *Sent.*, XXII, 1, 2, ad 1; *De pot.*, VII, 5, ad 1; *S. th.*, I, 13, 3, ad 2). This is so vital a point that I hope I will be pardoned for digressing beyond the normal bounds of a footnote.

For St. Thomas it is absolutely impossible, even with the aid of such attributes as goodness, justice, wisdom, power, to conceive what God is in Himself. There are many texts in St. Thomas which clearly state that all knowledge, imperfect or perfect, of the essence of God *secundum se* is radically inaccessible to man in this life. (E.g., see *In Epistolam ad Romanos*, I, 6; *C.G.*, I, 30, end of chapter: "We cannot grasp what God is, but what He is not, and what relation all other things have to Him.")

There may be grounds for suspecting, as Gilson suggests, that some commen-

After quoting a perfectly correct statement of this distinction, Patterson proceeds to write as if no such distinction existed. To know that God is good, wise, intelligent, etc., proportionately by analogy of proper proportionality, of course is not to know Him quidditatively, or as He is in Himself. Having missed this point, however, Patterson continues:

Had he [St. Thomas] maintained that our knowledge of the divine essence, though genuine, is imperfect, because while we can understand what is meant by the proposition, *God is good*, we cannot realize how good He is . . . his position would not have been self-contradictory. But self-contradictory it is. The doctrine of degrees of being does not save him, on the contrary, it condemns him; for it was formulated to sustain the view that goodness in God and goodness in man have something in common beside the name, that there really is a resemblance between the creature and the

tators do violence to the texts of St. Thomas in order to obtain from them the conception of analogy as a source of knowledge which is in some degree positive even *quantum ad modum significandi*. Perhaps Professor Gilson had this notion of "positive knowledge" of God in mind when dealing with this question in *Le Thomisme*, 5th ed., pp. 153 ff. In any case there is clearly no need to force any Thomistic text in order to see that, thanks to the principle of analogy, we can acquire some positive knowledge of God and can know Him more or less confusedly, not as He is in Himself but as He presents Himself to the human intelligence through certain created perfections which are realized proportionately in Him. This is the clear doctrine of St. Thomas. All our knowledge of God is analogical (*De ver.*, II, 11, *et alibi passim*); it is imperfect or "confused" (e.g., *De Trin.*, VI, 3); it is positive or affirmative *quantum ad rem significatam*, but negative *quantum ad modum significandi* (e.g., *De pot.*, VII, 5, ad 2). God infinitely transcends every created intelligence, angelic as well as human: "Deus est potior omni nostra locutione et omni cognitione, et non solum excedit nostram locutionem et cognitionem, sed universaliter collocatur super omnem mentem, etiam angelicam, et super omnem substantiam" (*De div. nom.*, I, 3). Nevertheless through immaterial perfections found in creatures we can acquire *some* true knowledge of Him: "Omne quod est perfectum in creaturis oportet Deo attribui, secundum id quod est *de ratione* illius perfectionis absolute; non secundum modum quo est in hoc vel illo" (*De pot.*, IX, 5; cf. *I Sent.*, XXII, 1, 2, ad 2). Thus, although our knowledge of God is "minuscule" (*quantulacumque cognitio—IV Sent.*, XLIX, 2, 7, ad 7), it is more precious than all our other knowledge (*C.G.*, III, 25; on this whole question, see Maritain, *Degrés*, pp. 827-43).

Creator in this particular respect that, in so far as the creature is what we call good, it is like God; from which the corollary inevitably follows that we know that God is good.[14]

Here indeed is a clear statement that goes to the root of the misunderstanding. It is only too evident that for Patterson a "real" resemblance must be a *univocal* resemblance; so that, to his mind, for something to be "in common" in any non-verbal sense is to be "in common" univocally. There is no suggestion of an analogical community between things. This, essentially, is the same illusion under which Father Descoqs labors. And it is to him that Patterson appeals in support of his own mistaken views on analogy.[15] Patterson seems to have derived his notion of Thomistic analogy mainly from Descoqs. But if in the course of this book we have already succeeded in fairly representing the doctrine of analogy as St. Thomas understood it, then we must say that Father Descoqs does not teach that doctrine. For example, he holds that being has no real unity, that the analogical unity which belongs to being as such is purely conceptual.[16] Indeed he believes that analogy of proper proportionality (which, we have maintained, is the Thomistic analogy par excellence) is a mere novelty invented by Cajetan,[17] and that with respect to God and creatures, this analogy is "purely fictive." [18]

14 *Ibid.*, p. 257. (See also pp. 255 f. for Patterson's quotation of the distinction in question.)

15 Cf. pp. 248 f. The "resemblances" which Patterson sees between the philosophy of St. Thomas and that of F. H. Bradley (pp. 103, 184–87, 381, 443) derive largely from a misunderstanding of Thomistic analogy: the two philosophies differ *toto coelo*.

16 P. Descoqs, *Inst. Meta. Gen.*, Vol. I, esp. pp. 143 f.

17 *Ibid.*, p. 277: "L'analogie de proportionnalité ne commencera d'encombrer la scolastique qu'avec Cajetan et son *De nominum analogia*."

18 *Ibid.*, p. 270.

The whole history of thought could be written from the standpoint of the principle of analogy alone, and the various great systems and types of philosophy evaluated metaphysically in the light of that principle. Of course a study of that sort, made from but a single perspective, would have a very limited significance; many important things would necessarily have to be left out. But a balanced, careful study of this kind would be worth-while. It would reveal (without discounting the elements of truth in any philosophy) certain perennial metaphysical errors, shared by philosophies which appear to be and which are in many respects very different. Thus Neo-Platonic agnosticism, pluralistic empiricism, nominalisms of all sorts, the old and the new philosophy of becoming: all, for the purposes of that study, could be grouped together because they exemplify a common error, namely, the idea that being has no real unity in beings, the notion that the concept of being as applied to beings is essentially equivocal. In one way or another those philosophies are all opposed to true metaphysical analogy; for they either deny the reality of being—in which case obviously there is no analogy—, or they deny that being has any real unity in things—in which case also there is no analogy: being, as common analogous perfection, and beings, as analogates, are thereby eliminated.[19] So in the last analysis such philosophies do away with that which they are especially eager to preserve: the actual manyness of things. For if being (not as a thing, of course, but as a proportionately common *act* present in all

[19] Cf. G. M. Manser, O.P., "Das Wesen des Thomismus" in *Divus Thomas* (Frib.), VII (1929), 11.

things) is not real, then there are not and cannot be any beings. However, unless it is granted that being is real, that it has a real (though proportional or analogical) unity in things, the whole effort of scientific thought will end in frustration, because it would then in fact be groundless.

At the opposite extreme (the other side of the same false coin) is the doctrine of the univocity of being. The following section is a brief commentary on the Scotist doctrine of univocity. Some observations on the theory of univocity in general will be made in section 4.

3. The Univocity of Being in Duns Scotus

If John Duns Scotus (1265–1308) is the Subtle Doctor par excellence, he is also the Difficult Doctor. In the latter role he is probably pre-eminent among all first-rate thinkers in the history of Western culture. And his theory of univocity, which has a central place in his system, is the focal point of a multitude of arduous problems. Omitting a host of difficult questions, in this section I intend to do no more than indicate certain basic elements of that theory and point out what appear to be some of its chief implications and its ultimate source.

Scotus held that the proper object of the human intelligence is not the essences of material things; neither is God that object, nor even substance, as such—but *ens in quantum ens,* that which is most universal in all things.[20] For Scotus, being (*ens*) is an absolutely universal form having a simple unity in all things: "*Ens* is included quidditatively in all quidditative inferior concepts; hence no

---

20 Cf. Duns Scotus, *Opus Oxon., In I Sent.,* prol. q. 1, n. 1.

inferior concept can be conceived distinctly apart from the concept of being. But being cannot be conceived unless it be conceived distinctly, because it has an absolutely simple concept; hence being can be conceived distinctly apart from other concepts, but the others cannot be conceived distinctly apart from this distinct concept; therefore being is the first distinctly conceivable concept." [21]

Now, according to Scotus our natural knowledge of God requires a middle term which applies "univocally" to Him and to His creatures; otherwise He would not be knowable by a simple concept, and the concept of being is such a concept: "God is not naturally knowable by us unless being is univocal with respect to the created and the uncreated," and the same argument, he says, applies in the case of substance and accident.[22] But if *ens*, having a simple unity, is "univocal" in respect of creatures and God, substance and accident, it would seem that it must be a genus. Yet Scotus maintains that being is not a genus, as this term is commonly understood in logic.

For Scotus, being is univocal but, logically speaking, it is not genus, because it has no specific differences: it is "specified" by its own "modes." Nevertheless "being" is said "univocally" of God and creatures. For Scotus, a notion is *univocal* when the law of contradiction can be ap-

21 *Op. Oxon.*, I, d.3, q.2, n.24: "Ens includitur quidditative in omnibus conceptibus quidditativis inferioribus; ergo nullus conceptus inferior distincte concipitur nisi concepto ente. Ens autem non potest concipi nisi distincte, quia habet conceptum simpliciter simplicem; ergo potest concipi distincte sine aliis, et alii non sine eo distincte concepto; ergo ens est primus conceptus distincte conceptibilis." Cf. I, d.1, q.4, n.15; d.3, q.3, n.8.

22 *Op. Oxon.*, I, d.3, q.3 n.26 (chol. 9): "Deus non est nobis cognoscibilis naturaliter, nisi ens sit univocum creato et increato, ita potest argui de substantia et accidente."

plied to it and when it can serve as the middle term of a syllogism without involving the argument in a *quaternio terminorum*.[23] If being were not univocal, Scotus argues,[24] we could not form any natural concept of God, and natural theology therefore would be impossible: we would have only a supernatural revelation of God's existence and no natural knowledge of Him. But as a matter of fact this is not the case.

Thus, according to Scotus, it is perfectly clear that all our natural knowledge of God is founded on the univocity of our concept of being; it is this concept alone which enables us to apply to Him those predicates which belong to being so far as it is "indifferent" to infinity as well as to finitude. For Scotus, properly speaking, it is not by (or in) a concept analogous to the concept of creature that God is conceived, for He is absolutely diverse from everything in the created order, but by a concept which is univocal with respect to Him and the creature.[25]

Scotus hoped to steer a middle course between (1) the error of subsuming the Divine Being under the categories and so denying Its transcendent nature, and (2) the error of overemphasizing the transcendence of God and thereby

---

[23] E.g., *Op. Oxon.*, I, d.3, q.2, n.5 (Comment.): "Conceptum univocum dico, qui ita est unus, quod ejus unitas sufficit ad contradictionem, affirmando et negando ipsum de eodem. Sufficit etiam pro medio syllogistico, ut extrema unita in medio sic uno, sine fallacia aequivocationis, concludantur inter se unum." Also note *Op. Ox.*, I, d.8 (Quarrachi, 1912), n.626: "Principia illa sempiterna sunt causa veritatis in aliis; si enim accipitur in minori quod illa principia sunt principia aequivoca *vel* analoga, erunt quatuor termini in syllogismo."

[24] *Ibid.*, n.8.

[25] *Ibid.*, n.5.

removing Him altogether from the reach of human reason. He believed that the theory of a purely analogical knowledge of God courted the latter error, laying too much stress on the negative aspect of our knowledge of God. Scotus always upheld the divine transcendence, insisting not only upon the imperfection of created being as compared with the Uncreated Being but upon the absolutely radical diversity between them. Moreover, he maintains "analogy" without abandoning univocity: there is analogy in the being of things inasmuch as there are real relations between them and an actual order among them.[26]

This position has given rise to the theory that entitative analogy in Scotus is perfectly reconcilable with his doctrine of univocity, which, it is held, requires only that measure of unity which is necessary for any valid argument; for (as we have seen in the case of the "univocal" concept of being), the law of contradiction, according to Scotus, forbids us to affirm and deny the same (univocal) predicate of the same subject. It is true that without unitary concepts signifying objects having a real unity in themselves, the human intelligence can acquire no positive knowledge. But Scotus held that the conceptual unities in question, and especially the unity of the concept of being, must be univocal, because such unity alone provides a basis for positive knowledge. This univocity has been attenuated and minimized by some modern Scotists, but it is generally held that, in the last analysis, analogy must be grounded on univocity, for otherwise human

26 Cf. *Super Libros Elenchorum*, 16, 4, 2; 24 b.

knowledge would have no positive basis, the assumption being that only a univocal unity can supply such a basis.

The supposition that all valid argument requires an at least minimal univocity in the conceptual objects involved, is untenable, because contradiction does not consist merely in affirming and denying the same univocal predicate of the same subject. The proportional unity of our notion of being suffices to render contradictory any simultaneous affirmation and denial of that concept; and the analogical concept, in the Thomistic sense, can very well serve as middle term in valid arguments; in fact, the demonstration of God's existence requires it.[27]

The claim that Scotist univocity is not really opposed to Thomist analogy [28] may seem plausible on the argument that the one is purely logical while the other is purely ontological. But such a reconciliation is actually impossible; for, according to Thomism, nothing is predicated univocally of God and creatures; and Thomistic analogy does not contain nor does it admit any slightest element of univocity.

The metaphysical root of the Scotist doctrine of the univocity of the concept of being lies in an essentialist conception of being. This means, at least implicitly, that *ens* is emphasized at the expense of *esse*. Grammatically speaking, *ens* is being considered as a noun, while *esse* is being considered as a verb: the one denotes thingness, the other, act of existence; the one says *that which,* the other says *is;*

27 Cf. chap. 13, note 1; chap. 19, sect. 4.
28 Cf. M. S. Belmond, "L'univocité scotiste" in *Revue de philosophie,* August 1, 1912.

ens signifies being in its essence-aspect, while *esse* signifies the act of existing itself. Being *qua ens* is substantival being; it is the ultimate ground of logical intelligibility, and hence of univocal conception; being *qua esse* is being-in-act; it is the ultimate ground of metaphysical intelligibility, and hence of analogical conception. To make the concept of being "univocal," even in a tenuous sense, is to confuse these two orders or aspects of being.

Scotus, it is true, held that the concept of being is not generic and therefore cannot be defined logically; yet, since it is an absolutely simple concept, it is for the logician univocal.[29] This univocity was considered necessary to allow for a sufficiently positive knowledge of God and thereby to avoid the pitfalls of agnosticism.[30] But the fact is that the concept of being is not univocal even in a minimal sense. The unity of all our properly metaphysical and theological concepts is purely analogical or proportional. Univocal unity in these orders is neither necessary nor possible.

4. GENERAL OBSERVATIONS ON THE UNIVOCIST ERROR

Despite numerous differences, there are certain doctrinal links between Scotus and Suarez. They do not share the same conception of being, but they both tend toward an essentialist view, and this accounts for the irreducible element of univocity in their fundamental teaching on the character of the real. The doctrine of Suarez and his school

---

[29] Cf. *Reportata Parisiensia*, prol., q.3, n.4.

[30] Cf. E. Gilson, "Avicenne et le point de départ de Duns Scot" in *Archives d'histoire doctrinale et littéraire du Moyen Age*, II, 1927, pp. 100–17.

was treated in Part Two, where [31] it was pointed out that certain Suarezians, notwithstanding their so-called analogy of intrinsic attribution, were unable to avoid falling back to the univocist position because, following their master,[32] they have assumed that being must have a simple unity, like that proper to logical concepts. This assumption is the result of attempting to grasp being logically: it reveals the mentality of the logician who would like to subsume all things under clear and distinct ideas. But no transcendental object can be conceived logically; it can be seen only metaphysically. Being is the chief of such objects, and it is not itself an intelligible essence; it is an act, really common to all that is or can be.

In addition to Scotism and Suarezianism, there are of course many other cases of the error of conceiving being univocally: in divers forms and degrees we found this error in Plato and Plotinus, in certain medieval Neo-Platonists, in Spinoza, Hegel, Bradley. There are "monisms" which are monistic only in a qualified sense, and the same applies to "pantheism." Indiscriminately used, such terms are mere epithets. But they do have certain proper senses. The general point I wish to make here is that all systems which are really and essentially monistic or pantheistic (even though they may not be so in the actual intention of their authors or even from the standpoint of a strictly historical type of exegesis), all systems of this kind exemplify the common metaphysical mistake of conceiving reality univocally. In fact, every essentialism which pur-

[31] Chap. 9, sects. 3–5; chap. 10, sect. 1.

[32] Cf. Suarez, *Disp. Metaph.*, esp. disp. 28, sect. 3, nos. 18, 11; disp. 2; sect. 2, n. 34.

ports to be a metaphysics is based on a univocal idea of being. In those philosophies, "being," as *summum genus*, has many different names, but they are all fundamentally univocal: the supreme category, or the class of all classes, is still a logical intention.

Great "vigilance" is required, Cajetan observes,[33] lest one fall into univocity. This pitfall is omnipresent because, in their primary imposition, almost all the words we use are univocal; hence it is not unreasonable to suppose that they all have univocal meanings, that all or nearly all of them really stand for "clear and distinct" ideas. So the search for "scientific" knowledge becomes a search for such ideas. In philosophy this quest generally issues in system-building. But it is metaphysically fruitless. Univocity is the ruination of metaphysics; it is the ruination of every philosophical science, including ethics and political philosophy, the basic concepts of which are intrinsically analogical.[34]

Lack of vigilance in this matter of univocal ideas largely accounts for agnosticism, whether explicitly symbolist or not. It is responsible for the denial of the metaphysical value of the principle of causality; [35] for the assertion of

---

[33] *De nom.*, V, p. 50; see cap. XI, "De cautelis necessariis circa analogorum nominum intellectum et usum."

[34] E.g., consider the terms *right, wrong, duty, person, individual, end, justice, law, the common good.*

It is important to bear in mind that logic is not itself a philosophical science; it studies reason as the tool of knowledge and is thus a propaedeutic to philosophical science. Cf. Maritain, *An Introduction to Philosophy*, Eng. tr. (New York: Sheed and Ward), pp. 147 ff.

[35] In Kant, *cause* is univocal: it is a category and as such it cannot apply outside the order of "experience." For this reason alone it was inevitable that Kant should have found any speculative demonstration of the existence of God impossible.

the equivocity of the divine names, such as just, wise, good, living, person, indeed even of the names being, essence, and one. Thus we have Plotinus, Maimonides, Eckhart, Spinoza, and many of their predecessors, contemporaries, and heirs.

The univocist error generally lies at the basis of the equivocist error. To guard against univocity in all its forms, subtly deceptive as many of them are and will always be, is a prime rule of the metaphysical art. No matter how magnificent they may be as literature, no matter how exquisitely articulate as works of human reason, systems of philosophy built on univocal foundations are philosophical failures. For philosophy seeks knowledge of that which *is;* and the being of things cannot be known through univocal concepts because it is not as such univocal. The attempt to grasp the real by means of logical categories is bound to fail. A priori intellectual forms may help us to order our experiences, but they will not enable us to apprehend things in their actual existence. Being as such is not a logical entity and it cannot therefore be enclosed in our logical univocal frames. This is why no metaphysically sound philosophy is or can ever be "systematic" in the sense proper to a system of logic or to a "dialectical" or an idealist ontology. The idea of being is a transcendental-analogical idea. But being itself is not any sort of idea.

5. Analogy Is Based on Simple Diversity in Act of Being

Univocity, the bête noire of metaphysics, is itself a logical intention. No two things are univocal with respect to their actual being, because no two things exercise the same act of being. Every single thing is diverse, simply, from every other one in point of its *esse:* the "is" of A is not the "is" of B, though both may be identical in essence. What possible significance for a philosophical doctrine of analogy could a fact so elementary possess? This: it completely excludes univocity from the order of existence and makes the "analogy of being" immediately evident. For (to slightly paraphrase St. Thomas) where there is diversity in act of existing, univocity is impossible.[36] In its primary and elementary sense, the phrase "analogy of being" is only shorthand for the statement that, although all things are distinct from one another in their very act of existing, they are nevertheless all brought together in a community of relations through their proportionate sharing in that act. Is it not then clear that being (*esse*), said of two or more beings, is in no case univocal, not even in the case of individuals belonging to the same genus or species? For example, the act of being of this match is not the act of being of that match. But we are not speaking equivocally when we say that this match exists and that match exists, although the act whereby this match exists is simply diverse from or other than the act whereby that match exists. So we see there is something common here, for we can say that as the nature of this match "is to" its act of existing, so the nature of that match "is to" its act of existing. If we like, we may represent this community of relations in a mathematical

36 Cf. *De pot.,* VII, 7. Most of the argument of this section, and parts of sections 4 and 5 in chapter 20, are reproduced, with some minor changes, in my article, "The Basis of Metaphysical Analogy," *The Downside Review* (no. 203, January 1948, pp. 38–47).

form (while abstracting completely from its mathematical meaning): This match : its act of existing : : that match : its act of existing. The act of existing in each case is absolutely or simply diverse (*simpliciter diversus*), but relatively the same (*secundum quid idem*). Of course the two matches are specifically the same because they have the same essence or definition. But they are not the same *secundum esse*.

Being (*esse*), predicated of two or more beings, is never univocal: [37] it is always analogical, and analogical by analogy of proper proportionality. Perhaps we can now begin to see the deep metaphysical significance of the following statements of St. Thomas: "All univocal predications are reduced to one non-univocal, analogical principle, which is being"; [38] "Being is not a genus, but is predicable analogically of all things in common." [39]

St. Thomas, clearly, allows no exceptions. Some, however, hold that *being*, predicated of specifically identical

[37] Here I wish to call attention to E. L. Mascall's work, *He Who Is: A Study in Traditional Theism* (Longmans, Green and Co., 1943, reprinted 1945). This interesting book, "put forward as a small contribution to the reconstruction of Anglican theology" (p. xi), is explicitly based on the Thomism of St. Thomas himself and of some of his chief modern expositors, in particular Gilson, Maritain, and Father Garrigou-Lagrange.

The author explains that the problem of analogy has received inadequate consideration in his book (Preface, p. xi), although he is aware of its importance as well as of its difficulty. I agree that "the great work of the Abbé Penido . . . has [not] said the last word on the matter" (*ibid.*), but I believe that Mr. Mascall would not have found this problem so difficult and forbidding had he not assumed, as he apparently did, that the problem of analogy is properly designated by the expression *analogia entis* in the sense used by Pryzwara (cf. pp. xi, 126). For the analogy of "being" is not the analogy of *ens* (of being *qua* thing) but of *esse* (of being *qua* act). See chap. 19, note 6.

[38] St. Thomas, *S. th.*, I, 13, 5, ad 1: "In praedicationibus omnia univoca reducuntur ad unum primum non univocum, sed analogicum, quod est ens."

[39] St. Thomas, *De nat. gen.*, I, *in fine:* "Ens genus non est, sed de omnibus communiter praedicabile analogice."

material individuals, can in no proper sense be called analogical. This opinion, in fact, seems quite generally held, though seldom explicitly formulated. One important source of it is found in John of St. Thomas, who argues [40] that, although *being*, predicated of such things, is transcendental in a restricted and accidental way, it is not actually analogical because those things are specifically one and the same and distinct from one another only materially; whereas analogy requires inequality and diversity. There is a sense in which this argument is logically sound despite the fact that it is metaphysically false. It holds for the logician's "being," but not for the metaphysician's; because individuals of the same formal species are distinct precisely as existents: "The act of existing of each and every thing is proper to that thing and is distinct from the act of existing of each and every other thing." [41] Here we

40 *Logica*, II, q. 13, a. 3; q. 14, a. 2. Thus we read (q. 13, a. 3): "Transcendens de se et per se ad plura extendi, quae et specie et genere differunt, respectu quorum analogum est, et sic non coactatur ad illa tantum individua; *respectu tamen illorum praecise analogum non est*, licet transcendens sit, sed hoc est per accidens, quia non sumitur ratio transcendens secundum se totam, sed cum restrictione ad duo inaequalitatem formalem non habentia, sed tantum materialem, quae non est diversitas inaequalis, et ideo *secundum restrictionem ad illa, non exercetur inaequalitas et diversitas simpliciter analogiae*, licet transcendentia remaneat, sed restricte, et per accidens considerata, non secundum quod habet ex se." And again (q. 14, a. 2): "Non repugnat aliquod analogum, si restricte sumatur in ordine ad aliqua inferiora, non exercere ibi analogiam, quia illa non sunt simpliciter diversa, sicut sanum dictum de duobus animalibus non est analogum; sic *ens restricte ad duo individua non exercet analogiam*, licet exerceat transcendentiam, quia illa singularia ejusdem speciei ita sunt unum quod *diversitatem simpliciter non habent, sed tantum materialem*, quae extrinseca est naturae, in qua omnino conveniunt. Unde inclusio in talibus differentiis non solvit unitatem conceptus simpliciter, licet ex vi sui conceptus transcendens illud sit analogum, quia ratio transcendentiae postulat non coactari ad illa duo individua, et consequenter diversitatem simpliciter. Quare ex hoc argumento, nihil deducitur pro univocatione transcendentium secundum se." (Italics mine.)

41 "Esse uniusque rei est ei proprium, et distinctum ab esse cuiuslibet alterius rei" (St. Thomas, *De pot.*, VII, 3).

reach the ultimate in metaphysical concreteness and simplicity. It very evidently follows from this most evident
fact that our knowledge of the *existence* even of specifically
identical things cannot not be analogical. If we say such
knowledge may in some sense be considered univocal, we
are "logicizing" existence. This is what has happened in
John of St. Thomas' analysis of *being*, predicated of material individuals. It is an "essential" analysis, as opposed
to an "existential" one: the view of the logician rather than
that of the metaphysician. I speak of *the* logician rather
than of *some* logicians, because the approach in question
is essential to the logical art.

The statement that "being," predicated of specifically
identical individuals, is logically univocal but metaphysically analogical, is in a sense a paradox, but it is no contradiction. For it is precisely the office of the logician to
consider the "being" which things have in and through
second intentions. Now the second intention, being the
formal object of logic, is what makes logic to be specifically
that which it is: a reflexive science which considers being
under an aspect in which it cannot exist except in the
mind. Without going into technicalities, the relevant point
is this: that the second intention *is* the essence, in an intentional mode. Therefore, when the logician says that
"being" is univocal with respect to specifically identical
individuals, he means being in the sense of specific essence;
and he is perfectly correct.[42] When the metaphysician says

---

[42] It should be noted that in the *concept* of existence, *esse* is considered from
the point of view of an essence, namely, as a certain intelligible object. It is
therefore truly said that existence does not exist, "existence" being merely an

that "being" is analogical with respect to specifically identical individuals, he means being in the sense of act of existing; and he is perfectly correct.

There is no doubt that as a principle of knowledge, analogy is first and foremost a problem of predication. Whence the assumption readily follows that analogy is fundamentally, if not exclusively, a logical problem. In the order of knowing, we are indeed confronted with the problem of the modes of unity enjoyed by different types of concepts; and in this order we find that some concepts have no univocal unity at all. Thus arises the problem of the analogy of concepts and, in consequence, the problem of the analogical predication of certain terms. It is the business of logic, then, to treat of the nature and functions of analogical concepts. But it is the province of the metaphysician alone to treat of the analogy of beings in act of existing. Logic, so to speak, parallels metaphysics. But a logical consideration of the actual analogy within the being of things is in the nature of the case impossible. To say that "being" is intrinsically analogical is to say that existence is diverse in every individual being and in every mode of being, yet proportionately the same. From this fact it follows that being is predicated analogically "of all things in common" (*de omnibus communiter,* in St. Thomas' phrase).

----

ens rationis which we form of the act of an essence in order to speak of it. We cannot do otherwise, for nothing is conceivable except as an essence. But it is imperative to realize that in so doing we are viewing an act as an essence; and an act is no essence. Whence the necessity, under pain of divesting metaphysical objects of all actuality, for constantly correcting by our own interior judgments everything we say about them.

The metaphysical necessity of this analogy may be brought home to us by the reflection that, apart from it, even the univocal predication of a common term of several actually distinct things would be impossible. For were there no analogy of beings in being, there would not be several things distinct in act of being, but only one Thing, One Essence; and we should be back with old Parmenides. Univocal predication itself clearly presupposes simple diversity of act of existing of diverse existents. This act, which is the root and flower of every perfection, since it proceeds from Him alone who is Pure Act, St. Thomas calls esse—"to be."

Any two beings sharing a common nature will serve to illustrate the point that univocal predication rests on esse; hence on the "real distinction": "If the essence man and the act of being a man did not differ in Peter, it would be impossible to predicate man univocally of Peter and Paul, since the act of being of the one is diverse from the act of being of the other." [43] Obviously, in that case there would not be Peter and Paul but only Peter, who would himself be man, a pure essence. This patent fact concerning the nature of univocity has tremendous implications: it means that the whole logical structure of every human science rests on the analogy of being. For without the actual multiplicity and distinctness of beings, no logical operations of any sort—no definitions, divisions, classifications, etc.— would have any grounding in the real. It is therefore exact

[43] De ver., II, 11: "Si enim in Petro non differret homo et hominem esse, impossibile esset, quod homo univoce diceretur de Petro et Paulo, quibus est esse diversum." (Cf. I Sent., XXXV, 1, 4.)

to say that the doctrine of metaphysical analogy is *demanded* by the actual multiplicity of beings.[44]

In general terms, then, the upshot of the matter is this: "Pluralism" spells equivocity; "monism," univocity; "analogism," neither equivocity nor univocity, but a type of thought which, based on the being of things, surmounts both these positions without partaking of the errors of either. For although analogy is a mean between opposing extremes, it does not bring them together in a hybrid synthesis; it transcends them.[45]

[44] G. M. Manser, "Das Wesen des Thomismus," *Divus Thomas* (Frib.), VI (1928), 389 f.
[45] Cf. Penido, *Le rôle,* pp. 77 f.

CHAPTER XXI

OBJECTIONS AND REPLIES

THE doctrine of Thomistic analogy has been attacked so many times from so many different angles that a book would be required to deal adequately with all these charges. Numerous difficulties, some very reasonable, also have been found; but at present we are not concerned with difficulties as such, but with definite objections. In this chapter, only two major objections (which are prototypes of many others) will be considered. The first, treated in the following two sections, comes from a non-scholastic source; the second, treated in section 3, from a scholastic source.

1. A "VICIOUS CIRCLE"?

According to Thomism, everything that can be properly said of God can be said of Him only analogically by analogy of proper proportionality. Analogy of this sort contains at least four terms, and in theology it has always the follow-ing form: $\dfrac{\text{created (a)}}{\text{participated being}} = \dfrac{\text{uncreated (x)}}{\text{unparticipated being}}$.[1] X designates any predicate attributed to God, *a* its created analogue. What *x* is, is of course unknown: to discover this *x* is the object of our theological investigation. This is

[1] Cf. Penido, *Le rôle*, p. 136.

merely a statement of the factual situation. The objection
follows.

That is all very well, it is said, but you have failed to see
that you have on your hands not only one "x" but two; for
"being," said of your "unparticipated being" (which you
call God) has not at all the same sense as "being," said of
your "participated being." Consequently, if the third term
of your proportion is by definition an *x*, the fourth term
must also be an *x*. As Edouard Le Roy puts it,[2] "a proportion is enlightening only if three of its four terms are
known independently of it, and here there are two un-
knowns: God and His attribute."

If you insist that the fourth term is not indeterminable
because it is not purely equivocal but "analogical," this
will profit you nothing, for, our objector will say, you will
then be caught in a vicious circle. Each attribute, you
claim, is analogical and can be known by the aid of your
master proportion. But that is impossible. As you yourself
admit, the fourth term, on which all the others depend, is
itself already analogical, since it designates the "divine"
existence; obviously, therefore, you base analogy on analogy, and this is a *petitio principii*. Moreover, if you place
the *divine existence* in your second proportion (as you
must), then your third and your fourth terms make only
one term, since, by hypothesis, God *is* His own existence.
Hence your proportion is actually reduced to the follow-
ing: $\dfrac{\text{created being}}{\text{participated being}} = \dfrac{\text{uncreated X}}{\text{X}}$. It is evident that
nothing but sophisms can issue from such a matrix. The

---

[2] *Dogme et Critique*, pp. 146 ff. Quoted by Penido, *op. cit.*, p. 137, note 1.

whole of your "theology," both natural and revealed, is therefore a veritable "Niagara of paralogisms." [3]

2. Why the Objection Does Not Hold

There are a number of reasons why this whole argument

[3] Cf. Penido, *Le rôle*, p. 137. In a much less positive form, essentially the same objection (though apparently in this case it is rather a difficulty than an objection) is raised by Austin Farrer in his book, *Finite and Infinite: A Philosophical Essay* (Westminster: Dacre Press, 1943): "The scheme of proportionality looks as uninformative as it is unexceptionable. Whatever mode of activity is referred to God (e.g. intelligence) must be referred through this scheme; but we cannot do the sum which the formula appears to propose to us. As 5 to 13, so X to 117. Then X = 45. And the theological proportionality would be equally handy if the notion of absolute existence were a notion of what the absolute mode of existence is. In that case, we could, so to speak, write down its number and work the sum. But *ex hypothesi* we do not know what the absolute mode of existence is; it is precisely this that the proportionalities are called in to begin determining. And so the scheme of proportionality has something fraudulent about it, when it is given this mathematical appearance. Only God could use it; and He does not need it" (p. 53). But Farrer proceeds to defend proportionality, suggesting that it "at least sketches out an area or a direction in which the truth lies, and that this may be the best information that we can get" (p. 53). He adds (p. 54): "Further there is the general consideration that this puzzle arises only in the (finite) terms with which we are bound to express the unique Divinity if we are to have any discourse about Him at all. That which originally comes to bear on the mind is not the scheme of proportionality, but God as active in us, a reality which drives the mind to such straits as these in the effort to comment upon it." Moreover, he states that, "although proportionality does not offer us, in the notion of absolute being, the 'number by which the sum can be worked,' it does offer in that notion certain factors which can be applied to the finite analogue to fit it better for its analogic function."

Farrer apparently assumes that analogy of proper proportionality purports to be an instrument whereby we can "begin determining" the absolute mode of existence. But that mode as such is absolutely unknowable to man in his present state. Fundamentally, analogy is not a logical procedure but a metaphysical principle; and this principle does not in any degree help us to determine the divine mode of being—to know God as He is in Himself; it merely makes it possible for us to know that certain immaterial perfections which come within our own experience are realized in Him *suo modo*, that is, in a manner commensurate with His Being.

The "mathematical appearance" of analogy of proportionality is merely an appearance: the analogy itself is in no sense mathematical. Perhaps the very term *proportionality* invites misunderstanding, as well as the mathematical-seeming illustrations commonly given of it. A better term would be welcome; but any other term might be equally susceptible of erroneous interpretations.

is groundless. A detailed rebuttal is unnecessary, and it will be sufficient to consider only the main points in a summary fashion. First of all it should be pointed out that *being*, said of participated and of unparticipated being, is not equivocal, as our objector holds; it designates something which is proportionately common to both these (infinitely) diverse modes of being. Consequently there are not four terms in our "master proportion," but only three: the middle term (being) is analogically the same in both relations. Need we repeat that the middle term in every metaphysical and every theological argument (and all such arguments rest on analogies of proportionality) is analogical? Of course, the fourth term of our proportion is already analogical; analogy is already explicitly present in the demonstration of God's existence. Moreover, it should be observed that the third and fourth terms do not "make one term," because they are logically distinct; and a distinction of reason is a sufficient basis for a relation.[4] (See below, sect. 3.)

Behind our objector's arguments lies the assumption that *being* is an equivocal term—at least equivocal as applied to participated and to unparticipated, to finite and to infinite, being. It follows necessarily that for the equivocist no demonstration of the existence of a First Being, in the sense of a being radically diverse from all finite beings, is possible. For him, there is no demonstrable reason why there should be a First Being. This position, however, is open to a fundamental *reductio ad absurdum*. In the

---

[4] Cf. Penido, *Le rôle*, pp. 137–42. I am indebted to Penido for the main points of the argument presented in this and in the preceding section.

simplest terms, it is as follows: If there is no First Being, then this concrete being here before me must vanish at once. But it does exist. Of course this *reductio* needs to be completed by a number of subsidiary arguments; yet it expresses a basic metaphysical insight. From another angle, this same insight is expressed in a less absolute form by the proposition that, if there is no First Being which is the *raison d'être* of all other beings, then unintelligibility lies at the very heart of the "real."

No matter how this First Being is characterized, if it is admitted that *It* exists, not only in the mind but in the nature of things; if it is admitted that there is truly an X which exists by itself, then we can proceed to reason about it and its attributes without becoming involved in a vicious circle. There will be no leap into the unknown if it is conceded that this X is the ultimate sufficient ground of the being of this concrete thing here before me. Into this simple, initial affirmation, namely, that the existence of any limited being points to the existence of some, single, unlimited Being, analogy does not enter at all, at least not explicitly. Hence, since all the derivative analogates rest on this affirmation, there is no question of a "vicious circle." Of course it does not follow that theological argument moves in a vicious circle because the fourth term of our model proportion is already analogical. All metaphysical thought is analogical from the outset; so this alleged difficulty is not peculiar to theology. Metaphysical arguments are in fact all based on analogy, on the analogy of being. No other basis is possible; for being is analogical in itself.

Let us suppose that the existence of a First Being has not been demonstrated. In that case we can nevertheless show a priori that some of our concepts (concepts of simple perfections, such as being, unity, goodness, justice, wisdom) have a transcendental value, an extra-predicamental or analogical value, and hence that no contradiction would be involved in attributing them to the First Being—if indeed It does exist. So if we can proceed to show that those concepts are not "mere" concepts but of their very nature demand realization in a transcendent principle, and if we can demonstrate that the very being of things requires the existence of that Principle, then we can affirm that the latter exists, is one, good, etc. Thus, before even attempting to demonstrate the existence of God, we will have shown that some of our concepts are, so to speak, naturally apt to be attributed to Him because they have a transcendent and analogical value in themselves. Clearly, therefore, the imputation that there is a vicious circle, a radical incoherence, in this procedure is without foundation.

3. THE CHARGE OF "VERBALISM"

One critic writes that it was only with Cajetan and his *De nominum analogia* that analogy of proper proportionality "began to encumber scholasticism." [5] This analogy,

[5] P. Descoqs, S.J., *Inst. Metaph. Gen.*, p. 277. Cf. chap. 20, note 17. Aloys Goergen has assembled a vast number of texts on analogy from the works of St. Thomas and of Cajetan, has analyzed them very carefully, and has shown clearly that both men taught essentially the same doctrine. Far from having invented analogy of proper proportionality (or any other mode of analogy recognized by St. Thomas), Cajetan expounded and developed the doctrine St. Thomas himself taught. (Aloys Goergen, *Kardinal Cajetans Lehre von der Analogie; ihr Verhältnis zu Thomas von Aquin:* Inaugural Dissertation presented to the Faculty of Philosophy of the University of Munich, 1938. See especially Kaput V, pp. 39–57.)

the critic contends, is a mere verbal *tour de force:* "The relation of God to His being is purely verbal: far from opposing two terms, it must be reduced to a pure, absolute, formal identity. . . . Whence this necessary consequence: in the classic proportion $\dfrac{\text{God}}{\text{His being}} = \dfrac{\text{creature}}{\text{its being}}$, the first relation being nul, the proportion itself will be purely logical, without any basis, purely fictive." [6]

The notion that analogy of proper proportionality is a mere innovation, foreign to the thought of St. Thomas, is itself "fictive"; for St. Thomas refers to this analogy many times, explains what it is, and shows that it is the only analogy that properly applies to creatures and God. For instance, St. Thomas points out that although there is not, strictly speaking, any *proportion* between the creature and God, the finite and the infinite, nevertheless there is a proportional likeness between them; they are *proportionable* in virtue of the equality of the two proportions in which they each stand in relation to their own being. This, he explicitly states, is what is meant by *proportionality,* and it is this mode of likeness which exists between the creature and God.[7]

Although St. Thomas does not always use the term "proportionality," this analogy is clearly referred to and explained in the following texts, among many others: I *Eth.*, VII, 95 f.; I *Sent.*, XIX, 5, 2, ad 1; *De pot.*, VII, 7; V *Meta.*, VIII, 879; *De ver.*, II, 11; V *Meta.*, V, 939 f.

[6] Descoqs, *op. cit.*, 270, note 6: "La relation de Dieu à son être est purement verbale: loin d'opposer deux termes, elle doit être réduite à l'identité pure, absolue, formelle. . . . D'où cette consequence obligée: dans la proportion classique: $\dfrac{\text{Dieu}}{\text{son être}} = \dfrac{\text{créature}}{\text{son être}}$ le premier rapport étant nul, la proportion elle-même sera purement logique, sans aucun fondement, purement fictive."

[7] *De ver.*, XXIII, 7, ad 9. Cf. *S. th.*, I, 14, 3, ad 2; IV *Sent.*, XLIX, 2, 1, ad 2, *et alibi passim.*

The charge that the relation of God to His being is "nul," is also groundless; for, although there is no real relation here, there is a logical one. This relation is indeed based on a purely logical distinction, because God is absolutely identical with His being. In the proportion stated above, the term "God" stands for the Divine Essence, the words "His being" stand for the Divine *Esse*. Between them, there is no real distinction at all. But *essence* and *being* signify different concepts; and when we apply these concepts to God, we know that they signify absolutely the same Thing, namely, God Himself, not different "aspects" of God. But we are also aware of the fact that these concepts do not signify Him in the same way: hence, while the distinction between them has no basis whatever in God, it does have a basis in us—in our creaturely mode of conceiving—and this purely logical distinction is sufficient to found a relation.[8] Thus our "theological proportion" (God/His being = creature/its being) merely signifies that the *commensuration* between essence and existence in the creature is found also in God, *suo modo*.[9] In fact, the following proposition clearly implies that, for St. Thomas, the identity of two of these terms, coupled with a real distinction between the other two, does not prevent the setting up of a proportion: "God is related to being (*se habet ad esse*) in a way other than any creature, for He is His own being, and of no creature is this true." [10]

[8] Cf. Balthasar, *L'être et les principes métaphysiques* (Louvain, 1914), p. 88, note 2.

[9] Cf. Penido, *Le rôle*, p. 145.

[10] *De pot.*, VII, 7: "Deus alio modo *se habet* ad esse quam aliqua alia creatura; nam ipse est suum esse, quod nulli alii creaturae competit."

The point is that analogy of proper proportionality does not require that the terms of the similar relations be really distinct. When we say that God "is to" His being as the creature "is to" its being, the first relation is an identity; yet analogy of proper proportionality remains in effect, because it concerns only the likeness of relations involved and simply abstracts from the fact that this instance of proportional likeness requires in the case of the first relation, identity, and in the second, distinction. The analogy itself likewise abstracts from the "distance" not merely between the terms of the relations, but between the relations themselves. Thus St. Thomas points out that likeness which consists in agreement of proportions holds in the case of things which are very "distant" from one another, as well as between things which are relatively "close"; for example, the likeness of *proportionality* between 2 and 1, and 6 and 3, is no greater than that between 2 and 1, and 100 and 50.[11] Of course this example is not to be taken as an illustration of *analogy* of proportionality itself, since mathematical proportions are not analogies but univocities in the form of analogies. The illustration merely serves to indicate a general property of proportionality, namely, its complete indifference to the natures of the terms related and indeed to the character of the relations themselves.

11 *De ver.*, II, 11, ad 4.

CHAPTER XXII

THE ESSENCE OF METAPHYSICAL ANALOGY

1. VIRTUAL QUANTITY, PROPORTION, PROPORTIONALITY

WE HAVE pointed out [1] that analogy means proportion, and that according to the first imposition of the term, proportion is nothing other than a certain relation of one dimensive quantity, continuous or discrete, to another such quantity, and further, that quantity of this sort (i.e., of mass or extension) is the proper subject of mathematics. Moreover, it was shown [2] that philosophical analogy is not defined in terms of mathematical quantity, because in that case analogy would be reduced to univocity. If dimensive quantity were the only kind of quantity, then analogy would be basically mathematical. However, in the order of perfection or completion, that is, of the realization of the essential natures of things, there is a certain *virtual* quantity.[3] From the fact that a thing *is*, it has virtual quantity as regards its perfection in the order of being.[4]

Therefore, while dimensive quantity exists only in corporeal things, virtual quantity exists in all things. Thus

[1] Introduction, sect. B, no. 4.
[2] *Ibid.*
[3] Cf. St. Thomas, *S. th.*, I, 42, 1, ad 1; *De ver.*, XXIX, 3 ("ad cujus evidentiam . . . ").
[4] *De ver., loc. cit.*

the term proportion, which was first invented to signify the relation of one dimensive quantity to another (e.g., the relation of a surface to a surface or of a number to a number), was extended to signify any relation whatever of virtual quantity to virtual quantity. But in this sense, quantity is transcendental: it "wanders through" all the categories, because it is bound up with the very being of things. Virtual quantity resides first of all in the perfection of the form or nature of a thing. Thus heat is called *great* because of its intensity or perfection. Since the act of being, the *esse,* of a thing is in a sense determined by its form or nature, virtual quantity is found also in this order. Moreover, since every agent acts *through* its nature, and its power of acting is more or less perfect relatively to its nature, it is evident that virtual quantity exists in the order of operation as well.[5]

If virtual quantity has such a broad, indeed transcendental, meaning, it is clear that *proportion* does also. Yet there is no compelling reason why this term should be limited even to relations between virtual quantities; and in fact "proportion" has been extended to designate any relation whatever of one thing to another.[6] Thus matter may be said to be proportionate to form; the knowable object to the knowing faculty; the effect to its cause; potency to act, and conversely.[7]

[5] Cf. St. Thomas, *S. th.*, I, 42, 1, ad 1; I–II, 52, 1; V *Meta.*, XVIII, n. 1037 f. See also I *Sent.*, XIX, 3, 1, where St. Thomas shows that only virtual quantity exists in God.

[6] Cf. St. Thomas, *S. th.*, I, 12, 1, ad 4; *De ver.*, VIII, 1, ad 6.

[7] Cf. St. Thomas, *De ver.*, loc. cit.; *S. th.*, III, Suppl., 92, 1, ad 6; *S. th.*, I, 12, 1, ad 4.

Composite (as distinguished from simple) proportion requires at least four terms and is called *proportionality*. In mathematics, proportionality designates the strict equality of two relations, taking equality according to the first imposition of the term as referring to mathematical quantities. When St. Thomas defines proportionality as the equality of two proportions,[8] therefore, he is giving primarily its mathematical definition; but when he speaks of proportionality as the likeness of two proportions,[9] he is giving its properly metaphysical definition.

Just as there is a simple proportion between 4 and 2, and 20 and 10, in the order of dimensive quantity, so there is a simple proportion between matter and form in the physical order, and in the metaphysical order between essence and existence. And just as there is equality in the proportions between 4 and 2, and 20 and 10, so there is likeness in the proportions between matter and form, and essence and existence. Indeed, proportion is itself proportional. Thus proportion of virtual quantity : proportion of dimensive quantity : : proportionality of virtual quantity : proportionality of dimensive quantity.[10] Analogy has no univocal basis: all the modes of analogy are themselves mutually analogous.

It is convenient to express metaphysical and theological analogies in the form of geometrical proportions; e.g.,

---

8 V *Eth.*, V, n. 939 f.

9 *De ver.*, XXIII, 7, ad 9; IV *Sent.*, XLIX, 2, 1, ad 6.

10 Cf. St. Thomas, *S. th.*, III, Suppl., 92, 1, ad 6; *De ver.*, VIII, 1, ad 6; *C.G.*, III, 54, *in fine; De Trin.*, I, 2, ad 3; III *Sent*, I, 1, 1, ad 3; Cajetan, *De Dom.*, IX; Ramirez, "De Analogia . . . ," *La Ciencia Tomista*, XXIV (July–December, 1921), 23–25.

$$\frac{\text{matter}}{\text{form}} = \frac{\text{potency}}{\text{act}} \; ; \; \frac{\text{the created}}{\text{participated being}} = \frac{\text{The Uncreated}}{\text{unparticipated}}$$
$$\text{being.}$$

If such formulas are interpreted in a mathematical or quasi-mathematical sense, however, they will only serve as obstacles to understanding analogies of that sort.[11] All school children are acquainted with "proportions" and they know that they are all based on terms which have identically the same meaning in the case of each proportion. It is therefore "natural" to look for a univocal idea at work in any allegedly philosophical analogy expressed in the form of a mathematical proportion. Consequently one may feel that there is something fictitious or "fraudulent" about the claim that there are certain proportions or proportionalities which are not founded on any univocal notions at all but on ideas which are only "analogically" or "proportionately" common to the terms involved. Little wonder, then, that some critics persist (often unwittingly) in seeking a univocal foundation for every conceivable analogy.

Proportion can be understood either strictly or broadly. Strictly, proportion designates the relation of two quantities, dimensive or virtual, according to a determinative excess or adequation. If you have more than two terms, therefore, or even if you have only two terms the relation between which is not determinate or finite, then in either case you will not have proportion in the strict sense. Hence when St. Thomas denies that there is any proportion between the finite and the infinite, between God and

11 Cf. above, chap. 21, note 3; also Penido, *Le rôle*, pp. 22 f.; Le Rohellec, "De Fundamento . . . ," *Divus Thomas* (Placentiae), 1926, p. 79.

creatures, it is because they are not proportional to one another in this strict, determinate, or finite way.[12] Broadly considered, however, there is a proportion between two terms which are even infinitely distant, and in this sense St. Thomas admits a proportion between the creature and God. That is to say, when the term "proportion" designates any relation whatever of one thing to another, it can be truly said that there is a *proportion* between the creature and God.[13]

2. "PROPORTIONAL LIKENESS"

To conceive proportion-in-general univocally is to mathematize the doctrine of analogy. If the mathematical notion of quantity is expanded so that it will apply to all things, we have a "metaphysical" mathematics. This is easily accomplished by arguing that quantity, and therefore mathematics itself, is really transcendental for the simple reason (among others) that all things whatever can be numbered. This last phrase is true; but the argument fails to take into account the fact that number, in what may be called the transmathematical sense, is itself analogical, inasmuch as it cannot be predicated univocally of diverse orders of beings, such as immaterial forms and material individuals. Mathematical number in the strict sense applies only to the latter type of entity: it implies the division of matter, and it is univocal. The univocal idea of proportion, that is, the mathematical notion of equality

[12] This is evident, e.g., in De ver., II, 3, ad 4, and in II, 11 ("unde dicendum est . . . "). Cf. De ver., III, 1, ad 7.

[13] S. th., I, 13, 1, ad 4. See also De ver., VIII, 1, ad 6; XXIII, 7, ad 9; De pot., VII, 10, ad 9; C.G., III, 54, in fine; IV Sent., XLIX, 2, 1, ad 6; S. th., III, Suppl., XCII, 1, ad 6 ("Vel dicendum . . . ").

of ratio, may also be converted into a philosophical principle or at least considered as a useful tool in cosmological
and even metaphysical investigation.[14] In philosophy
such transpositions are not legitimate, because mathematical proportion is univocal and cannot be validly applied
outside its proper order. But the principle of proportion
itself is not univocal. In all things (indeed in all sciences)
there are proportions, analogies, because there are relations and comparisons. There are in fact as many modes of
proportion as there are modes of being. This means that
proportion is itself proportional; that analogy is itself
analogical. But there is something proportionately common to all proportions. If we abstract from all particular
proportions and types of proportion, we are left with a
notion in the highest degree universal: the notion of proportional likeness. This notion expresses the essence of
analogy as such.[15] It is the only kind of likeness we have in
the only metaphysical analogy, analogy of proper proportionality.

Whereas in a case of mathematical proportionality the
common notion is univocal in the two proportions or relations, in a case of metaphysical proportionality the
common notion is analogical in the strict sense in the two
proportions. For instance, in the proportionality, matter
is related to form as essence to existence, the common no-

[14] Cf. Plato, *Timaeus*, 31b 10–32c 3; and Socrates' remark to Callicles
(*Gorgias*, 508a 6) to the effect that geometrical equality, that is, equality of
ratio, is "most potent in heaven and on earth." Interesting remarks on Plato's
use of μάθημα, μαθήματα, and ἀναλογία, are found in Heath, *History of Greek
Mathematics*, I, 10 f., and in A. E. Taylor, *A Commentary on Plato's Timaeus*
(Oxford, 1928), pp. 95 f.

[15] Cf. Ramirez, *art. cit., La Ciencia Tomista*, XXIV (July–December, 1921),
30.

tion is that of potency-act, which is realized diversely in both proportions, because it is a question of two different orders of reality, the physical and the metaphysical, hence of two essentially diverse modes of being.[16] The community here is only relative or proportional. The same applies to truth as attributed to the divine intelligence, the human intelligence, and to things: "The divine intellect is a measure that is not measured; natural things are measures which are at the same time measured; but our intellect is not a measure; it is only a thing that is measured." [17]

Therefore, when we use the expression "proportional likeness" to designate the very essence of analogy, we are saying that the character of analogy as such is not that of something common to the terms in any given analogy, but to the relations between them. Analogy, then, is likeness of proportions, proportional likeness: *similitudo ad invicem proportionum*.[18] The essence of metaphysical analogy lies in proportionality.

---

[16] Form, considered in itself, is metaphysical, whereas form-matter is physical (cf. *De ente et essentia*, IV, V). "The analogous is divided according to diverse modes" (St. Thomas, I *Sent.*, XXII, 1, 3, ad 2).

[17] St. Thomas, *De ver.*, I, 2, c. ("Sic ergo . . . ").

[18] Cf. St. Thomas, *De ver.*, II, 11; XXIII, 7, ad 9, *et alibi*.

Le Rohellec argues (in *Divus Thomas*, Placentiae, Vol. XXIX, 1926; pp. 91 f.) that if we hold that the analogous term directly signifies the relation itself of proportionality or the likeness itself of the proportions, then we shall not be able to distinguish between proper and improper proportionality. But Penido points out that this argument ignores the fact that analogy of proportionality dominates its modes; therefore we must have a definition which applies both to proper and to improper proportionality, and this definition, Penido says, can only be *likeness of proportions*. Hence he correctly states that the analogous term, as analogous, directly signifies the likeness of *proportions* (emphasis on "proportions"), while connoting the form according to which that term is found intrinsically but in diverse modes in all its inferiors (*Le rôle*, pp. 25 f.).

3. The "Participation" of Analogy

In the case of univocals, we have the same name applied to different things according to a formality that is absolutely the same in them all. Of such a character are universals strictly so-called, that is, generic and specific concepts.[19] Things designated equivocally are not only absolutely diverse in essence; there is no order between them, and likeness only in name. Equivocation is of course a barrier to all rational argument. In the case of analogy, however, we have the same term applied to diverse things according to a formality that is partly the same and partly different in each of them.[20] Since analogy partakes both of the identical and of the diverse, it is said to "participate" in univocity on the one hand, and pure equivocity on the other. It is of crucial importance to understand precisely what this participation is; for the nature of analogy itself is involved. As far as I know, Father Ramirez has analyzed this participation more closely than anyone else. He shows that there are four possibilities.[21]

First, if the participation were absolutely equal, then analogicals would be defined as things designated by a single term, the concept signified thereby being at once absolutely the same (as participating in univocity) and absolutely diverse (as participating in equivocity). In other words, the concept would be at once absolutely the same and absolutely different as applied to its analogates.

19 On the properties of univocal concepts, see *C.G.*, I, 32; cf. F. A. Blanche, "La notion de l'analogie . . . ," p. 171.

20 St. Thomas, XI *Meta.*, III, n. 2197; IV *Meta.*, I, n. 535. Cf. Cajetan, *De nom.*, VI, pp. 53 f.

21 Ramirez, *art. cit., loc. cit.,* pp. 34 f.

This is plainly self-contradictory. Such participation, then, is not even a possibility in the sense of a real possibility.

Secondly, if this participation were relatively equal in both extremes, then analogicals would be defined as things designated by a single term, the concept signified thereby being at once relatively the same (as participating in univocity) and relatively different (as participating in equivocity). Nor is this a real possibility, although at first sight this definition may appear plausible. Nothing is purely or merely relative. Not even relation is relative. (If a purely relative relation is conceivable at all, it would perhaps be equivalent to the thought of nothingness or of "pure being" in the Hegelian sense.) The point is that there can be no analogy where participation is simply relative and equal, because in that case the "analogy" would be reduced to relations with nothing related.

Thirdly, if this participation were absolutely or simply unequal, but consisted in sharing more in univocity than in equivocity, then analogicals would be defined as things designated by a single term, the concept signified thereby being essentially the same (as participating in univocity) and relatively diverse (as participating in equivocity). It is evident that this definition would turn analogy into a fundamental univocity: analogy would be absorbed into univocity or confounded with it. Moreover, if the word *"ratio"* designates the root of intelligibility in things, and if this is the same in all things, then there would be no substantial or essential diversity in things. But, as we have seen, even univocal predication presupposes a plurality of substances really distinct. So if this definition were the true one, univocal as well as analogical predication would be impossible: all propositions would be tautological and all terms essentially synonymous. This definition, in fact, would apply only if reality were truly pantheistic, i.e., if reality were essentially and substantially only one.

Lastly, if this participation is simply unequal, but consists in sharing in equivocity more than in univocity, then analogicals will be defined as things designated by a single term, the concept signified thereby being simply or absolutely diverse and relatively the same. This definition is the only really possible one. For, as compared with univocity, analogy entails a certain diversity. Indeed, the very existence of analogy lies in the fact that the *ratio* signified by the analogous term is, logically speaking, equivocal in itself, yet in some way (i.e., proportionately) applies to all its inferiors.

This is true of all properly metaphysical ideas; for they all flow from being and are reducible to being, the concept of which is simply diverse in respect of all beings, yet relatively or, more precisely, proportionately, the same.

4. THE ULTIMATE BASIS OF ANALOGY

All beings are proportionately one in being: they are all brought together in a community of relations in virtue of their common participation in existence. Yet every being, in respect of its very act of being, is diverse simply from every other being. Thus analogy is not a weak univocity; nor is it merely the least common denominator between univocity and equivocation. On the contrary, analogy is based on the diversity of the acts of existing exercised by existing things, and the similarity of the relations between those acts (*esse's*) and the subjects receiving them (*supposita*). The relations in which any two essences stand to their own acts of existing immediately establish an analogy of proper proportionality. (As we have seen, this holds even in the case of material individuals of the same species.) If we reflect upon this elemental "analogy," it should not be difficult to see that it embraces all beings; for all (even possibles, privations, and negations) are united through the fact that, in some way, they *are*. But if we see this, we shall also perceive that this unity is, and can only be, proportional, because it consists solely in the analogical community of relations which all entities maintain with one another through their act of being, in any order and mode exercised.[22] Analogy is the unique bond of union between everything that is.

Only a genuine analogy has scientific, demonstrative value, and we have such an analogy only where the members of the analogy are somehow unified through the actual possession of a common entity. Without this internal, entitative unity, the argument-by-analogy lacks a true middle term.[23] The analogous form, as common term in which all

[22] Cf. St. Thomas, *De nat. generis*, I; I *Sent.*, XXXV, 1, 4.

[23] Cf. Manser, "Das Wesen des Thomismus," *Divus Thomas* (Frib., 1929), pp. 397 f.
It is interesting to note that Bishop Butler's famous *Analogy of Religion* was not intended to be demonstrative in the strict sense, because the Bishop fully realized that, although arguments based on similarities might indeed have a high degree of probability (and hence of persuasiveness), they could not be advanced as *proofs*. (Cf. Joseph Butler, D.C.L., *The Analogy of Religion, Natural and Revealed, to the Constitution and Course of Nature*, ed. by the Right Hon. W. E. Gladstone (Oxford: Clarendon Press, 1897), esp. pp. 7, 9, 13.

the analogates share, must be present in the analogates formally and likewise actually. And of such a character is being.

Being is in the highest degree "formal" in all things,[24] in all degrees, kinds, differences, and properties of things, so that without it they would be nothing at all. If being were univocal, there would be only one essence, hence only one being, hence no multiplicity, hence absolute monism. If being were univocal, it would be a genus. But being is essentially included in everything of which it is predicated; consequently it cannot be limited or determined by any differentiating element or formality, and for that reason it cannot be a genus.[25]

The analogates of being, that is, all beings, are mutually diverse and have unity only in virtue of the fact that being is present in them as their act. Thus metaphysical analogy is rooted in the transcendental-ontological relation in which all beings stand in respect to their own acts of being. This is why it is said that "the ultimate metaphysical basis of every analogy is the doctrine of potency and act." [26] But it is more accurate to say that the ultimate basis of every analogy is the *division* of being by potency and act.[27] To see the truth of this proposition, we need only bear in mind the fact that all analogy presupposes multiplicity. Remove multiplicity, and you remove analogy—and indeed, univocity as well. But without the real division of being

24 Cf. St. Thomas, *S. th.*, I–II, 94, 2; *De pot.*, III, 16, ad 4, *et alibi.*

25 Cf. *S. th.*, I, 3, 5; *C.G.*, I, 25; Manser, *art. cit.*, p. 402.

26 K. Feckes, "Die Analogie in unserem Gotterkennen . . . ," p. 162; cf. Manser, *art. cit.*, p. 398.

27 Cf. Le Rohellec, "De Fundamento . . . ," *Divus Thomas* (Placentiae, 1926), p. 686.

by potency and act, the multiplication of beings is impossible, and Parmenides' dilemma remains.

The first or primary composition of potency and act is
the composition of essence and act of existence—of existing (*esse*) [28]—by which finite being is distinguished from
infinite being, participated or received from unparticipated or unreceived being.[29] Of itself, act is unlimited in
the sense that it signifies nothing other than *esse* itself,
apart from any admixture of potentiality, that is, of capacity for being. Act is limited only by a potency distinct from
it, and it is limited if the act is itself in potency to some
higher act. Thus *esse* is limited by essence, and form by
matter. But form is the act of matter and, along with
matter, is in potency to existence. No actuality is limited so
far as it is actual or in act, but only so far as it is in some way
potential or in potency.

Since limitation comes from potency, which of its very
nature is an imperfection and a restriction, it follows that
multiplicity stems from the potential element. If a perfection (an essence or a form) is multiplied, it is divided, and
if it is divided, it is limited. Being received in a subject
which limits it, it is not a complete perfection; it is not
self-subsistent or independent. There can be a multiplication of acts, or perfections, or of forms only if the subjects
which receive them are multiplied correspondingly. This
subjectivity is precisely the receptive capacity we call potentiality. So, wherever there is the finite and the multiple,

[28] Since *existence* is a substantive, it is less misleading to use the word *esse*
to signify being itself, that is to say, the *act* "to be."
[29] Cf. St. Thomas, VIII *Phys.*, XXI, n. 13. See also *De Heb.*, II; *De ver.*,
XXVII, 1, ad 8; *De pot.*, I, 2; *De ente*, V; *C.G.*, II, 52; *S. th.*, I, 3, 7, ad 1, *et
alibi passim.*

there is an act that is received, a capacity or subjective potency which restricts that act in receiving it and divides it in communicating it to a plurality of subjects. In a word, wherever there is the finite and multiple, there is real composition of potency and act; where act is pure and unreceived, there is only the limitless and the unique.[30]

The distinction between essence and act of existing is analogically the same as the distinction between potency and act. If, outside God, there is a real distinction between the first two, there is also, of course, a real distinction between the second two. If there is no real distinction between essence and act of existing in things other than God, then there is no analogy of being: if being were not realized in many modes, then being would not be predicated in many modes; it would be attributed to all things —to God as well as to creatures—univocally. Thus we should have to say that just as God *is*, inasmuch as He has being really identical with His essence, so the creature *is*, inasmuch as it has being really identical with its essence.

For where there is no diverse order to being, predication remains entirely univocal. Yet if being is univocal in this sense, then so likewise are all other perfections. Moreover, if being is univocal, it is a genus; and if it is a genus, then it is as such a purely logical entity. But if being is a purely logical entity, then there is no existential analogy, for such analogy requires diversity in modes of existing. Remove the analogy of being, and you remove all diversity in modes of existing, and hence all actual analogy. It is

[30] Cf. St. Thomas, *C.G.*, I, 43; *Comp. theol.*, XVIII; *C.G.*, I, 28; II, 52; *De ente*, V; *De subst. sep.*, VIII, *in fine;* I *Sent.*, XLIII, 1, 1–2; *De ver.*, II, 2, ad 5, etc.

therefore clear that analogy is based on the real division
of being by potency and act.

This real division is the result of creation: the continuous divine act of giving existence to things. Therefore
the relation of the world to God established by creation
is the single, positive basis of the analogy between the
world and Him. It is this real causal relation which alone
prevents equivocation in our statements about Him; for
He is truly an Agent, and His effects are linked to Him
through real relations of likeness, even though that likeness is in fact purely analogical.[31] This causal relation also
obviously prevents univocation, since God and the world
are essentially diverse.

If God is Pure Act, in whom alone essence and act of
existing are identical, it follows that if any other beings
exist, they are dependent upon Him and receive their
being from Him. All the Thomistic arguments for creation are based on the principle that God alone is pure act,
all other things being composed of potency and act, of
essence and *esse*.[32] The act of creation is the positing in

[31] Cf. Josef Habbel, *Die Analogie zwischen Gott und Welt nach Thomas von
Aquin*, pp. 67 ff.

[32] The doctrine of creation in St. Thomas is a special application of the doctrine of potency and act. Arguing from the proposition that God is *ens a se* (the
result of the Five Ways), in whom alone essence and *esse* are identical,
St. Thomas, in opposition to two of the keenest thinkers of his time, Albertus
Magnus and Maimonides, showed that the creation of all things *ex nihilo*
(i.e., from no pre-adjacent matter) is philosophically demonstrable. (Cf. Manser,
art. cit., *Divus Thomas*, Fribourg, Vol. IX, 1931; pp. 335 f.)

St. Thomas uses a number of arguments to demonstrate creation (e.g., in
C.G., II, 15), but they are all derived from the principle referred to above.
The following texts are among the most significant in this connection: II *Sent.*,
I, 1, 2; *S. th.*, I, 44, 1; *De subst. sep.*, VII; *Comp. theol.*, LXVII; *De pot.*, III,
5, 6; cf. also *S. th.*, I, 44, 2; *C.G.*, II, 16.

Although creation (which is distinct from all other forms of production,
such as generation and emanation) is philosophically demonstrable, the doc-

existence of analogues of the Author of that act. Since the existence of every being is given to it by Him who is Existence, every existent is a created analogue of its Author; and, as such, it participates in Him and imitates Him existentially. But existential participation (the only possible mode of metaphysical participation in God open to the creature, for there is no community of essence whatever between them) is intrinsically analogical. Now, since creation introduces essential diversity and actual multiplicity, it clearly establishes "the analogy of being," which in turn founds the analogy of the predication of being: *ens est multipliciter, ergo ens dicitur multipliciter.*[33]

But the fact that the analogy of being follows, so to say, automatically from the very act of creation, really signifies that the ultimate ground of that Analogy is none other than the divine act of existing itself: the unique act which, in and through *itself,* is imitable analogically in infinite ways, since its existence knows no bounds.

5. SUMMARY AND NOTE ON ANALOGY AS A PRINCIPLE OF BEING

Only in analogy of proper proportionality is the common analogous character actually and by intrinsic necessity present in all its analogates. It is for this reason that proper proportionality is the only metaphysical analogy.[34]

---

trine of creation was never philosophically formulated prior to the Christian era. Gilson has shown (*L'esprit de la philosophie médiévale;* Paris: Vrin, 1932, 1st series, pp. 77 ff.) that the notion of creation, while not in itself unattainable by human reason, was, as a matter of historical fact, a contribution of Christian revelation to the treasury of philosophical ideas.

[33] Cf. St. Thomas, IV *Meta.,* I, n. 535 f.

[34] Cf. Cajetan, *De nom.,* III. "Without a knowledge of this analogy," Cajetan

Metaphysical analogy bears on the likeness of proportions or relations between diverse modes of being of proportionately the same reality. The proportional likeness which is the basis of metaphysical analogy is a "likeness of unlike things" (*similitudo dissimilium* [35]) that is not, as in the case of univocal likeness, founded on any specific or generic unity, however tenuous or remote this may be, but on diverse and unequal participation in an essential perfection which is proportionately common to all the members of every such analogy.[36]

Analogical likeness is opposed to all degrees of univocal likeness; analogical unity is opposed to all degrees of univocal unity. Popular analogies, experimental analogies, linguistic analogies, logical analogies (in the modern arguments-by-analogy), pseudo-analogies of inequality: all are based on some sort of univocal likeness, whether specific or generic, distant or close. Nor, despite the fact that they bear on the relations between terms and not on the terms related, do mathematical analogies realize the notion of true analogical likeness, because they are by their very nature based on univocal concepts. Moreover, despite certain differences (which have been considered at length in the chapters devoted to these analogies), both analogy of attribution and analogy of metaphor involve concepts which are univocal in themselves and which are only employed "analogically." Analogy of proper proportion-

---

says (*ibid.*, n. 29), "metaphysical arguments are . . . artless": *sine huius analogiae notitia, processus metaphysicales absque arte dicuntur.*

[35] St. Thomas, *Commentary on Psalm XXXIV*, v. 7.

[36] Cf. St. Thomas, *De ver.*, II, 11, ad 2; *De pot.*, III, 4, ad 9; I *Sent.*, XLVIII, 1, 1.

ality, therefore, is alone properly analogical, if for no other reason than that this analogy alone has to do with a concept which is analogical in itself, in the sense that it can be realized intrinsically and formally (though proportionately) in each and every one of the subjects of which it is predicated. Only the properly analogical concept has a properly analogical unity, a unity of proportionality; yet in analogy of attribution and in metaphorical analogy, there is not even this sort of unity, imperfect though it is.[37]

While the term "analogy" elicits and stands for many problems, in metaphysics it primarily and fundamentally designates a principle and not a problem. For an "existentialist" (in the sense that St. Thomas was an existentialist) metaphysical analogy is intrinsically evident, like the principle of identity, for example. The inner connection of these two principles, in fact, may be indicated by the following propositions: the principle of identity (which, understood metaphysically, is no tautological axiom) signifies that being is not non-being, that that which exists, exists, that being is be-ing; while the principle of analogy signifies that, though every being is diverse from every other in point of its own act of being, all beings are (proportionately) one in be-ing. In its root meaning, therefore, metaphysical analogy could be considered problematical only were the existence of things considered problematical.

If a sound existential metaphysics is a science ordered to the *esse* of things (unintelligible, because non-existent,

[37] Cf. Maritain, *Degrés*, p. 823.

apart from the *Esse* who is God), there is no escaping the consequence that metaphysical analogy is a first principle of that science: a principle not made by the human intelligence but inscribed in the existence of beings by Being.

What folly, then, to conceive philosophy as essentially an endless search for dialectical solutions of dialectical problems rather than an effort (conclusive at points but never completely achieved) to penetrate the real ever more deeply through a progressive understanding of the *actual* significance of principles of being!

CHAPTER XXIII

ANALOGY AND THE POSSIBILITY OF SCIENCE

1. On "Being as Being"

THIS ancient phrase [1] is held to designate the "formal object of metaphysics." But it is an apparently meaningless repetition of a word which, closely scrutinized, seems to have no actual content at all. For presumably "being as being" is being as such, and being as such is being in general. But being in general is no thing at all; it is a mere abstract idea. It may be granted that *being* is the most universal of all universal ideas, yet even so, it obviously does not stand for anything real, and consequently it cannot be the "object" or the "subject" of any kind of science properly speaking. As a matter of fact, Berkeley showed that abstract general ideas do not give us any real knowledge of things as they are; Kant proved that "being" is not a real predicate; Hegel pointed out that Pure Being is indistinguishable from Nothing. Therefore, since every science requires a definite subject-matter, it is clear that metaphysics, as a science of "pure being" or of "being as being," is a non-existent science.[2]

Certainly, if metaphysics is concerned with "being"

[1] Cf. Aristotle's *Metaphysics,* Bk. III (Γ), 1. St. Thomas refers to it as Book IV.
[2] Cf. R. G. Collingwood, *An Essay on Metaphysics* (Oxford: Clarendon Press, 1940), chap. 2.

in that sense, it is the name not of a science but of a mistake. But metaphysics has nothing to do with being in that sense. *Being as being* means being in the sense of essence (that in virtue of which every being is *what* it is), as *existing* or as capable of *existing;* hence metaphysics is concerned with that which really is or really can be, and not with the idea of pure being or being in general or existence as such.[3]

The emphasis falls on the word "existing"; for metaphysics bears primarily on the *act* of being. It is in virtue of *esse,* not of *essentia,* that beings *exist.* And metaphysics is not a philosophy of form or essence, that is to say, of being *qua* intelligible or possible: "It is a philosophy of whatever is or can be in any manner whatever, considered specifically in the light of the ultimate existential actuality of all reality, the act of being (*esse*)." [4]

[3] Aristotle's "being as being" has nothing in common with Collingwood's version of it as "the limiting case of the abstractive process" (*op. cit.,* p. 14): the notion of "pure being," which indeed is equivalent to the thought of nothingness. Having shown, quite correctly, that there cannot be a science of "pure being," Collingwood advances the theory that metaphysics is an historical science of "absolute presuppositions" (*op. cit.,* chap. 6, *et alibi*). Yet, since his refutation of Aristotle's alleged metaphysics of Pure Being merely disposes of a misconception of what that metaphysics is about, Collingwood's proposed reduction of "first philosophy" to a type of historical study is itself without historical basis.

[4] G. B. Phelan, "A Note on the Formal Object of Metaphysics," *The New Scholasticism,* XVIII (April, 1944, no. 2), 199.

"It is this ultimate formal constituent of being as such, namely, the act of being (*esse*) which, when grasped by the intellect, specifies the habitus of metaphysical wisdom and differentiates it from every other habitus of knowledge. The act of being (*esse*) in itself cannot strictly speaking be defined by any finite mind. It needs to be linked with some, at least vague, notion of a thing which exercises this act. But when the metaphysician thinks of being, he thinks primarily of the act by which all being is (*esse*) and only secondarily of the thing or quiddity which exercises this act and which is, at it were, but the vehicle by which the knowledge of that act (*esse*) is transported to the mind and the staff or stay or prop which upholds it in conception" (p. 198). Dr. Phelan goes on to point out (p. 199) that whereas, in the initial act of the

2. THE UNITY OF ANALOGY

The unity of metaphysics, and hence its very existence as a science, is made possible only through the reduction of its multiform objects (substance, accident, becoming, the opposites—even non-being) to the analogical unity of being. This reduction can be effected, for, though being is diversely participated in all things, it nonetheless in some way exists in them all.

The unity of analogy is a unity of relation: *habitudo ad esse*. All entities, however different, are *ordered to being*, and consequently to all the other transcendentals. Thus all efficient causes agree in that they produce effects; all effects in that they are produced; all final causes in that they are ordered to the good; and everything potential is ordered to act, and thereby to being and unity. All causes therefore entail an intrinsically necessary relation to being. We are able to attain an analogy in which essentially diverse things are somehow "made one," because they all stand in the same transcendental relation (*habitudo ad esse*); because they are all beings and, as such, are one, true, good; because, in various ways, they are all causes, and, with the exception of God, are all effects; because they are all potential in respect of their changeable character, and are ordered to *act* as to their end. All beings, then, have a relation, a proportion, to being, and

---

intellect, the concept of being is, so to speak, wrapped up in the concrete apprehension of sensible qualities and only vaguely grasped, in the metaphysical concept of being as being, the reverse is true, viz., "the quidditative substream" of the act of being is only vaguely and implicitly conceived, while the act of being is itself explicitly envisaged and "stands at the focus of intellectual intuition."

herein they all are one. Even non-being stands to being in
a certain relation; for, though its "being" is purely mental,
it is nevertheless said to *be*, analogically.[5] "In analogicals
we do not consider different realities, but different modes
of being of the same reality"; [6] and that *same reality* is a
reality which is proportionately one in all its inferiors.
Such is being; such is every metaphysical object.

3. SCIENCE AND THE ANALOGY OF BEING

The statement that the "salvation of metaphysics" lies
in analogy [7] has a hyperbolical tone, but it is literally true
that without this principle metaphysics is lost; it is fin-
ished; indeed, it cannot even begin unless analogy is at

---

5 Cf. St. Thomas, *De ver.*, II, 11, ad 5; " . . . ipsum non ens, ens dicitur
analogice."

6 Cf. Penido, *Le rôle*, p. 54, note 2.

7 Cf. *ibid.*, p. 97.

Not only is analogy a first principle in metaphysics, it is equally important
for a "sane philosophy of culture," as Maritain shows (*True Humanism;* New
York: Scribner's, 1938): "It is this principle of analogy which dominates all
Thomist metaphysics and according to which the highest ideas are realised in
existence in a way which is essentially diverse, while all the while keeping
their proper formality, which must be our guiding star" (p. 131). "St. Thomas
and Aristotle," he goes on, "made use of it in their political philosophy, and
that in the most far-reaching way, apropos of the various political systems and
specifically different types of *common good* which correspond to each of these."
. . . "It is a like analogical diversity which it seems to me valuable to bring
to light with regard, not to political systems, but to types of culture and Christian civilization" (p. 132). Maritain therefore argues that a vitally Christian
society today must be realized in terms of a "new concrete analogue" (p. 133),
"founded on the same principles (analogically applied) as those of the Middle
Ages," yet implying a *"secular Christian,* not a consecrational, conception of
the temporal order" (p. 156). Hence he develops his conception of a "pluralist
commonwealth," bringing together in an organic unity a vast number of
diverse social groupings and structures, based on positive liberties and realizing
in different ways the common principles of a true Christian society (pp. 157 ff.).
The principle of analogy is employed also in his theory of economic and jurid-
ical pluralism (pp. 158 f.). The significance of this principle in Maritain's
political philosophy is also seen in *The Rights of Man and Natural Law*
(Eng. tr.; New York: Scribner's, 1943; e.g., pp. 51 f.).

least implicitly at work from the start. For being is analogical in itself: being is "realized" diversely, yet proportionately, in all things whatever. Since the formal object of metaphysics, namely, *ens in quantum ens,* is analogical, it follows that all properly metaphysical notions are analogical, for they all stem from, and are reducible to, being. And if all science treats of being, under one aspect or another,[8] it follows that every science *presupposes* the analogy of being. This is evident from the fact that any sort of scientific knowledge requires the reduction of a multiplicity of objects or of data to some kind of unity: the multiple, as multiple, is not intelligible. This is another way of saying that for us there is no science of particulars or individuals as such: they can be known intellectually only through universals, that is, through certain unitary concepts which reveal something that is common to each class of them. Thus scientific knowledge requires that the *same* notion apply to *several* things. Now if those things are simply heterogeneous, having nothing whatever in common, then they cannot be known scientifically in any legitimate sense of the term. On the other hand, if they are all homogeneous or identical in essence, then our "knowledge" of them would consist of a number of propositions all having essentially the same meaning; and in the last analysis our "science" would be reduced to a tautology.

Ontological *equivocity* means diversity without unity; ontological *univocity* means unity without diversity. In

---

[8] St. Thomas, IV *Meta.,* I, 530: "Scientiae aliae, quae sunt de entibus particularibus, considerant quidem de ente, cum omnia subjecta scientiarum sint entia, non tamen considerant ens secundum quod ens, sed secundum quod est *hujusmodi* ens." Cf. Aristotle, *Meta.,* IV, 1.

either case, scientific knowledge is impossible; for the first abolishes all actual oneness in things, while the second abolishes plurality and real differences. A purely heterogeneous world would be unintelligible, since it would offer no basis whatever for concepts expressing any kind or degree of community between things; and a purely homogeneous world would likewise be unintelligible, since it would offer no basis for concepts expressing the diversity in the being of things and in their operations. Only an analogical world, i.e., a *universe* embracing irreducible individuality and manyness, is scientifically intelligible; such a world alone offers a real basis for concepts expressing the "way" things actually *are* and *behave*.[9] This argument may be summed up aphoristically as follows: No real multiplicity and essential diversity, no analogy; no real unity in multiplicity or identity in diversity, no analogy; no analogy, no science.

4. THE CHARACTER OF ANALOGICAL KNOWLEDGE

In a philosophy of being (of *esse*), analogy is indeed "axiomatic" [10] and, as such, it is on the same level as the principle of identity or of non-contradiction. It is quite generally assumed that the "doctrine of analogy" is an extremely recondite metaphysical theory. But in truth analogy is itself an obvious fact: the phrase, "analogy of being," is merely a conveniently brief way of saying that things are really diverse yet at the same time really one. In itself, this is no doubt an eminently simple and even self-evident

---

9 Cf. Penido, *Le rôle,* pp. 77 f.
10 Cf. Phelan, *St. Thomas and Analogy,* p. 2.

proposition; but, like the principle of identity and all other metaphysical simplicities, analogy has far-reaching consequences and significant implications; and, while analogy may be intrinsically "axiomatic" and "self-evident," it is not necessarily so *quoad nos:* In any case there is surely just as much need in this age as there was in Cajetan's [11] to try to show what this principle actually means and to at least indicate its role in philosophical thought. There would be no occasion to devote a book to this topic if analogy were not, like the axiom of identity, largely ignored and indeed widely unknown as a principle of being and not merely of thought. For although analogy may be considered logically or dialectically [12] (in the "order of knowing" and of "signifying"), it is primarily a metaphysical principle; first and foremost it concerns the order of being (*ordo essendi*).

[11] Cf. *De nom.,* I, p. 3. The opening words of Cajetan's treatise are these: "Invitatus et ab ipsius rei obscuritate, et a nostri aevi flebili profundarum litterarum penuria, de nominum analogia in his vacationibus tractatum edere intendo." This might well have been written by someone today, though the *obscuritas ipsius rei* is dubitable. Cajetan continues: "Est siquidem eius notitia necessaria adeo, ut sine illa non possit metaphysicam quispiam discere, et multi in aliis scientiis ex eius ignorantia errores procedant."

[12] It is surprising to find analogy reduced to a logical problem in a distinguished metaphysical work by L. B. Geiger, O.P., *La participation dans la philosophie de S. Thomas d'Aquin* (Paris: Vrin, 1942); e.g., pp. 51 (note 1), 317 f. (note 3), 429, 453.

John of St. Thomas treated analogy in his *Logic,* and the very title of Cajetan's study (*De nominum analogia*) might seem to indicate that he was primarily concerned with analogy as a grammatico-logical problem. (Of course it is important to consider analogy from the standpoint of the order of knowing and of signifying, but, as Cajetan fully realized, analogy is primarily and fundamentally a metaphysical problem. Cf. *De nom.,* I.) There is evidence that John of St. Thomas did "logicize" the doctrine of analogy (cf. his theory that being, said of individuals of the same species, is not analogical), yet this cannot be said of Cajetan. Nevertheless the facts alluded to above have, I believe, helped create the impression in some Thomists' minds that analogy is essentially and primarily a logical doctrine, being part and parcel of the problem of predication or of attribution. (Cf. Geiger, *op. cit.,* pp. 274-77.)

It is the principle of analogy which alone "saves" metaphysics, and behind every science there lies the analogy of being *in-exercised-act*. Without this analogy no science would be possible. It is the principle of analogy which alone solves the "antinomy" of the one and the many, conducting us over and between (not around) monism and anthropomorphism on the one side, pluralism and agnosticism on the other.

If analogy points the way to knowledge on the higher levels, it also at the same time discloses the extreme poverty of that knowledge. For by this principle we are able to know merely that a given entity is realized proportionately, that is, through a certain likeness of relations between nature and being (*esse*), in the terms in question. For instance, we know that God exists in a manner commensurate with or proportionate to His nature; but we are absolutely ignorant of what that mode of existence is in itself; we have a purely relational knowledge of it. This does not mean that analogical knowledge is *relative* in the ordinary sense; it does however mean that analogical knowledge is extremely *thin*. It is only through analogical concepts that we can attain any scientific knowledge in metaphysics or in theology. This knowledge (as knowledge) is certain and formal and proper, yet it is slight indeed, and may even be said to be minimal. For whatever we know in metaphysics we know through the concept of being, and that concept has a very imperfect sort of unity and consequently can convey only a very imperfect sort of knowledge. The unity of being is only a unity of proportionality, consisting solely of a community of relations between nature and act of being throughout the entire realm of existence. Since all metaphysical concepts are based on and develop from the concept of being, they will all have only that relational type of unity characteristic of the latter, and they will therefore be similarly deficient as vehicles of knowledge. Univocal concepts are clear and distinct: they have a simple unity in relation to their inferiors, whereas analogical concepts have a merely proportional unity, embracing their inferiors "confusedly," indistinctly, indifferently, implicitly. Univocal concepts are quidditative: they signify the generic or specific natures or quiddities of things. Analogical concepts are non-quidditative: they do not signify natures or quiddities, but existences or modes of being, actual or possible. Univocal concepts are proper to a Cartesian mode of thought and to essentialist philosophy in general. They are out of place in a metaphysics of being.

To sum up: All analogical knowledge is imperfect, because analogical concepts do not abstract perfectly from their inferiors and therefore they have not, like univocal concepts, a simple unity, but only a proportional one. All analogical knowledge is incomprehensive, inexhaustive, non-definitive. (Only generic or specific objects can be defined.) Analogical knowledge is in the highest degree general, that is to say, *common,* and for this reason it is indistinct, as compared with the clear-cut, quidditative knowledge acquired through univocal ideas. But despite its radical deficiencies *as knowledge,* analogical knowledge is the highest and best knowledge of which we are naturally

capable. What St. Thomas says [13] about our knowledge of
"divine things" is true also of our knowledge of metaphysical things: "Of divine things, the human intellect can
ascertain but little; yet it takes keener delight in that
knowledge and desires and loves it more than the perfect
knowledge which it has of the lowest things."

[13] *C.G.*, III, 25 (*Amplius, unumquodque maxime* . . .): "Intellectus . . .
humanus magis desiderat et amat et delectatur in cognitione divinorum, quam-
vis modicum quidem de illis percipere possit, quam in perfecta cognitione
quam habet de rebus infimis."

EPILOGUE

IT IS an implied thesis of this essay that, although other philosophers have said various intelligent things about analogy and have developed various types of analogical doctrines of varying degrees of universality, it was St. Thomas alone who as a matter of historical fact made full use of this principle: a principle which indeed he found in Aristotle but which Aristotle did not develop into a full-fledged metaphysical doctrine. I did not deal directly with Aristotle's theory of analogy; an adequate account of it would require a book in itself. I here advance the hypothesis that Aristotle was chiefly concerned with analogy in predication and did not exhibit its metaphysical basis. This hypothesis I believe can be verified, but only through a fundamental critique of his First Philosophy. To have attempted any such verification in this study would have taken me too far afield.

The research behind this book, however, has not had as its object the establishment of that or any other hypothesis about analogy, but the discovery of what analogy is and how it functions. That search was conducted primarily in the field of Thomistic doctrine. It developed into a search in many other fields. But it wound up where it began, in Thomism. For all along the line it appeared increasingly clear to me that it was only in the doctrine of St. Thomas, as set forth in numerous scattered texts (he never wrote a treatise on analogy) and in the writings of some of his expositors, that analogy had a truly metaphysical status.

I started out with the belief that this was so; I ended convinced that it was. Is not this an obvious case of antecedent belief determining one's "reasoned" conclusions? Yes, in a very real sense, but in a sense broadly true of anyone's thinking. For an "open" mind, one absolutely undetermined by prejudices, that is to say pre-judgments, is not a mind, but a vacuum. But all this is psychology. The truth or falsity of a man's thinking is not determined by its psychology, nor by its history, but solely by its accord or disaccord with that which is. An analysis of all the factors, external and internal, conditioning the origin and development of a philosophical doctrine would leave completely untouched the question of its truth. Nor are those judgments philosophical (in any properly speculative sense), which in an analysis of the aforesaid sort bear upon the theological background (if any), or the psychological and sociological "determinants," of a philosophical doctrine. That is, in the nature of the case, such judgments are extra-philosophical.

Among the solid findings of modern research into the doctrinal relationships between Aristotle and St. Thomas is this fact: that the metaphysics of St. Thomas is not the simple echo of Aristotelian thought, but a new, and in certain fundamental respects, an original development. It is likewise true that Thomistic analogy is not reducible to Aristotelian analogy. Nor is Aristotle the only historical source of Thomas' teachings on analogy. There were many other influences (Arabic, Jewish, Platonic-Christian) which made it imperative in St. Thomas' eyes to establish

the principle of analogy on firmly metaphysical foundations, in order to save both philosophy and theology from
the ultimately destructive and essentially irrational consequences designated roughly by the words pantheism
and monism, anthropomorphism and agnosticism.

In exploring a wide range of systems I found a number
of cases of highly universalized symbolisms in metaphysical
and theological garb, posing as philosophical analogies.
But outside Thomism I discovered no doctrine of analogy
which was philosophical or metaphysical in the sense that
it was rooted in the very existence of things. The facts
seemed to point to the conclusion that it was only in
Thomism [1] that a metaphysical doctrine of analogy, rightly
so called, was to be found. To *demonstrate* that conclusion
would call for a speculative, historical study of vast dimensions. This essay is but a kind of propaedeutic, yet it contains, I believe, at least some of the necessary materials
for such a demonstration.

The reader will have noted that, whereas certain aspects of the philosophies of Spinoza and Leibnitz have
been dealt with, other no less important "moderns"
(Hegel and Kant, for example) have only been alluded to
in passing, while such relatively unimportant thinkers as
Bradley, Vaihinger, Höffding and Berdyaev have received
some detailed attention. I trust it is clear that not one of

[1] By "Thomism" I understand that line of philosophical and theological
thought inspired by the fundamental principles (supra-historical in themselves) operative in the actual thinking of St. Thomas Aquinas: principles
which, if true, are *eo ipso* operative, at least implicitly, in all true philosophical
and theological thinking. Of course, mere abstract titles, like the various intellectual ones ending in "ism," are frequently misleading and could well be
eliminated from philosophical discourse, if equally handy concrete substitutes
were only available.

the philosophers mentioned need have been included. That is to say, all of them (as well as some of the non-moderns) could have been omitted without affecting the main drift of the discussion; their role in this work is illustrative and therefore incidental. The basic reason for these "arbitrary" selections is the conviction that since the Renaissance the philosophers wielding the greatest general influence have done their thinking outside the tradition of existential philosophy, in the full theistic sense, with the result that analogy as a metaphysical principle and problem has no place in their systems. It is hoped that this book furnishes some evidence of the objective validity of that conviction.

BIBLIOGRAPHY

THIS bibliography includes: 1. the main original sources of the Thomistic doctrine of analogy; 2. some secondary or subsequent works respecting that doctrine; 3. other works concerning analogy, but not directly or specifically the Thomistic doctrine of analogy. The latter I have ranged in three groups: (a) ancient and medieval; (b) modern "scholastic"; (c) other modern.

Titles of articles are enclosed in quotation marks; the names of the periodicals or other works in which they are found are italicized.

I. MAIN ORIGINAL SOURCES

ARISTOTLE. *Metaphysics*, Books Γ, Δ, Θ, K, Λ (esp. Γ, 2; Λ, 4, 5).

————. *Nichomachean Ethics*, Books II; V, 6, 7.

————. *Physics*, Books IV, 8; VII, 4.

AQUINAS, St. Thomas. Commentary on Aristotle's *Metaphysics;* esp. Books IV, V, VII, IX, XI, XII (according to the numbering in St. Thomas' *Commentary*).

————. Commentary on Aristotle's *Nichomachean Ethics*, Books I, IV, V.

————. Commentary on Aristotle's *Physics*, Books I, VII, VIII.

————. Commentary on Peter Lombard's *Sentences;* esp. Book I.

————. *Summa theologica.*

————. *Summa contra Gentiles.*

————. Disputed Questions, *De potentia Dei.*

————. Disputed Questions, *De veritate.*

————. Disputed Questions, *De anima.*

————. Opusculum, *On Dionysius' "De divinis nominibus."*

————. Opusculum, *On Boethius' "De Trinitate."*

————. Opusculum, *De ente et essentia.*

————. Opusculum, *De principiis naturae.*

————. *Quodlibetal Questions.*

CAJETAN (Thomas de Vio Cardinalis Caietanus). Scripta philosophica: *De nominum analogia; De conceptu entis*. Ed. by P. N. Zammit, O.P. Rome: Institutum "Angelicum," 1934.

————. *Comment. in "Summa theologica" D. Thomae Aquinatis* (Prima pars, q. 13, a. 5).

————. *Comment. in "De ente et essentia" D. Thomae Aquinatis.* Turin: Marietti, 1934.

JOHN OF ST. THOMAS (Joannes a S. Thoma, O.P.). *Cursus philosophicus: Logica*, II (q. 13, a. 3, 4, 5). Turin, 1930.

SYLVESTER OF FERRARA (Fr. de Sylvestris Ferrariensis). *Comment. in "Summa contra Gentiles"* (Lib. I); in S. Thomae Aquinatis: *Opera omnia;* Leonine edit. Rome, 1882.

II. Secondary Works

ALVAREZ-MENENDEZ, Fr. S., O.P. "De diversitate et identitate analogica iuxta Caietanum," *La Ciencia Tomista*. Salamanca, 1934.

BALTHASAR, N. *L'être et les principes métaphysiques.* Louvain, 1914.

————. *L'abstraction métaphysique et l'analogie des êtres dans l'être.* Ed. by Em. Warny. Louvain, 1935.

BITTREMIEUX, J. *De analogica nostra Dei cognitione et praedicatione.* Louvain, 1913.

BLANCHE, F. A., O.P. "Note sur le sens de quelques locutions concernant l'analogie dans le langage de saint Thomas d'Aquin," *Revue des sciences philosophiques et théologiques.* Paris: Vrin, 1921.

————. "La notion de l'analogie dans la philosophie de saint Thomas" (*ibid.*).

————. "Une théorie de l'analogie: Eclaircissements et développements," *Revue de philosophie.* Paris: Téqui, Vol. XXXII, 1932.

————. "L'analogie," *Revue de philosophie,* 1923.

CHOLLET, A. "Analogie," *Dictionnaire de théologie catholique* (Vacant-Mangenot). Paris: Letouzey et Ane, 1908.

DEBRAISIEUX, M. *Analogie et symbolisme.* Paris: Beauchesne, 1921.

DEL PRADO, N., O.P. *De veritate fundamentali philosophiae christianae.* Fribourg (Switzerland): St. Paulusdruckerei, 1911; Lib. II, cap. xi; V, cap. i.

DE MUNNYNCK, M. "L'analogie métaphysique," *Revue néo-scolastique de philosophie,* Louvain. Editions de L'Institut Supérieur de Philosophie, 1923.

―――. "Intuition et analogie," *Atti del V Congresso intern. di filos.* Naples, 1925.

DESBUTS. "La notion d'analogie d'après saint Thomas d'Aquin," *Annales de philosophie chrétienne.* Paris: Bloud; Vol. I, 1906.

DESCOQS, P., S.J. *Institutiones metaphysicae generalis.* Paris: Beauchesne, 1925, Vol. I. Good bibliography on analogy, pp. 180–82.

DIGGS, B. J. *Love and Being.* New York: Vanni, 1946. Penetrating applications, throughout this work, of the principle of analogy to the metaphysics of love in St. Thomas Aquinas.

FECKES, K. *Die Analogie in unserem Gotterkennen, ihre metaphysische und religiöse Bedeutung.* Veröffentlichungen der Albertus-Magnus Akademie zu Köln, B, II, Heft 3. Munster, 1928.

GARDAIR, J. "L'être divin," *Revue de philosophie,* Vol. VIII, 1906.

GARDEIL, A. "Faculté de l'être ou faculté du divin?" *Revue néo-scolastique de philosophie,* 1911.

―――. "La structure analogique de l'intellect," *Revue Thomiste.* Saint-Maximin (Var.), 1926.

GARRIGOU-LAGRANGE, R., O.P. *Dieu, son existence et sa nature.* Paris: Beauchesne, 6th ed., 1933. Eng. tr. by Bede Rose: *God, His Existence and His Nature.* St. Louis, Mo.: Herder; 2 vols., 1934.

―――. "La première donnée de l'intelligence d'après saint Thomas d'Aquin," *Mélanges Thomistes.* Paris: Vrin, 1923.

GENTIL, P. "L'analogicité de l'être," *Revue Augustin,* July, 1909.

GILSON, E. *L'esprit de la philosophie médiévale.* Paris: Vrin; 2 vols., 1932; 1e série, esp. chap. 5. Eng. tr. by A. H. C. Downes: *The Spirit of Mediaeval Philosophy.* London: Sheed & Ward, 1936.

BIBLIOGRAPHY

331

———. *Le Thomisme.* Paris: Vrin, 5th ed., 1944; esp. First Part, chap. 5, sect. 2. Eng. tr. by E. T. Bullough: *The Philosophy of St. Thomas Aquinas.* Cambridge: Heffer, 2nd ed., 1929.

GOERGEN, A. *Kardinal Cajetans Lehre von der Analogie; ihr Verhältnis zu Thomas von Aquin.* Speyer: Pilger-Verlag, 1938.

GREDT, J., O.S.B. *Elementa philosophiae aristotelico-thomisticae.* Freiburg (Germany): Herder, 1937; Vol. I, pp. 131 ff.

HABBEL, J. *Die Analogie zwischen Gott und Welt nach Thomas von Aquin.* Regensburg, 1928.

LANDRY, B. "L'analogie de proportion chez S. Thomas d'Aquin," *Revue néo-scolastique de philosophie,* 1922.

———. "L'analogie de proportionnalité chez S. Thomas d'Aquin," *ibid.*

LAURENT, E., C.Sp.S. "Quelques réflexions sur l'analogie," *Acta Pont. Acad. Rom. S. Th. Aq. et Rel. Cath.,* Vol. V, 1938, Marietti, 1939.

LE ROHELLEC, J., C.Sp.S. "De fundamento metaphysico analogiae," *Divus Thomas* (Piacenza, Italy), 1926–1927 (also in "Problèmes philosophiques," articles et notes recueillis et publiés par C. Larnicol et A. Dhellemmes. Paris: Téqui, 1933).

MANSER, G. M., O.P. "Das Wesen des Thomismus," *Divus Thomas, Jahrbuch für Philosophie und spekulative Theologie.* Fribourg (Switzerland): St. Paulusdruckerei; VI (1928), VII (1929), IX (1931).

MARC, A., S.J. "L'idée thomiste de l'être et les analogies d'attribution et de proportionalité," *Revue néo-scolastique de philosophie,* Vol. XXXV, 1933.

MARÉCHAL, J. *Le point de départ de la métaphysique.* Paris: Alcan, 1926–1927; cah. I, liv, ii, iii; cah. V, liv. ii, iii.

MARITAIN, J. *Distinguer pour unir ou les degrés du savoir.* Paris: Desclée de Brouwer, 2nd ed., 1932 (Annexe II, "De l'analogie").

———. *Sept leçons sur l'être.* Paris: Téqui, 1933; esp. 4e leçon. Eng. tr., *A Preface to Metaphysics: Seven Lectures on Being.* New York: Sheed & Ward, 1940.

MORE-PONTGIBAUD, Ch. de. "Sur l'analogie des noms divins," *Recherches de science religieuse.* Paris, 1929–1930.

PATTERSON, R. L. *The Conception of God in the Philosophy of Aquinas.* London: Allen & Unwin, 1933; chaps. 5, 6, and esp. 7.

PENIDO, M. T.-L. *Le rôle de l'analogie en théologie dogmatique.* Paris: Vrin, 1931.

————. "Cajetan et nôtre connaissance analogique de Dieu," *Revue Thomiste,* Vol. XVII, 1934–1935.

PETAZZI, J. "Univocità od analogia? *Rivista di filosofia neo-scholastica.* Milan, 1911–1912.   •

PHELAN, G. B. *Saint Thomas and Analogy.* Milwaukee: Marquette Univ. Press, 1941 (The Aquinas Lecture, 1941).

RAMIREZ, J., O.P. "De analogia secundum doctrinam aristotelico-thomisticam," *La Ciencia Tomista,* 1921–1922, 1923.

ROUSSELOT, P., S.J. *L'intellectualisme de saint Thomas.* Paris: Beauchesne, 1924; 2e partie, chaps. 2, 5.

SANTELER, J. "Die Lehre von der Analogie des Seins," *Zeitschrift für katholische Theologie.* Innsbruck, 1931.

SERTILLANGES, A. D., O.P. *Agnosticisme ou anthropomorphisme.* Paris: Bloud, 1908.

SUAREZ, Fr., S.J. *Disputationes metaphysicae,* in *Opera omnia,* Vivès edit. Paris, 1877; disp. ii, xxviii, xxxii.

VAN LEEUWEN, A., S.J. "L'analogie de l'être," *Revue néo-scolastique de philosophie,* Vol. XXXIX, 1936.

III. References

A. Ancient and Medieval

EUCLID. *Elements.* Eng. tr. by Sir Thomas Heath, *The Thirteen Books of Euclid's Elements.* Cambridge Univ. Press, 2nd ed., 1926; Books V, VII, in Vol. II.

PLATO. *Dialogues,* Jowett ed. London, New York: Macmillan, 3rd ed., 1892; esp. *Phaedo,* VI, *Republic,* VI, *Sophist, Parmenides, Timaeus, Gorgias, Philebus, Politicus, Laws,* I, III, VI.

MAIMONIDES (Moses ben Maimon). *Guide for the Perplexed.* Eng. tr. by M. Friedländer. London: Routledge; New York: Dutton, 1936; esp. Part I, chaps. 1, 5, 26, 50–59.

SCOTUS, John Duns. *Opera omnia,* Wadding-Vivès edit. Paris, 1891–1895; esp. the following:

———. *Quaestiones in librum Elenchorum,* q. 1, 15, 16.

———. *Quaestiones in librum Praedicamentorum,* q. 3, 4, 6, 7.

———. *Quaestiones super universalia Porphyri,* q. 12, 28.

———. *Quaestiones quodlibetales,* q. 3, 14, 21.

———. *Quaestiones subtilissimae in metaphysicam Aristotelis,* I, q. 1; II, q. 3; IV, q. 1; VI, q. 1, 3.

———. *Quaestiones super libros Aristotelis De anima,* q. 19, 21.

———. *Opus Oxoniense,* I, d. 3, 8.

———. *Reportata Parisiensis,* Prol., q. 1, a. 2; I, d. 8, q. 5.

B. Modern "Scholastic"

BELMOND, S. *Dieu, existence et cognoscibilité* (Etudes sur la philosophie de Duns Scot). Paris: Beauchesne, 1913; 3e partie.

BIARD, A. *De l'analogie en théodicée* (thèse de doctorat). Grenoble: Brotel et Guirimand, 1909.

BOIRAC, B. "Proportion," *Grande Encyclopédie* (Ladmirault).

CHOLLET, A. "Anthropomorphisme," *Dictionnaire de théologie catholique* (Vacant-Mangenot).

CHOSSAT, M. "Agnosticisme," *Dictionnaire apologétique* (Arles).

DE LA BARRE, A., S.J. "Agnosticisme," *Dictionnaire de théologie catholique* (Vacant-Mangenot).

GILSON, E. *La philosophie de saint Bonaventure.* Paris: Vrin, 1924; chap. 7. Eng. tr. by I. Trethowan and F. J. Sheed. London: Sheed & Ward, 1938.

LANDRY, S. "La notion de l'analogie chez S. Bonaventure," *Revue néo-scolastique de philosophie,* 1922.

LE DANTEC. "Homologie et analogie," *Revue philosophique,* 1900.

MARITAIN, J. *Humanisme intégral.* Paris: Aubier, 1936; chaps. 4, 5. Eng. tr. by M. R. Adamson, *True Humanism.* London, Geoffrey Bles, 1938.

————. *Le songe de Descartes.* Paris: Correa, 1932, chap. 4. Eng. tr. by M. L. Andison, *The Dream of Descartes.* New York: Hubner & Co.

————. *Trois réformateurs: Luther, Descartes, Rousseau.* Paris: Plon, 1925. Eng. tr., Sheed & Ward, 1928.

————. *Eléments de philosophie,* Vol. II, L'ordre des concepts, I. *Petite logique* (logique formelle). Paris: Téqui, 7th ed., 1923. Eng. tr. by I. Choquette, *An Introduction to Logic.* New York and London: Sheed & Ward, 1937.

PHELAN, G. B. "A Note on the Formal Object of Metaphysics," *The New Scholasticism,* Vol. XVIII, April, 1944.

PRZYWARA, E., S. J. *Analogia entis.* Munich: Kosel u. Pustet.

SCHIRCEL, C. L., O.F.M. *The Univocity of the Concept of Being in the Philosophy of John Duns Scotus.* Washington: The Catholic University of America Press, 1942.

SOUILHÉ, S.J. *La notion platonicienne d'intermédiaire dans la philosophie des dialogues.* Paris: Alcan, 1919; esp. 1ᵉ partie, chap. 5, with conclusion.

VALENSIN, A. "Une théorie de l'analogie," *Revue apologétique.* Paris: Beauchesne, December 15, 1921.

C. Other Modern

ADAMSON, R. "Analogy (in logic)," *Dictionary of Philosophy, Psychology and Scientific Method* (J. M. Baldwin). New York, 1911, Vol. I.

ASHLEY, M. "The Nature of Hypothesis," Decennial Publications of the University of Chicago (*Studies in Logical Theory*), Vol. XI. University of Chicago Press, 1903.

BOSANQUET, B. *Logic, or the Morphology of Knowledge.* Oxford: Clarendon Press, 2 vols., 2nd ed., 1911; Vol. II, chap. 3.

BUCHANAN, S. "An Introduction to the 'De Modis Significandi' of Thomas of Erfurt," in *Philosophical Essays for Alfred North Whitehead.* London, New York, Toronto: Longmans, 1936.

BUTLER, J. *Works.* Ed. by W. E. Gladstone, 2 vols. Vol. I: *The Analogy of Religion,* etc. Oxford: Clarendon Press, 1897; esp. Introduction.

COHEN and NAGEL. *An Introduction to Logic and Scientific*

Method. New York: Harcourt Brace, 1934; chaps. XI, 6; XIV, 4; XVIII, 5.

DARWIN, C. *Origin of Species*. London, 1897; Vol. I, chap. 5; Vol. II, chap. 14.

FARRER, A. *Finite and Infinite: a Philosophical Essay*. Westminster: Dacre Press, 1943; esp. parts of chaps. 2–5 and chap. 8.

HEATH, Sir T. *A History of Greek Mathematics*. Oxford: Clarendon Press, 2 vols., 1921; esp. I, 325–27, 384 f.

HÖFFDING, H. *Der Begriff der Analogie*, ed. Reisland. Leipzig, 1924. Danish original: Copenhagen, 1923. French tr. by R. Perrin, *Le concept d'analogie*. Paris: Vrin, 1931.

JASTROW, J. *Fact and Fable in Psychology*. Boston and New York, 1900; chap. entitled "The Natural History of Analogy."

JESPERSEN, O. *Language, Its Nature, Development and Origin*. London: Allen & Unwin, 1922; pp. 70, 93, 129, 130, etc.

JOSEPH, H. W. B. *An Introduction to Logic*, 2nd ed., revised. Oxford: Clarendon Press, 1916; chap. 24.

JOYCE, G. C. "Analogy," *Encyclopaedia of Religion and Ethics* (Hastings), 1908; Vol. I.

KANT, I. *Kritik der reinen Vernunft*. Berlin; Tillgner, B. I, pp. 95 ff.

LALANDE, A. *Vocabulaire technique et critique de la philosophie*. Paris: Alcan, 1928; I, 45.

LEIBNITZ, G. W. *The Monadology and Other Philosophical Writings*, ed. by R. Latta. Oxford, 1898; esp. *Monad.*, nos. 61 ff.

LOCKE, J. *An Essay Concerning Human Understanding*, Bk. IV, chap. 16, sect. 12.

MASCALL, E. L. *He Who Is: a Study in Traditional Theism*. London, New York, Toronto: Longmans, 1943, 1945; esp. chap. 8.

MERCIER, C. *A New Logic*. London, 1912; esp. pp. 345–49.

MILL, J. S. *A System of Logic*, 7th ed. London, 1868; Vol. II, Bk. III, chap. 20 ("Of Analogy").

SCHILLER, F. C. S. *Formal Logic*. London: Macmillan, 1912; chap. 22, sect. 4.

———. *Logic for Use*. London: Bell, 1929; chap. 16, sect. 13.

STEBBING, L. S. *A Modern Introduction to Logic.* London: Methuen, 1930; sect. 3, entitled "Analogy."

UEBERWEG, F. *System of Logic.* Eng. tr. by T. M. Lindsay. London: Longmans, 1871; sect. 131.

VAIHINGER, H. *The Philosophy of "As if": A System of the Theoretical, Practical and Religious Fictions of Mankind.* Eng. tr. by C. K. Ogden. London: Kegan Paul, 1924; esp. pp. 28 ff., 172 ff.

WHEELER, B. I. "Analogy (linguistic)," *Dictionary of Philosophy, Psychology and Scientific Method* (J. M. Baldwin).

WOLF, A. "Analogy," *Encyclopædia Britannica,* 14th ed.

INDEX